The Project as a Social System

The Project as a Social System

Asia-Pacific Perspectives on Project Management

Edited by Henry Linger and Jill Owen

Monash University Publishing
Building 4, Monash University
Clayton, Victoria 3800, Australia
www.publishing.monash.edu

Monash University Publishing brings to the world publications which advance the best traditions of humane and enlightened thought.

Monash University Publishing titles pass through a rigorous process of independent peer review.

National Library of Australia Cataloguing-in-Publication entry:
    Author: Henry Linger and Jill Owen (eds).
    Title: The project as social system : Asia-Pacific perspectives on project management.

    ISBN: 9781921867040 (pb)
    ISBN: 9781921867057 (web)

    Subjects: Project management--Pacific area.

www.publishing.monash.edu/books/pss.html

Design: Les Thomas

Printed in Australia by Griffin Press an Accredited ISO AS/NZS 14001:2004 Environmental Management System printer.

The paper this book is printed on is certified by the Programme for the Endorsement of Forest Certification scheme. Griffin Press holds PEFC chain of custody SGS - PEFC/COC-0594. PEFC promotes environmentally responsible, socially beneficial and economically viable management of the world's forests.

Contents

Section 2: Strategic Aspects of Project Management

Section 3: Managing Socio-Technical Projects

Introduction

Keynote address

Rethinking information systems project risk: Implications for
research

Chris Sauer

University of Oxford, UK

Andrew Gemino

Simon Fraser University, Canada

Blaize Horner Reich

Simon Fraser University, Canada

Introduction

This is a research conference so I'm going to talk about what seems to me
a very significant issue in research into projects and project management. I
want to discuss risk – 'discuss' is code for manhandling it, roughing it up,
kicking its legs from under it and seeing whether it can still stand up. And
I shall draw out what I think should be some very discussable – code for
possibly contentious – implications for research.

Risk is at the heart of the study and practice of project management.
Some even equate project management and risk management though I do
not go that far. So, the centrality of risk makes it important that we are
confident that our research is robust.

One of the seductive features of research into project risk is that it seems
to offer an empirically objective domain for research. That is we can attach

numbers! Combine this with the central place of risk in our field's thinking and it is easy to slide into the assumption that project management is relatively easily studied by empirical methods to secure an objective understanding.

This objectivist view has been put on notice by, among others, Mark Winter and those colleagues who contributed to the Rethinking Project Management project in the mid-2000s (Winter et al. 2006). Their stance, that project management is a social process and therefore subject to all the arguments that militate in favour of interpretivist approaches in other fields, offers an important corrective to what I would term the traditional or conventional wisdom of project management. According to that 'wisdom', project management is a technical field with mechanistic relationships governing cause and effect. Witness Rodney Turner's quixotic attempt to formulate an axiomatic theory of project management (Turner 2006a; 2006b; 2006c; 2006d), a position I have argued against (Sauer & Reich 2007). The conference theme and many of the papers in this conference indicate that there is no need for sermonising on this point.

Notwithstanding this corrective, it remains relatively easy to think that risk is independently objective: project size can be measured in dollars, person-years etc; project performance can be measured in percentage variance against objectively stated targets. Risk therefore can be understood independently of all those problematic, sophisticated explanatory accounts you find in interpretivist case analyses.

So behind the critique that I'm going to offer of our thinking about risk is a more philosophical concern about the very nature of the field of project management. I'll return to this at the end.

Before I launch into risk, let me make a couple of qualifications, an admission of guilt and an acknowledgement.

First, my research domain is principally that of information technology (IT) projects by which I mean IT-enabled business process change projects. Don't ask me to define it precisely. I think we all know what we mean. Nothing in my argument hinges on it. Indeed, I think that while IT projects are thought to be intrinsically more risky than other types of project, the arguments I shall advance should be more generally applicable.

Second, this is very much work in progress. I have been thinking about it and bouncing it around with Andrew Gemino and Blaize Reich for a couple of years and we have one conference paper that was our initial stake in the ground prior to this (Sauer et al. 2008). The arguments here are intended to be indicative not exhaustive.

Third, my admission of guilt. I shall criticise what I take to be our normal understandings of and research into risk. In doing this, it may look as though I'm setting up a straw man. If it does, it's because I am or have been that straw man. I am one of the guilty parties (Sauer et al. 2007). I think that the Standish Group stands accused alongside me – and implicitly many of those who have cited Standish Group findings in their papers.

Maybe some researchers have always had more sophisticated views than I have but I suspect there are plenty of others in the same camp as me. In this connection, perhaps it's worth saying that although many of my early publications related to information system (IS) project failure (e.g. Sauer 1993; Sauer et al. 1997), it is only in the last six years that I have published papers that explicitly examine risk. It has been in writing these that I have become increasingly uneasy about the concept.

Now the acknowledgement – I have recently happened upon a paper by Paul Bannerman of NICTA and UNSW (Bannerman 2008). In it, he starts to critique risk. His conclusion is that project risk researchers have not paid adequate attention to the needs of practitioners and that practical tools have taken too little heed of research. While there is some overlap between his critique and mine, mine is more extreme and more extensive in its implications.

So, I'm going to start by examining the concept of risk, the research construct and its constituents. Then I shall turn to the problem of data to support our understanding of risk. Then I want to ask about the analysis of data and its interpretation. Finally, I shall turn to the implications in relation to four avenues for research. And for good measure, I'll sign off with a philosophical speculation to give us something to talk about over morning tea.

The concept of risk

Starting with the concept of risk, the traditional definition looks something like:

Project risk = probability of outcome x impact

So, for example, there's a 30 per cent probability that the project will incur a loss of $1m would imply that the project risk is $300,000.

Does anybody know what that means in language I can understand?

It seems to mean something like on average I should expect to lose $300,000 on a project with this set of characteristics (risk factors). Except of course that on seven occasions in ten I lose nothing and on three occasions

I lose $1m. So, I worry that the idea of risk as the product of an outcome's impact and its probability has no necessary correlate in reality.

I also worry that the outcome/impact in this case is rather specific and does not reflect the range of other outcomes that might occur. For example, there are non-budgetary considerations such as job satisfaction, image etc. But there may be many other budgetary outcome possibilities. For example, there may be a 70 per cent probability of losing $100,000 alongside the 30 per cent probability of losing $1m. And many other possibilities besides.

So let's try to be more helpful to risk.

I'm at the capital projects funding committee with my wish list of 10 projects and their business cases including net present values (NPVs). The business case allows us to factor in both costs and benefits. For ease of argument, let's pretend that all costs and benefits can be translated into monetary values.

Project 1 has a business case with NPV of $4m.

Project 2 has a business case with NPV of $5m.

Project 3 has a business case with NPV of $3m.

Etc.

Therefore,

Project 1 has risk to the business case of 30 per cent.

Project 2 has risk to the business case of 45 per cent.

Project 3 has risk to the business case of 20 per cent.

So, if we adjust the NPVs for the risk weighting, Project 1's risk adjusted NPV is $4m x (100–30%) = $2.8m

That is, if we did enough of these projects, on average we'd end up with $2.8m per project rather than the projected $4m.

Project 2's risk adjusted NPV is $5m x (100–45%) = $2.75m.

Project 3's risk adjusted NPV is $3m x (100–20%) = $2.4m.

Etc, etc …

Note that as I have constructed the concept of risk I have surreptitiously conflated the frequency with which downside outcomes occur with their impact. Even in the context of project portfolio investment decisions, we would want to know whether my 30 per cent risk to the business case was derived from a data set of 100 projects in which all 100 missed their business case by 30 per cent or whether 90 per cent hit their business case target but 10 per cent had negative NPV of $8m. Both distributions of data would generate us 30 per cent risk to the business case but would probably have different implications for decision makers. I'm going to set this complication aside. In principle, we could accommodate it.

So what risk gives us is the ability to compare the likely outcomes of different projects and if we were economically rational to choose from among them. I'm gambling, but at least I know the odds!

But, this assumes many things including:

- I have confidence in the business cases.
- I have confidence in the risk benchmarks.
- The projects are totally independent of each other.

Actually, I only refer to confidence rhetorically, because we all know that in practice business cases are dodgy dossiers. We also know that in practice most risk assessment falls short of being rigorous (one of Paul Bannerman's key points). What I'm interested in is not so much how things may fall short in practice and more whether we ever could expect to develop sufficiently accurate measures of risk that it would be rational to have confidence in them.

Let's take stock. So far I have implied three things. One, it is not easy to be clear what the meaning is of risk, especially in the context of a single project. Two, that it is seemingly more useful to apply risk at the portfolio level – it is a probabilistic concept so not surprisingly it is hard to relate it to the reality of a single project. Third, that it is all too easy to be slack in our use of the concept.

Risk data

Let me turn now to the data that might support the discovery of sufficiently accurate measures of risk – what I shall refer to as risk benchmarks.

So the data question is something like – what data could we use to justify our saying that – 'a project with this set of characteristics (risk factors) would on average miss its business case by such and such a percentage'?

First, I'm going to need sufficient projects with similar characteristics to be able to draw statistically significant conclusions. What exactly are similar characteristics? How similar in size is a project costing $1m and another costing $2m and another costing $10m? We'd probably say it depends. On what? The duration of the project might be one factor, the number of team members another, the labour-capital ratio, that is it manpower intensive or is a lot of the cost the purchase of hardware/software? So a particular $1m project might be more like another $10m project than the $2m.

Apparently similar objective attributes do not necessarily support the presumption that they are similar projects.

What about things like complexity and uncertainty of requirements? These are far more problematic in that we do not have objective measures. Researchers at best use subjective measures, typically Likert scales, often as undiscriminating as 1–5.

Second, I need to be able to calculate levels of risk for projects with a given set of characteristics. How do I do that? So for each project that fits the criteria I need to be able to identify the degree to which the project outcome delivered the business case. Two problems worry me: Problem A and Problem B.

Problem A is the problem of measuring the achievement of the business case. This has several sub-problems such as how to identify which performance effects in the organisation result from the project and which result from parallel initiatives; how to treat non-financial outcomes; when to assess the performance outcomes, e.g. one month after implementation, five years after implementation.

Problem B is the problem of using *the* business case as a baseline. What if the business case changes during the project – for example, the project runs into trouble and as the result of a gateway review the objectives are scaled back and a revised business case is developed? Well, you might say you should stick with the original business case. But what if the objectives are scaled back because the organisation decides that it wants to redirect some of its investment to a more urgent need? Surely I don't stick with the original business case? As yet nobody has developed (or even tried to develop) a satisfactory decision rule for identifying the appropriate business case as a baseline.

As a digression I would mention that my colleague at Oxford, Bent Flyvbjerg, argues that the original business case is the gold standard for estimating risk (Flyvbjerg et al. 2003). But, he is interested in showing how business cases are fictions dreamt up by the incurably optimistic and the unscrupulously manipulative. While I accept that his observation of what he calls strategic optimism reflects a common project experience, I do not think that it constitutes a reason for believing that changes to a business case during the course of a project might not sometimes be perfectly legitimate and reasonable. So to properly understand and measure risk we would need to account for such cases.

A sub-problem here relates to the question of when the original business case was created. Across organisations this can vary from being at a very early stage before any groundwork has been done through to the point when a project team has been established and an initial prototype created.

That's probably a soluble problem. But there are further complications. If there have been multiple business cases developed (certainly possible in an environment with a strict gateway discipline), if you ask project managers about the *original* business case, which one are they thinking of? My colleague, Andrew Gemino, has asked about this. He found that project managers vary quite considerably as to what they are thinking about when asked about original targets. For some it was the first ever, for others it was the most recent or 'live' targets (see Figure A).

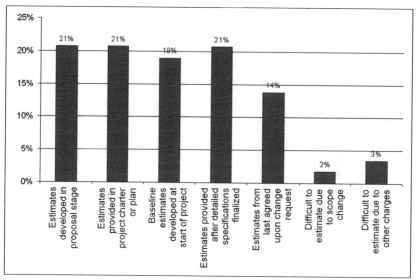

Figure A. Relative frequency of initial estimate definitions

So, there are plenty of problems associated with the task of collecting data that would allow us with a large enough sample to calculate risk benchmarks. I do not say that they are all insuperable. My point is to paint a picture of the distance we would have to travel in our research to get me, as a rigorous researcher, to say that I have confidence in the numbers we hawk around as levels of risk.

Analysing data to generate risk benchmarks

My next step, as promised, is to examine what we would need to do to analyse the data to generate accurate risk benchmarks. Let's start by assuming that the problems about the data themselves can all be overcome. We have a set of risk factors that we can measure accurately and are unambiguous in what they mean.

The obvious approach is to correlate risk factors with project performance outcomes – achievement of the business case. For example, we examine projects of a certain size (100–200 person months). We find that on average they achieve 45 per cent of their business case.

So what? Examine another 200 projects and would it be reasonable to expect that approximately 90 of those would achieve their business case? This would only be so if the original 45 per cent had already been shown to model some aspect of reality such as, for example, that there was a functional relationship between size and business case achievement. So as size increases there is a correlative reduction in the frequency with which business cases are achieved. But I have to tell you that with two samples of 400 and 200 we have found it very hard to detect a definite size-performance relationship. So if you did sample another 200, my guess is that you'd get quite a different number the second time.

The problem is not merely that our data might not have been sufficiently well-defined and rigorous. Two other considerations apply. First, risk factors are rarely solo artists. They usually perform in bands. They appear also to be interdependent. So size and complexity are often associated as are volatility and requirements uncertainty. In principle we could perhaps identify types bearing similar combinations of risks at similar levels of measurement. Then we might have a better basis for expecting the second 200 to have the same success rate as the first. Except … !

Except that none of this takes account of project management. If we believe that project managers do something useful and can make a difference then we surely believe something more like: risk factors are managed/moderated by project management to achieve outcomes (see Figure B).

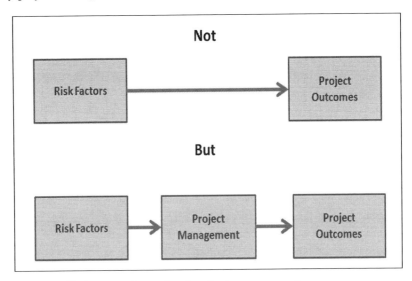

Figure B. The intermediate role of project management

Moreover, I think we believe that the quality of project management varies from project to project. So, on this model, the best we could ever say is that projects with such and such attributes managed to a given level have X per cent risk of not achieving their business case. This requires us to be able to predict the level or quality of project management. This in turn requires a predictive model. And that model would need to be developed and validated against performance outcomes such as achievement of the business case and in the presence of combinations of risk.

You can probably sense that I'm worrying about the possibility of a circular argument. I think we can avoid it. If we can detect a relationship between a given type of project and level of risk and differing qualities of project management leading to consistently different levels of project performance, then we could specify differing levels of project management and if all goes well we may be able to identify antecedents of those levels of project management that would then enable us to predict the level or quality of project management.

I'm making an assumption here – that project management is uniformly effective. That is that in all projects certain management practices are effective. Put crudely, if methodological discipline is good, more methodological discipline is better *in all cases*.

But what if project management is contingent? Certain project management practices work well in certain contexts; other project management practices work well in other contexts. This has been Barki, Rivard and Talbot's claim (2001). And whether you are persuaded by the analysis or not, it's hard not to feel a sneaking sympathy with the idea that for example in a hotel building project you need tight formal control whereas in a new product development project in high tech you might achieve a better outcome with looser formal control.

So if you wanted to predict the level of project management to be applied under given conditions of risk in a world where the impact of project management is contingent, you would also have to predict whether it would be applied contingently.

My point here is that if we are to develop rigorous assessments of project risk, some heavy duty modelling and theorising about project management is required.

By this stage you're probably dropping with exhaustion at this catalogue of difficulties. Bad luck, I'm going to kick you while you're down! Two further points:

One, suppose we did all of this research perfectly. Could we be confident of its validity across time? Would data collected in 1990 or 2000 be a robust basis for applying risk benchmarks in 2010? Would it translate from IT to construction to new product development to policy-making etc? I don't know the answer but we'd need to have one.

Two, what if project management turns out to be much more contingent than any of us imagines? That is, we can't model the contingencies and responses on a two by two matrix! Or even worse, what if there are no clear relationships between risk factors, project management practice and performance outcomes? I'll come back to this.

Review and conclusions

Let's take stock again. I have presented a series of reasons for doubting that we shall have rigorously based risk benchmarks in my lifetime or probably ever. There is too much work to do requiring degrees of resource, rigour and research excellence that are not readily available. It seems a thesis of despair.

What are the implications for us as researchers?

I draw four conclusions. One relates to the pursuit of scientifically rigorous project risk benchmarks. The second concerns what we might do pragmatically that would be helpful to practitioners. The third suggests reducing our ambitions. The fourth argues for the value of qualitative research.

Finally, I want to return to those philosophical roots I referred to earlier and speculate a little about the nature of project management as revealed by today's discussion and connect that to the question of 'what can we ever hope to know about project management?'

Let me start with the pursuit of scientifically rigorous project risk benchmarks. I have suggested that there are issues as to what exactly we are talking about when we talk about risk and what it refers to in reality. I have queried the measures and the data that we'd expect to use. I've raised questions about the lack of underlying theory to justify the logic by which risk benchmarks might be calculated. If I were starting a research career, I would not view this as a promising avenue on which to build a reputation.

Let us move on to a different point. What would be helpful to practitioners? I don't know. I have my prejudices but little evidence on which to base them. Why? To the best of my knowledge, there has been little or no work carried out within the project management field examining how executives use risk in making project investment decisions, or how project managers think about risk and apply their knowledge, or how sponsors, gateway reviewers and other stakeholders use risk benchmarks. Do they use whatever information they have rationally? Do executives in practice want all of the possible information about risk? Are there some risk metrics that are used more than others? Are they the most appropriate metrics for making effective decisions? There is an ample literature on the limits of human cognitive capacity in decision-making (Simon 1955; 1977) to suggest that only a limited set of metrics is likely to be employed in most information system project investment decisions. The interesting question for researchers is to discover what could be useful short of our scientifically rigorous benchmarks. Now, if I were starting a research career, I'd view this area as much more promising.

I guess that this connects to my third conclusion – about limiting our ambitions as researchers. The fundamental point is that the complex relationships between risk factors at the start of a project and final outcomes make it practically impossible to develop scientifically rigorous benchmarks. There's too big a gap between independent and dependent variables. Which is partly why I see focus on smaller slices or segments of projects such as the practice of investment decision-making as a better prospect for research – at least quantitatively based research.

Finally, we are left with the qualitative avenue for research. Might it be the case that the best we could do is to demonstrate through longitudinal studies the causal webs that link the starting conditions of projects with the events and actions that make up the project with its final outcomes? We might choose to acknowledge the riskiness of projects, that is there is an indeterminate probability that the organisation will not get what it wants/expects, without attempting to put numbers on the risks. Instead, we show how projects are risky without committing to any underlying beliefs about objectively detectible patterns of measurable conditions. In effect, I'm suggesting that we might bring into the foreground in all their horrific majesty the reality of the devils that lie in the detail.

All of which leads me to that speculation about the nature of projects and project management. I have argued that the promise of scientifically rigorous approaches to IT project risk research is not encouraging. Some of the reasons behind this conclusion are based on our recognition of the distance in time and activity between independent and dependent variables and on the complexity of the setting which includes all kinds of moderating or mediating activity – viz project management and the events and actions to which it responds. In short, we all know that most projects other than the most trivial are highly complex. We also know that to call something a project is to apply a social construction. It is to project a human interpretation on to social and organisational phenomena. It is not the same as identifying physical phenomena as of a particular natural kind. So we cannot take for granted that projects will exhibit much by way of regular patterns of behaviour. While calling something a project may be handy for the purposes of organising and allocating resources, it does not follow that it is therefore handy from the point of view of research. While I would not recommend trying to build a research career on addressing this question, it does seem a salutary thought with which to leave this conference on research into project management.

References

Bannerman, P. 2008. 'Risk and risk assessment in software projects: A reassessment'. *Journal of Systems and Software* 81: 2118–2133.

Barki, H; Rivard, S; Talbot, J. 2001. 'An integrative contingency model of software project risk management'. *Journal of MIS* 17 (4): 37–69.

Flyvbjerg, B; Bruzelius, N; Rothengatter, W. 2003. *Megaprojects and Risk: An Anatomy of Ambition*. Cambridge: Cambridge University Press.

Sauer, C. 1993. *Why Information Systems Fail: a Case Study Approach*. Henley-on-Thames: Alfred Waller.

Sauer, C; Southon, G; Dampney, CNG. 1997. 'Fit, failure, and the house of horrors: Towards a configurational theory of IS project failure'. In Proceedings of the18th International Conference on Information Systems, edited by Kumar, K; de Gross, J I. Atlanta, Georgia, December, Association for Information Systems Atlanta, GA, USA 349–366.

Sauer, C; Gemino, A; Reich, B. 2007. 'Managing projects for success: The impact of size and volatility on IT project performance'. *Communications of the ACM* 50 (11): 79–84.

Sauer, C; Gemino, A; Reich, BH. 2008. 'Of what use is research on IS project risk? A proposal to make IS risk research fit for practice'. Paper presented at Administrative Sciences Association of Canada Conference, Halifax, Nova Scotia, 24–27 May.

Sauer, C; Reich, BH. 2007. 'What do we want from a theory of project management? A response to Rodney Turner'. *International Journal of Project Management* 25 (1): 1–2.

Simon, H A. 1955. 'A behavioral model of rational choice'. *The Quarterly Journal of Economics* 69 (1) (Feb): 99–118.

Simon, H A. 1977. *The New Science of Management Decision*. Englewood Cliffs, New Jersey: Prentice-Hall.

Turner, J R. 2006a. 'Towards a theory of project management: The nature of the project'. *International Journal of Project Management* 24 (1): 1–3

Turner, J R. 2006b. 'Towards a theory of project management: The nature of the project governance and project management'. *International Journal of Project Management* 24 (2): 93–95

Turner, J R. 2006c. 'Towards a theory of project management: The functions of project management'. *International Journal of Project Management* 24 (3): 187–189

Turner, J R. 2006d. 'Towards a theory of project management: The nature of the functions of project management'. *International Journal of Project Management*. 24 (4): 277–279

Winter, M; Smith, C; Morris, P; Cicmil, S. 2006. 'Directions for future research in project management: The main findings of a UK government-funded research network'. *International Journal of Project Management* 24 (8): 638–649.

Section 1
Socio-Technical Aspects of Project Management

Chapter 1

Illuminating the role of the project owner

Erling S Andersen

BI Norwegian Business School, Norway

The Norwegian Centre of Project Management has established a research and development project to gain a better understanding of the role of the project owner and contribute to more professional project owners in the future. The paper reports some early results.

The project has conducted two empirical studies: a questionnaire survey among project management professionals and a series of in-depth interviews with very experienced project owners and managers. The survey paints a picture of the present project owners as rather weak and not fulfilling the role as prescribed by theory. The interviews introduce a different view, showing a rather satisfactory performance by the project owners.

The paper proposes several propositions for further studies, focusing on investigating the effects of experiences, training, project work standards, and socialisation for creating better project owners. The paper further illuminates which areas of the role of the project owner are of importance in order to improve their performance.

The challenge: Better project owners

There are an infinite number of education and training offers for project managers. Extensive research has shown what is required of project managers to achieve project success (see for instance Zimmerer and Yasin [1998] and El-Sabaa [2001]). There has been less focus on what is required of the project owners. Many project managers complain that the lack of competence of the project owners has a negative effect on project results. This paper focuses on the role of the project owner.

We deliberately use the term 'project owner'. Some use the term 'project sponsor' and see the two as synonymous. The Project Management Institute

(2004) describes the sponsor as the person/group that provides the financial resources, in cash or in kind, for the project. This is a narrower concept than we find adequate. As we will discuss below, the role of the project owner is extended to cover many tasks beyond providing financial support for the project.

The Norwegian Centre of Project Management has, in response to requests from its members, taken on the challenge of making project owners more conscious of their tasks. This paper reports some early results from the work. We present two empirical studies: a quantitative survey and a round of qualitative interviews. The purpose of the studies is to gain a better understanding of how the project owners are handling their tasks and identify their challenges in order to create better project owners.

Our empirical studies examine the performance of project owners in the following areas:

- desirable attributes of project owners;
- relationship between the project owner and the project manager;
- project owner behaviour and the assumptions of agency theory.

The two first areas are easily understood: it is important to see first how the project owners behave and second how they interact with the project managers. The third area needs some explanation. One of the important tasks of the project owner is to control the progress of the project. Agency theory has been proposed to give the theoretical underpinning for the control function (Andersen 2008; Turner & Müller 2004) and therefore it will be interesting to see if the project owners behave as agency theory predicts.

Research design

Data about the Norwegian project owners are collected through survey and interviews.

It is our intention that the survey results should be representative of Norwegian projects. The survey is based on a convenience sample. It was conducted among students in part-time executive master's programs in project management. The participants in these programs come from a wide variety of enterprises; large and small, different industries, and different kinds of organisations. The enterprises all have several projects and the 'students' are familiar with the way project management is executed in their own enterprises. We consider that the responses represent a good cross-section of Norwegian projects.

As the base organisation of the respondents could have several projects running at the same time, they were asked to think of a specific project and the project owner. To be sure that the respondent had a certain project in mind, they were asked to identify the project owner by title. In this way we ensured that the responses were based on concrete observations and not loose thoughts.

The survey had 77 respondents. To ensure that the respondents only answered questions on which they were well-informed, the questionnaire facilitated 'Don't know' responses. By studying the results one can see that the number of responses on certain questions is below the maximum number.

In-depth interviews were carried out with eleven project owners and fourteen project managers from six enterprises in Norway. The enterprises were chosen because they had extensive experience with projects, more than the average, in fact. Contact persons familiar with the projects in these enterprises nominated potential interviewees. The chosen interviewees all had long experience of project work, usually ranging from 10 to 25 years. In most cases the interviewed project owner and the project manager belonged to the same project. The interviewees were not representative of Norwegian project owners and managers in general. The way they were selected ranks them above average in terms of experience and knowledge.

The survey should ideally present the general or average situation of Norwegian projects, whereas the interviews should reveal how some of the most experienced professionals are operating and where they still see room for improvement. Using this research design we are able to compare the general situation with what might be a more desirable situation.

Desirable attributes of project owners

The first part of the investigation deals with the desirable attributes of the project owner. We take as the starting-point the findings of Helm and Remington (2005). Their findings are based on the results of 28 interviews of project managers which were conducted to investigate what they considered to be desirable attributes of project owners.

The article emphasises that in studies of project ownership one has to focus on both behaviour and structure. The project management literature tends to focus on structure rather than behaviour. Helm and Remington (2005, 52) argue: 'If the dynamics of the project are to be more fully understood, studies must combine analysis of structures with an understanding of the behaviour and practice of key agents, which arise out of and, in turn, influence the structure and history of the organisation within which the project is being managed'.

According to Helm and Remington (2005), it is important that project owners have the following attributes:

1. appropriate seniority and power within the organisation;
2. political knowledge of the organisation and political savvy;
3. ability and willingness to make connections between the project and the organisation;
4. courage and willingness to battle with others in the organisation on behalf of the project;
5. ability to motivate the team to deliver the vision and provide ad hoc support to the project team;
6. willingness to partner the project manager and project team;
7. excellent communication skills;
8. personal compatibility with other key players;
9. ability and willingness to provide objectivity and challenge the project manager.

From the perspective of the project, the project owner has both an internal and an external role (Crawford et al. 2008). The external role is as the representative of the base organisation, defining its needs and ensuring that it supplies the project with the necessary resources and decisions. The internal role is as a support person for the project manager and the project team. Items 1, 2 and 3 in the list of desirable attributes above relate to the external role of project owners, while items 5 and 6 relate to their internal role. Communication skills (item 7) and personality compatibility (item 8) are important in the execution of both the external and internal roles.

Bryde (2008) confirms that project ownership can be classed in terms of externally focused client-representing activities and internally focused supporting/championing activities. His research confirms that the role of the project owner consists of a role with external focus, representing the base organisation and being the focal point between users and project, and a role with an internal focus, supporting the project. His research further indicates, however, that a delineation of project ownership based solely on externally focused activities and internally focused activities may be an oversimplification. A third factor, namely, championing projects, including making resources available, seems also to be vital to the work of the project owner. This may in extreme situations also involve the action of cancelling a project. This could, according to Bryde (2008), be viewed as a logical extension of the concept of project champion. The champion is a person who breaks down resistance to a project and uses all the weapons available to see a project succeed. In situations where resistance cannot be broken down or, despite the champion employing all weapons at their disposal, the project is still doomed to failure; a decision to cancel the project has to be taken. The role of the champion is addressed by items 5 and 9 in the list above.

Bryde (2008) investigates whether effective project ownership influences project success. His analysis provides some support for the hypothesis that the greater the project ownership effort the greater the perceived level of project success. The results suggest that internal activities comprising wide-ranging supportive actions coupled with the activities associated with the traditional project ownership role of the client representative may predict levels of overall project success.

The results of our survey are shown in Table 1.1 and the interviews in Table 1.2.

Attributes	N	Yes (%)	No (%)
1. Appropriate seniority and power within the organisation	71	94.4	5.6
2. Political knowledge of the organisation and political savvy	72	87.5	12.5
3. Ability and willingness to make connections between project and organisation	63	79.4	20.6
4. Courage and willingness to battle with others in the organisation on behalf of the project	52	76.9	23.1
5. Ability to motivate the team to deliver the vision and provide ad hoc support to the project team	65	56.9	43.1
6. Willingness to partner the project manager and project team	56	66.1	33.9
7. Excellent communication skills	63	60.3	39.7
8. Personal compatibility with other key players	55	27.3	72.7
9. Ability and willingness to provide objectivity and challenge the project manager	52	55.8	44.2

Table 1.1. The desirable attributes of the project owner – survey results

Table 1.1. reveals some common weaknesses of the project owners. It is especially noteworthy that close to half of the survey respondents say that project owners lack the ability to motivate (item 5), to communicate effectively (item 7) and to challenge the project manager intellectually (item 9). Many of the respondents see the project owner and the project manager as having different personalities (item 8) and this might make cooperation between them difficult.

Attributes	Project owners (N=11)	Project managers (N=14)
1. Appropriate seniority and power within the organisation	Eight interviewees agree. Three would have liked more seniority	Most agree. Some argue that the project owner could have had more decision power
2. Political knowledge of the organisation and political savvy	All agree	All agree
3. Ability and willingness to make connections between project and organisation	All agree	Most agree, some few say that the willingness is not always present
4. Courage and willingness to battle with others in the organisation on behalf of the project	They are willing to fight if the project/fight is worth it	They accept that the project owners must prioritise their efforts
5. Ability to motivate the team to deliver the vision and provide ad hoc support to the project team	All agree, but some add that they could probably do more than they actually do	The ability is there, but the project owners do not always do it (and maybe it is not their task)
6. Willingness to partner the project manager and project team	The willingness is there, but the implementation is not always optimal	Very often a good partnership, but owners and managers have different roles
7. Excellent communication skills	All agree that they have good or excellent skills	Some are very good, some good, some poor
8. Personal compatibility with other key players	All agree, but difficult to say	Find the project owners easy to work with
9. Ability and willingness to provide objectivity and challenge the project	All agree	Agree, good for project owners to have several projects for comparison

Table 1.2. The desirable attributes of the project owner – interview results

The survey showed that nearly all respondents thought the project owners had appropriate seniority and power. The interviews give a more differentiated view. We find among some project owners and project managers views suggesting that there would have been an advantage if the project owners had had more decision authority. One project owner said: 'I don't think all people have realised the importance of my role'. The statement implies that it would have been beneficial if the owner had had wider authority. A project manager said: 'The project owner is not given the necessary authority to exercise his role. This is not about the project owner, but it is an organisational problem'. The project managers say that it is of importance that the project owners have good experience, and some say that the project owners are getting better.

All project owners and managers agreed that the project owners have good understanding of how the base organisation works. In this sense we have the right project owners.

All project owners confirmed their ability and willingness to create contacts between the project and relevant members of the base organisation. The project owners stated that they are focused on interaction between the project and the base to 'sell' the project to the base organisation and to use all their available resources. The project managers confirmed that the project owners have the ability, but some think that the project owners do not always work intensively for the project.

All project owners said that they have the courage and willingness to fight for the project against others in the base organisation, but they added that this is also a matter of prioritising and they have to choose which fights to fight. Some said that the mandate should be so clear that there is no need for fights, but others observed that the role of the project owner is very often a fight over resources and this affects the priorities of the base organisation. The project managers understood that the base organisation has to set priorities and that the project cannot expect to win all the time or have project owners fight all the fights. Some said that it is an important task for the project manager to supply project owners with relevant information and arguments so that they know when to engage in such battles.

All interviewed project owners said that they had the ability to motivate and support the project team. The survey showed that close to half of the respondents thought the project owners did not succeed in this. Some of the interviewees said that they have potential for more than they are doing (confirming the results of the survey). Their excuse is that they do not have the time to do all they should do as project owners. Nearly all project managers thought that the project owners had the ability to motivate and support the project team. The actual efforts of the project owners may vary considerably. In some cases the project managers had experienced poor performances from the project owners, but we must also add that some of the project managers did not consider this to be the fault of the project owners; perhaps it was true at the start-up, but not all through the project. We should be aware that this is an area where the project owner and the project manager should agree at an early stage what kind of responsibility rests with the project owner.

All project owners said they are willing to be seen as a partner with the project manager and team, but some felt they should not fill this role exclusively. One project owner saw a conflict: 'The role of the project owner consists of two parts; setting the requirements and being the coach. I have to balance these two roles'. Many of the project managers confirmed this view. Most say they have a good dialogue with the project owner and receive valuable advice. As one project manager said, 'We have very different roles in the project. The project owner should represent the base organisation and has the responsibility for the value creation of the base organisation'.

The project owners said that it was difficult to evaluate their own communication skills, but they all thought they had good or excellent skills. They emphasised that the owner had to communicate with people at different levels both orally and in writing. The responses from the project managers were that the communication skills of the project owners varied from excellent to rather poor.

The survey revealed more scepticism regarding the communication skills of the project owners. More specific questions were asked about communication (see Table 1.3).

Communication skills	No	Avg.
1. Project owner's communication skills in general	67	4.06
2. Project manager's communication skills in general	71	4.87
3. Communication between project owner and project manager	57	4.68
4. Communication between project manager and project team	71	5.13
5. Communication between project manager and line management	59	4.27

Table 1.3. Communication in projects – survey results
(1=very poor, 4=medium, 7=very good)

The results in Table 1.3 suggest that the project owners had communication problem. It is easy to see that there is potential for improving the communication between the project owner and the project manager.

Regarding the personal compatibility of the project owners with other key players, the interviews revealed that it was difficult for the project owners to tell if their personality made it easy to cooperate with the project manager, but they believed so. The project managers confirmed that they usually found it easy to relate to the project owner. Among experienced project people the problems that should be expected from the survey results are not apparent.

All project owners thought they had the ability and willingness to challenge the project manager when necessary. Many said that they asked critical questions and demanded good reasons to ensure that the best solution is chosen. One of the project managers called attention to the fact that it was quite common for project owners to have several projects that allowed them to compare projects and see what suits the base organisation best. He says: 'We are constantly challenged on solutions and cost savings'.

In summary the survey and interview findings demonstrate how the project owners are performing in terms of desirable attribute. The survey presents a picture of a rather weak project owner lacking the ability to motivate, communicate effectively and challenge the project manager. The interviews show that the experienced project owners are doing much better. The project managers felt that there was still room for improvement, but they understood the priorities of the project owners.

The relationship between project owner and project manager

Our empirical investigations also focused more specifically on the relationship between the project owner and the project manager. Five different important tasks were listed and the respondents were asked who contributed the most. The questions were:

1. Who contributed the most to the project mandate (the description of the project task)?
2. Who defined the success criteria of the project?
3. Who is most committed to the project – burning with desire to see it executed?
4. Who was in charge of the start-up meeting or most engaged at the start-up?
5. Who sees to it that the project gets its resources?

Kloppenborg, Tesch, Manolis and Heitkamp (2006) identify the possible behaviours of the project owner and examine which ones have an impact on project results. Project success is measured by three different outcome measures: meeting agreements (time, cost and quality), customer satisfaction and use, and future success of the enterprise. They find that six behavioural factors are significantly correlated with at least one of the three outcome measures. The six behavioural factors are: establishing communications and commitment, defining and aligning the project, defining project performance and success, mentoring the project manager, prioritising and selecting, and establishing project teams. Two of the behavioural factors were associated with all of the success factors: defining project performance and success, and mentoring the project manager. They might be of special importance.

The factors defining and aligning the project and establishing project teams are connected to item 1, namely setting up the project mandate. The factor defining project performance and success is partly covered by item 2 (defining project success), but probably only partly. The factor should ideally consist of the following parts. The project owner must ensure:

- metrics to measure the project's success are established;
- the strategic value of the project is communicated;
- the project managers are empowered to do their job effectively;
- the expectations of the project manager's performance are defined.

Item 3 deals with start-up. Halman and Burger (2002) have studied the effectiveness of project start-up (PSU) practices. The emphasis is on the focal position of both project owner and project manager and on uncovering potential differences between the two. The research findings support the assumption that a PSU contributes to a better understanding of project purpose, scope and objectives. The study makes it clear, however, that there is room for improvement of the PSUs. In particular, the role of the project owner and the project manager during the PSU should be discussed and aligned prior to the PSU.

The survey results are shown in Table 1.4.

Behavioural tasks	N	Project owner (%)	Project mgr (%)
1. Who contributed the most to the project mandate (the description of the project task)?	63	42.9	57.1
2. Who defined the success criteria of the project?	53	37.7	62.3
3. Who is most committed to the project – burning with desire to see it executed?	70	27.1	72.9
4. Who was in charge of the start-up meeting or most engaged at the start-up?	50	26.0	74.0
5. Who sees to it that the project gets its resources?	68	60.3	39.7

Table 1.4. The involvement of the project owner and the project manager in important project behavioural tasks – survey results

The results shown in Table 1.4 reveal a situation where the project manager is the dominant person in most instances. This could have severe consequences. The project manager is probably as a consequence of the task given to him/her focusing more on short term results while the project owner would have a longer term perspective.

Table 1.5 gives a summary of the interviews.

Behavioural tasks	Project owners (N=11)	Project mgrs (N=14)
1. Who contributed the most to the project mandate (the description of the project task)?	Cooperative effort, defined by the project work standard	Cooperative effort, but the project manager is often in the leading role
2. Who defined the success criteria of the project?	Cooperation	Cooperation
3. Who is most committed to the project – burning with desire to see it executed?	Half of the project owners say they are	Half of the project managers say they are
4. Who was in charge of the start-up meeting or most engaged at the start-up?	Cooperation	Cooperation, many involved
5. Who sees to it that the project gets its resources?	Most of the project owners say they do	Half say the project owner does it, half say the project managers

Table 1.5. The involvement of the project owner and the project manager in important project behavioural tasks – interview results.

We need to look more closely at the results. First, we turn to the question of who contributed the most to the project mandate.

A small majority of the survey respondents said that the project manager was the main contributor. The interviews show that there are great variations, but all interviewees indicated some kind of cooperation between the project owner and the project manager. Many said that the project owner takes the initiative, the project manager comes up with adjustments and proposals for change, and then the project owner approves. A project owner said: 'The project owner initiates, the project manager does the job'. Most often there are some processes managed by the project owner before the project manager is brought in. Some also said that it is the customer or client who orders the project and who sets the requirements.

We find the same kind of process for defining success criteria for the project as we do for determining the mandate. A project owner said: 'Dialogue is based on a draft from the project manager. It may also be based on the commission we have been given'. Some projects distinguish between the project's mission (purpose, overall objective) and goals (often expressed in terms of the time, cost and quality of the delivery of the project). In one case the mission is determined by the project owner and the project manager sets the goals. In another case it is the project owner who determines the three aspects of the project triangle: time, cost and quality.

The survey showed that most of the respondents felt that it is the project manager who is 'burning' for the project to succeed; the interviews, however, gave a somewhat different view. About half of the project owners said they are the ones most engaged. The project managers actually confirmed this as half of them said they are the most engaged.

A project manager said this about who is burning for the project: 'It is not the project owner. He does not allocate enough time to the project. It is the project manager. But sometimes the project manager gets 'burned out'. There is no more passion'. One project owner argued that they had struggled for a long time to get the project in place, but to get it going, one needs a motivated and enthusiastic project manager, so in that sense both parties should be burning. In some cases, it was reported that nobody was really burning for the project. A project owner said this about his involvement: 'I am not burning for it. It is a piece of work. My duty is to implement the strategy the company has chosen. We are not burning for it. We are businesslike, engaged'.

The survey overwhelmingly showed that people felt that the project managers took care of the start-up meeting. The interviewees again had a more multifaceted view. Most of them looked at it as a cooperative effort, whereby the project manager puts into effect all the practical matters, but the project owner still has a role to play. A project manager said: 'I was the propeller, but the project owner was involved in all important preparations for the meeting'. Another project manager observed: 'The project manager arranged the meeting. But this meeting really belongs to the project owner. The project manager is only a secretary'. One project owner argued that it is of great importance that the project owner plays a vital role in the start-up meeting. He said: 'It is important that the project owner is visible in the meeting. He must become more than a name in documents'.

Some 60 per cent of the survey respondents said that the project owner arranges for the project to receive its resources. The majority of the interviewed project owners said that they provided the resources for the project. As one of them said, 'This is the main task of the project owner'. There are still a few project owners, however, who took a different view on this and see it as the responsibility of the project manager.

Half of the project managers said that the project owners provide the resources. The other half said they were responsible for obtaining the necessary resources. In many situations the project owner and manager cooperated. A project manager said: 'The project manager must get hold of the people; the project owner comes up with the money'. The project may struggle to get enough resources. Sometimes the project manager and the project owner may decide to take it to a higher level; as one of them said: 'It should be a team effort, but often it is a fight'.

In summary, we may say that the survey showed the project manager as the leading person in most tasks. The interviews partly confirmed this, but stressed that all the different tasks discussed should be seen as cooperative efforts whereby the project owner and the project manager have distinct but complementary roles. Some of the differences indicate that the project owner–project manager relationship depends on the corporate culture. In some organisations the project manager looks for resources and in others the owner; and the same thing with budgets.

The project owner and the assumptions of agency theory

Project management deals with the relationship between two organisations (Andersen 2008). The base organisation sets up a temporary organisation and assigns it to perform work on its behalf. We need a specific theory to discuss and understand this constellation. A relevant theory is agency theory. This theory is directed at studying a relationship in which one party (the principal) delegates work to another (the agent), who performs the work (Eisenhardt 1989).

Agency theory is primarily used in situations where two parties enter into a contract, but the reasoning of the theory is also relevant when no formal contract is signed. We will draw on agency theory to illuminate the relationship between the base organisation as the principal and the project as the agent. The base organisation will usually appoint a project owner, who then takes on the role as the representative for the principal. The project will be headed by the project manager, who will represent the agent. The theory will accordingly throw light on the relationship between the project owner and the project manager.

Agency theory specifically addresses the following questions: Which is the best way for the principal to control the relationship between the principal and the agent to ensure the optimal solution for the principal? Which issues affect the relationship?

Let us apply this theory to projects. The optimal solution for the project owner as principal is to secure maximum value creation for the base organisation. The project owner has established the project for this specific purpose. He wants to see certain changes to the base organisation and has engaged the project manager to help him bring about these changes and create better results for the base organisation. If the two parties (the principal and the agent) are completely alike (they think and behave the same way), there will be no problem if the work is left to the agent. The agent will do exactly what the principal would have done himself.

Problems arise when the two are not quite alike, if they differ in some way. Agency theory points to areas where the two parties may differ. They may at least be dissimilar in the following aspects:

1. preferences (the project owner and the project manager may have conflicting values or preferences);

2. available knowledge (the project owner and the project manager do not have the same knowledge; we say that the situation is characterised by asymmetry between the two parties);

3. attitude to risk (the project owner and the project manager may have different risk aversions, i.e. they dislike differently exposure to risks).

Is it reasonable to believe that the project owner and the project manager differ on these points? This question emerged from our interviews.

Turner and Müller (2004) discuss communication and cooperation between the project owner and the project manager. The best project performance requires good communication and high collaboration between the two parties. Unfortunately, this is not how it happens in many projects. There is distrust, even conflict, between owner and manager, and the owner sets tight constraints within which the manager must work. Project owners mouth partnership and empowerment, but implement conflict and tight control. The article makes use of principal-agency theory to explain why the problems come into being and argues that better communication between the project owner and the project manager may reduce or eliminate the problems. We followed this up by including the following question in the interviews:

Socialisation: have activities to form common preferences taken place?

Our discussion on the validity of the assumptions of the agency theory was not covered by the survey, only by the interviews. Table 1.6 shows a summary of the results of the interviews.

Assumptions of agency theory	Project owners (N=11)	Project mgrs (N=14)
1. The project owner and the project manager have different values or preferences	All disagree; see no conflicts in mission	Nearly all disagree; some say it may happen
2. The project owner and the project manager have different knowledge of the project	Disagree: same knowledge of project work, but different information about project progress	Many agree: different knowledge and different information
3. The project owner and the project manager have different attitudes to risk	No clear picture, partly disagree	No clear picture, partly disagree
4. Socialisation (activities to form common preferences) has taken place	Activities are arranged	Activities are arranged

Table 1.6. The relevance of the assumptions of agency theory – interview results

All project owners agreed that the project owner and the project manager had the same idea and understanding of the mission of the project. They pointed out that this was an essential part of the project task and that the project manager by taking on his assignment had directly or indirectly approved the purpose of the project. Most of the project owners did not see any goal conflicts between the two parties. Some said that they experienced some conflicts when the project had to prioritise time, cost and quality. The project manager was more willing to sacrifice scope or quality than the project owner, who was more faithful to the original concept.

The project managers to a large degree agreed with the project owners that there was no fundamental difference in opinions on mission and goals, but the project managers emphasised to a larger extent that problems may arise when the two parties see the way forward differently. They were especially worried that lack of resources may elicit differences in preferences.

The interviews did not reveal that the project owner and the project manager had different perceptions on how to reach the goals but several interviewees stressed that there were good discussions along the road and that the project had flexibility to choose what they saw as the best approach. A project owner said: 'I feel that within our organisation we share the same basic thinking. We are good at focusing on mission and goals. The road is secondary. We discuss; there is no dictatorship. Our organisation has some basic principles, besides that freedom. That's the way it should be: freedom and responsibility'.

It was the perception of the project owners that the project owners and project managers did not have different knowledge of project work. They claimed to have experienced and competent project managers, who spoke the same 'language' as themselves. The interviewees were from enterprises that had their own 'project schools' which, according to the interviewees, created a common platform of knowledge. Even if the knowledge of project work was common ground, however, there were differences in experience. A project owner said: 'My project manager has a technical background; I am more focused on concepts'.

The project managers disagreed with the project owners and thought that the two had different knowledge of project work. The project managers considered that in certain areas the project owners were more experienced and that it was useful to talk with them to get another perspective on the tasks they faced. In their opinion, project owners and project managers could supplement each other and together create a better team. Among some of the project managers, however, there was scepticism about the competence of the project owners. One said: 'It takes time to create a good project team. I haven't met any project owners with that kind of competence and the role of project owner is very important to projects'. Another said: 'The project owner should take on greater responsibility'.

Most of the interviewees thought that the two parties held different information about the project. As one project owner said: 'The project manager is best informed about the project – and that's the way it is supposed to be'. All were concerned about the importance of an open dialogue and how to share the information about the progress of the project and not hold back important information. One project manager said: 'The challenge for the project owner is to communicate downwards in an adequate way. The project manager has a similar responsibility for communicating upwards so that the project owner does not get any unpleasant surprises'.

The interviews did not reveal any distinct variations in attitude to risk between the project owner and the project manager. Most of the interviewees were more focused on identifying risks and discussing how to handle them. Project managers are not risk averters, but on the other hand they do not want to take any risk beyond what is described in the mandate and their authority allows them to do. One project owner said: 'We should take risks, but we should have control and take deliberate actions'.

The interviews further showed that most projects conduct certain activities to create team spirit and a common understanding of the purpose of the project. Start-up meetings are important in this sense. Some projects have special team-building sessions twice a year. Some have regular meetings for the sharing of information. The initiative usually comes from the project manager. Some complained that lack of time prevents such gatherings. One project manager acknowledged: 'No, we don't have time and resources to do it'.

In summary, our findings suggest that the assumptions of agency theory are only partly confirmed. This does not necessarily mean that agency theory is invalid. We saw that all projects had socialisation activities. This may have reduced or removed the basis for the differences between the project owner as the principal and the project manager as the agent. We also saw that information imbalance prevails; but that it is accepted by the parties and no explicit actions are in place to overcome this imbalance.

Conclusions and further work

Our empirical studies have illuminated the role of the project owner. Importantly, the findings from the two studies have given somewhat different pictures of the situation.

These differences might be due to different data collection methods. The survey respondents might have felt that their responses should be in accordance with the popular notion that the project owner is playing a weak role and because of this they overemphasised the negative behaviour of the project owner. The interviewees, on the other hand, might have suppressed negative reactions to the project owner to avoid conflict or an attitude of negativity towards colleagues. Even if some biases are present, the results seem very clearly to indicate that the experienced companies and professionals are doing better than the average.

This is not a very surprising conclusion, but the challenge for further work is to find out which aspects are the most important in fostering the best project owners. Our interviews have shown that experienced people are doing a better job as project owners. They are working for companies which have institutionalised training by establishing their own project schools and also implemented project work standards. The successful projects also reported socialisation activities as part of project work. These aspects should be studied further.

The behaviour which is reflected in agency theory can be seen as a certain governance structure. Project governance is 'the value system, responsibilities, processes and policies that allow projects to achieve organisational objectives and foster implementation that is in the best interest of all stakeholders, internal and external, and the corporation itself.' (Müller 2009, p. 4). Project governance coexists with the corporate governance framework (Müller 2009). Since we were not able to verify that professionals of experienced project-based companies behaved according to agency theory, other governance structures should be investigated.

The research project initiated by the Norwegian Centre of Project Management will investigate these aspects further in its continuing work.

References

Andersen, E S. 2008. *Rethinking Project Management – An Organisational Perspective*. Harlow, England: Prentice Hall.

Bryde, D. 2008. 'Perceptions of the impact of project sponsorship practices on project success'. *International Journal of Project Management* 26 (8): 800–809.

Crawford, L; Cooke-Davies, T; Hobbs, B; Labuschagne, L; Remington, K; Chen, P. 2008. 'Governance and support in the sponsoring of projects and programs'. *Project Management Journal* 39 (Supplement): S43–S55.

Eisenhardt, K M. 1989. 'Agency theory: An assessment and review'. *Academy of Management Review* 14 (1): 57–74.

El-Sabaa, S. 2001. 'The skills and career path of an effective project manager'. *International Journal of Project Management* 19 (1): 1–7.

Halman, J I M; Burger, G T N. 2002. 'Evaluating effectiveness of project start-ups: An exploratory study'. *International Journal of Project Management* 20 (1): 81–89.

Helm, J; Remington, K. 2005. 'Effective project sponsorship: An evaluation of the role of the executive sponsor in complex infrastructure projects by senior project managers'. *Project Management Journal* 36 (3): 51–61.

Kloppenborg, T J; Tesch, D; Manolis, C; Heitkamp, M. 2006. 'An empirical investigation of the sponsor's role in project initiation'. *Project Management Journal* 37 (3): 16–25.

Project Management Institute. 2004. *A Guide to the Project Management Body of Knowledge (PMBOK Guide)*. 3rd edn. Newton Square, PA: Project Management Institute.

Müller, R. 2009. *Project Governance*. Burlington, VT, USA: Gower.

Turner, J R; Müller, R. 2004. 'Communication and co-operation on projects between the project owner as principal and the project manager as agent'. *European Management Journal* 22 (3): 327–336.

Zimmerer, T W; Yasin, M M. 1998. 'A leadership profile of American project managers'. *Project Management Journal* 29 (1): 31–38.

Chapter 2

Cross-cultural complex project management

Balancing social and cultural complexity

Louis Klein

Systemic Excellence Group and

Humboldt-Viadrina School of Governance, Germany

Projects fail on the human side, they say. We are well-equipped to manage technical complexity; however handling the human side is not our strength. In fact we are laypersons when it comes to dealing with social and cultural complexity. Projects nowadays are increasingly cross-cultural and complex. Project management has to deal with genuinely different expectations and cultural perspectives of stakeholders, clients, project managers and team members. Managing social complexity is a key competence for successful project management. Engineering and scientific management is for technical systems; it is not an adequate paradigm for social systems. Additional models, methods and instruments are required referring to an alternative paradigmatic background. And it will never be an 'either/or', it will always be an 'as well as'. Future practices will be based on an ecology of paradigms.

This paper presents the initial findings of a global research project on cross-cultural complex project management (CCCPM). The project aims to address the connectivity between the different views and expectations inside and outside of projects. This paper focuses on the practical implications of the initial findings for project teams and concludes with some recommendations for future research.[1]

---

1 The German version of the paper was published as: Klein, Louis. 2009. 'Cross-cultural complex project management: Das management sozialer komplexität nicht nur in kulturübergreifenden projekten'. In GPM Deutsche Gesellschaft für Projektmanagement e.V. (ed.): Die Kunst des Projektmanagements. Inspiriert durch den Wandel. 26. Internationales Deutsches Projektmanagement Form – Tagungsband, 14–15. October 2009. Nürnberg: GPM, pp. 98–107.

Introduction

The aim of this paper is to present some insights and initial findings of the global Cross-Cultural Complex Project Management (CCCPM) research project. The CCCPM project focuses on the challenges of social and cultural complexity to project management, especially in regard to cross-cultural cooperation in complex projects. The CCCPM project consists of 14 single PhD research projects and an overarching Habilitation project. Following the research guidelines of the Humboldt-Viadrina School of Governance all research projects engage in praxeological reflection (Bourdieu 1998). The majority of the projects are genuine field and action research projects.

This paper summarises some of the initial findings from the individual projects to indicate the overall direction of the CCCPM project. Drawing on the work of Niklas Luhmann (1984), the fieldwork is counterbalanced with a systemic perspective. The aim of this approach is to increase the applicability of the Theory of Social Systems for cultural and cross-cultural matters. While this may be considered counter-intuitive, a distinction between social and cultural complexity does not seem to be fruitful in the end. Accordingly, a more universal framework incorporating both social and cultural complexity will be advanced. For the moment, this paper will put forward some ideas on a systemic perspective on social and cultural complexity, especially in the case of project management; initial research findings will be illustrated in their application for project teams; and some recommendations for further research will be provided.

Case for action: We are laypersons when it comes to dealing with social and cultural complexity

We, as a community of practice in project management, are laypersons when it comes to dealing with social and cultural complexity. By and large we are dilettantes in applying the knowledge at hand in the field. In the best cases we are amateurs. We have simply not learned how to do this. In developed western societies there is no cultural or educational tradition of dealing with social and cultural complexity. In dealing with technical complexity, however, we are professionals. We have learned how to do this. The western world defines itself through technology. Focusing on technological possibilities is an integral part of our culture. In dealing with social complexity, however, we allow ourselves to be unbelievably unaware with regular dramatic, if not catastrophic, results.

This is the unfortunate point of departure for this discussion of social and cultural complexity in project management. It is almost embarrassing for the informed observer when yet another project manager, after a long period of suffering, comes to the conclusion that a project failed because of 'the human side'. Solving technical problems regularly enters the histories of project managers as success stories. Great technical challenges are tough nuts to crack. They can cost time and money, but the end of the story entails a technical solution. The power plant functions, the space telescope sends incredible images and the new bridge connects continents. It is a different story when it comes to cultural complexity: the team does not function; the leadership is dilettante; no clear objectives are negotiated with the stakeholders; and anyhow, working together across cultural boundaries is considered impossible.

There are no success stories to be told here. Yet, still, there is hope. There are teams that function. There is successful leadership. There is politically sensible stakeholder management. However, these stories are conveyed as lucky strokes of fate and wondrous turnarounds. There are no clear references as to why the management of social and cultural complexity works in one context and fails in another. This lack of awareness easily allows itself to be ascertained as an economic disadvantage. This would, however, just be further evidence of a systematic deficit orientation in this regard. On a regular basis, one is relieved if nothing goes wrong. Thus, the possibilities, the emergence and complexity gains, which would lift project management to a completely different level of performance, remain largely ignored and unstudied within the professional community of project managers.

Initial findings: Balancing social and cultural complexity for project teams

The Cross-Cultural Complex Project Management research project (www.CCCPM.com) is a global research initiative that is concerned with exactly these issues. The research project is a co-operative endeavour by the Systemic Excellence Group in Berlin, Cape Town and Hong Kong, the Humboldt Viadrina School of Governance in Berlin, the Europa-Universität Viadrina in Frankfurt (Oder) and the International Centre for Complex Project Management in Canberra (Australian). The research is arranged in the form of an open group of doctoral candidates. In the individual research projects, a social systemic anthropological approach is used to examine and relate the capacities and capabilities for performance of diverse concrete practices of project management. The goal is to explore, through a multiplicity of field studies, the terms and conditions of the possibility that can turn the subject of social and cultural complexity away from the deficit orientation and provide models, methods and instruments that allow progress towards a totally different level of performance.

Research has been planned over a period of three years. Pre-studies began in the summer of 2008. At its core, the approach is that of praxeological reflection (Bourdieu 1998). This means that the approach is inductive. For the most part, in the form of participatory observation from within the praxis, the terms and conditions of the possibility of a proactive, performance-oriented management of social and cultural complexity will be compiled. Moreover, in a quasi-experimental way, the capabilities and effectiveness of currently available models, methods and instruments will be explored and tested. Underlying this is the consideration that efforts should not be directed to produce a new theory or new set of models, methods and instruments, but that the assumption can be made that those possibilities, which are currently available today, could account for substantial successes in the subject field through the manner in which they are combined and handled. And so, after one year of intensive research, a set of initial findings with direct practical implications can be presented. Furthermore, that which is currently possible today, and the direction further research and development should proceed in, will be introduced focusing on the five most essential areas of achievement.

A team is more than a sum of individuals

A team and its performance capabilities or capacities cannot be explained from a summative perspective towards individual behaviour. A team – like every social system – is characterised by its dynamic nature and by what emerges in the interaction between the actors. The whole is more than the sum of its parts.

For a scientific understanding of these issues, a glimpse into the sociological theory of social systems is helpful and more than illustrative (Lurhmann 1984). The sociological theory of social systems operates explicitly upon the established distinction between psychological and social systems. The less helpful observation of individual behaviour is thereby removed from the focus of explanations. This reveals the emerging dynamic of social systems and guides attention to the terms and conditions of the possibility of social systemic emergence. Thereby, awareness is spurred in two directions. One view is of the general framework and context of social systems, on the support and debilitation of specific social systemic developments and configurations. The other view points to the psychological system and the paradigmatic reference of individual aspects of behaviour. Paradigmatic reference means, at this point, that it is significant to see what models, methods and instruments for the orientation of individual behaviour are available.

What that means can be shown in the area of team development in the contexts of cross-cultural collaboration and co-operation. A behaviour-oriented approach, as is known for example from the context of inter-cultural training, regularly results in the attempt to orient individual behaviour towards cultural stereotypes. One way or another, this does not do the individual, the team, or the cultural space any justice (Breidenbach & Nyíri 2008). And how annoying is it to then find that Mr Wong is actually very different than how he should be as a Chinese man? And how astonishing is it that the engineer Mr Müller from Germany and Mr Kim from South Korea are closer to one another than Mr Müller is to his colleague Mr Meier from marketing?

Focusing on the team as a social system directs attention towards that which we like to label 'communities of practice' (Wenger 1998; Willke 1998), meaning occupational categories or disciplines. It is important to note that grounded in this systemic perspective we see something like a paradigmatic turn in understanding communities of practice. Any community of practice is determined by the paradigmatic frame it is operating in and by doing so reinforcing it. For example, engineers, as an occupational category based on their relative homogenous education, form a community of practice within which many possible issues are always already predetermined. They do not even appear as problems. As soon as one has to do with business people or controllers, that which was taken for granted suddenly becomes a problem. At this point it becomes important to understand the team as a social system which must first negotiate the terms and conditions of its own possibilities. This can remain implied and succeed – however, this is an exception. And so, the first fundamental requirement of balancing social and cultural complexity arises by making the collaboration model of a team the object of negotiation. The team can constitute itself herein as a community of practice, give itself objectives and rules and decide on a variety of issues or problems in advance so that these do not become a spanner in the works at a later time. A team that is aware of its own conditionality and that takes the time to explicitly negotiate a model for collaboration/co-operation, is clearly at an advantage.

Social systems have self-reinforcing tendencies

Social systems have their own self-reinforcing tendencies. They behave like self-fulfilling or self-destructing prophecies. Based on this, the necessity becomes very clear of distancing the scrutiny of social systems from the habitual ways of thinking in the natural sciences. Indeed, the central scientific criterion of trueness or falsehood proves itself to be of little help in the consideration of social systems. From a social science perspective, an observation and assessment of social systems can only be meaningful if made on the basis of the criterion of functionality. A social system is consequently not true or false, but functional or dysfunctional. The criterion of causality, from A follows B, also consistently proves itself to be of little help in the context of social systems. In this regard, social systems are not trivial machines (Foerster 1996). Depending on the general state and dynamic of a social system, B can follow from A once, then C can follow from A and then B again. An important figure of thought in dealing with social systems is self-creation or autopoiesis (Maturana & Varela 1980). A social system creates itself in accordance with its own standards.

McGregor's (2006) Theory X and Theory Y comparison provides a descriptive observation of this issue. The point of this theory is that management can operate on the basis of two fundamentally different hypotheses. Theory Y describes the basic assumption that people are self-motivated and self-responsible and on the basis of this, management sees itself as an enabler that gives shape to the general framework within which motivation and responsibility can unfold. As an alternative to this, Theory X writes another role for management based on the assumption that people deal with things in regularly unmotivated and irresponsible ways. Thus, management is responsible for motivating staff and securing responsibilities through control mechanisms. What is astonishing about McGregor's research is that both assumptions, both Theory X and Y, prove themselves to be true. The consequence of this is that whichever assumption management operates on, it becomes a self-fulfilling prophecy. If people are treated as motivated and self-responsible, they will also prove to be so.

Let us return to the subject of team building. It is apparent that on the basis of the self-creation of social systems, the negotiation of models of collaboration and co-operation are accorded an important quality. Besides being the operative self-organisation, the 'how' of the collaboration involves a dimension that is normative and strategic. Simply said, a team becomes a team, rather than being implicitly established. The chance that is offered here is obvious. A high-performance team becomes such by explicitly negotiating the conditions and terms of the possibility of becoming such a team in a consensus of its members.

Social phenomena are dealt with reactively

Social phenomena are dealt with reactively. We are so insecure and inexperienced in dealing with social complexity that we only act when it is actually too late. This does not have to be so. Fundamentally, three different modes of action can be differentiated: reactive, active and pro-active. The reactive mode is familiar to us. We only take action when the psychological strain is intense enough: the team stops making progress, a conflict is omnipresent and the shared undertaking is about to fail. Now, only what can be saved will be saved. One operates on the basis of a deficit orientation. This is classical heroic management (Baecker 1994). The cow is brought off the ice, the burning hut is extinguished and the child is pulled from the well; it is too late for anything more than damage control.

It is a difference case if an active mode of action is employed in dealing with team issues. Using this mode of action, at the moment in which the team constitutes itself, it makes itself the subject for the purpose of negotiating a collaboration model. That would be, so to speak, step number one in the agenda of the project. Luckily, one can find a number of examples today in which this happens and, with regard to the self-creative dynamic of social systems, in which the negotiation process is perpetuated (Klein 2009). Concretely, this could be done, after fixed periods of time, by examining those negotiated collaboration models in order to assess their functionality and performance and then further optimise them. The qualitative difference in the steering of the team at this point is a bit like the difference between ballistics and bicycling. In ballistics, a projectile is aimed and fired. Then, everything else depends upon the influence of contexts. In the steering and leading of teams, this means that a team is oriented at the beginning of its collaboration and then left to the dynamics of the contexts. The steering model of bicycle riding sets up the opposite extreme. In this case, a continual adjustment with the path on which the bicycle travels is made, so that the bicycle rider arrives at the place he would like to arrive at. In relation to the team situation, this describes a procedure in which the collaboration model is continually under close scrutiny and is further optimised as needed.

A proactive method, in these contexts, shifts focus the away from the team and towards the contexts of the surrounding social systems. Let us take the example of a project organisation of a firm whose business involves managing and realising projects. It is then possible within the framework of this organisation to make programs, rules and scripts available that predetermine and, if needed, prepare for an active handling of the team as a subject (Lurhmann 2000). Such a preparation could take place, for example, by fundamentally anchoring the subject of team building in the curricula of employee training and professional development. This would equip the individual with foreknowledge and a repertoire of skills that would, in a broader sense, make the subject of team building and the balancing of social complexity an accentuated competitive advantage of the organisation.

The conditions for the negotiation of social settings are heterogeneous

The conditions for the negotiation of social settings are regularly heterogeneous. As previously described, an eye for social and cultural complexity is not an integral part of our culture or educational system. In contrast to areas of language, mathematics, or technology, one cannot presuppose a common base or prior knowledge. Quite the contrary, one must assume that actively broaching the subject of social systemic conditions, for example in team building, is not only an area of not knowing for individual team members, but also an area that represents excessive mental demands. We are therefore dealing in this context with heterogeneity of individual set-ups, which advises that for every process of negotiation within social systems, the terms, conditions and possibilities be explored beforehand.

This becomes very transparent and clear in trans-cultural areas. The difference of diverse cultural spheres becomes most visible here within the subject of social complexity and in its handling (Klein 2006). Often the only preparatory training, with regard to conscious dealings with people cooperating with one another, is religious training consisting of a methodological reference that exists as a type of catechism. There is, therefore, the need for a careful introduction to that which seems acceptable and possible for the type and scope of negotiations of a social system in order to have it become the basis of further proceedings. In a manner of speaking, it is essential to explore the individual paradigmatic references of the team members. Up until now, the most proven means of doing this is by conducting individual interviews. These can be used to determine which models, methods and instruments make available the respective world outlook and, therefore, the perspectives on social settings and phenomena, in particular. The lateral view of such a survey, also known as systemic inquiry (Klein 2005), illustrates on which grounds and with which methods and instruments a social system, as such, can be negotiated. This stands in fundamental opposition to a method found in team building in North America. A 'trust the process' method should be approached with great caution. A procedure that may, for example, function superbly in a co-operation between German and US companies can in a different context, for example in Asia, have almost catastrophic consequences. Instead of achieving consensus, dissent and cultural alienation would be perpetuated.

Even if it is possible in the trans-cultural field to describe a careful introduction to social systemic processes of negotiation in a very tangible way, it is important to once again remark that the social systemic reference of a cultural sphere or a nation need not be the dominant dimension for a particular process of negotiation. On the contrary, it is regularly evident that, in the context of project management, professional cultures are the more decisive. It depends, therefore, on the particular individual case and on the participating actors how the particular team charter will be negotiated. It is helpful at this point to cast a glance at the differentiation between next practice and best practice (Klein 2009a). Best practice describes an ideal typical state of objectives, which do not regard the particular terms and possibilities of a social system. Next practice is different. It deals with the options of those possibilities that are deposited in a concrete social system and the realisation of those options. A process of development is arranged on the basis that with each realised practice, the social system's space of possibility naturally changes further and a new next practice comes into view. Thus the development of a social system describes itself as a progression from a next practice to a next practice to a next practice. The particular path of development is, thereby, an intensely conditional individual case.

For team building, it follows that the process starts with the exploration of paradigmatic terms and possibilities and not the reference to a designated method or a designated instrument. Based on this, a distinct successful development becomes possible.

Each system that increases its social and cultural complexity gains a sustainable competitive advantage

Every social system that increases its social and cultural complexity gains a sustainable competitive advantage. In the first instance it seems contra-intuitive to shift the focus from problems to solutions. It is initially just this reduction of complexity, however, that justifies itself as a problem of social systems (Luhmann 1984). At the same time, with a reference to Ashby's (1956) 'Law of Requisite Variety', it is apparent that in order to deal with environmental complexity, internal complexity must be constructed. Variety as a measure of complexity can be appreciated when it comes to team resilience based on social variety. Internal complexity enables teams to meet external complexity in a controlled manner. What sounds very academic here becomes very clear using the example of a football team. Let us take a children's team as an example. Here the game is quickly reduced to kicking what is round into what has corners. The individual child tries to participate in that he reaches the ball and then heads for the opposing goal or takes a direct shot. If all of the available players on the field follow this idea, it will appear, to someone watching from the outside, like a tangle of children moving back and forth across the field. With a glance towards professional football it becomes clear what can be meant by complexity gain. Here the individual player takes on a clear, well-defined role within which he moves. He can be a striker, or a midfield player, or a defender. And each of these roles is defined by rules and a repertoire of behaviour, which contributes as a whole to an increase in the total complexity of the game and brings forth that which regularly thrills large crowds of onlookers.

Scientifically, this subject area is discussed under the heading of 'Thriving on Diversity' (Beneke 1998). If social complexity in teams stays implicit and is not reflected, then a social system tends to orient its behaviour repertoire towards the smallest common denominator. This reduces complexity, but also makes the system, in regard to a dynamic environment, unstable and susceptible. Thriving on diversity can be described, in contrast, as the orientation towards the largest common multiple. This not only means that commonality is available to the team, but also the difference of the individual actors. With regard to a dynamic environment, the potential of a social system to react is clearly increased. The resilience of this team increases and hence, the stability with regard to the most diverse environmental influences or internal dynamics.

An example of this is represented, on a different level, by the success of specific cities. One example that is cited again and again is the success of the city of Berlin in the 16th and 18th centuries. At this time Berlin, advanced from an insignificant marketing spot in the Margraviate of Brandenburg to the capital city of the Prussian state. Compared to other European metropolises, Berlin's liberal attitude towards the diverse religious and national origins of immigrants enabled an increase in the internal complexity of the city and thereby an expansion of its capacities with regard to commercial prosperity. The more diversity a community allows or can allow, the bigger its repertoire of action becomes, the bigger the possibilities to use various environmental dynamics for its own development. What can be observed on this large scale is also valid for teams. The more diversity a team has available through the individual team members, the bigger the chance of a sustainable performance capability as a team.

Summary for practice and further research

Summarising the previous research at this point, it is especially remarkable, with regard to the management of social complexity, how near issues and solutions are to one another. In the age of Web 2.0, the knowledge around collective intelligence is almost commonplace (Surowiecki 2004; Shirky 2008). However, that the 'Wisdom of Crowds' can be applied with regard to the management and handling of social and cultural complexity is surprising. At the same time, it can indeed be ascertained that the management and respectively, the handling of social and cultural complexity, regularly succeed. And with all the justified lament, it can be recognised that social systems have an enormous knowledge about their own make up, about the conditions and possibilities at their disposal. This knowledge, and here the relevance of the research on hand becomes particularly important, regularly remains implicit. Transforming implicit knowledge into explicit knowledge, and consequently making it available for learning and further development, should weigh as a special challenge to social systemic research (Nonaka & Takeuchi 1995). Correspondingly at this point, in the sense of an interim result, the current research allows the differentiation between two levels of summarising. One level is that which produces, from the field on the basis of assertions, implicit knowledge. The second level is that of the partly inductive-combinational, partly deductive-analytical paradigmatic further development of available models, methods and instruments.

Practical application of results

In the terms of a practical application, the inductively gained results described above can again be summarised into five points:

1. Understanding teams as social systems makes it possible to further develop them as communities of practice. Hereby the reflection of concrete practice in contrast to an ideal-type profile of requirements is enhanced. The focus shifts to the 'how' of what the individual brings into the social systemic dynamic. This is more fruitful than an individual-diagnostic perspective, which only looks at what skill set the individual is equipped with. Smart is as smart does.

2. An understanding that teams behave like self-fulfilling prophecies accords significant importance to the qualitative processes of negotiation as an additional level of a team charter. Only teams that conceptualise themselves in consensus as high performance teams have a chance to become high performance teams as well.

3. Shifting the management and handling of social and cultural complexity from reactivity to pro-activity opens up a path to the sustainability of specific levels of performance in and of teams. The practice of regularly renegotiating a team as such is one side of the story. On the other side, and this seems to be of great significance, it comes down to creating an organisational or respectively, a social systemic framework that precisely supports these continual processes of negotiation.

4. The exploration, recognition and explanation of difference are fundamental to the structure of team resilience. Team resilience signifies a clear advantage with respect to environmental dynamics, possessing a far-reaching repertoire of reaction and action that secures the performance of the team, even when the original fit between system and environment has fundamentally changed.

5. Thriving on diversity describes a process of the complexity gains of a social system or a team with respect to the environment. And the complexity gain is not only in the enhancement of team resilience, but also in the possibility of transitioning, in a systematic and sustainable way, from a mode of reaction to a mode of pro-activity and thereby shaping the environment.

High performance teams are possible, but do not exist as a matter of course. They succeed on the grounds that a management of social and cultural complexity can be transformed into operational practice.

Systemic application of results

A social scientific reflection of the results described above brings three research and development foci near: ecology of paradigms, social innovation and competitive social design.

(a) Ecology of paradigms

When one deals with the paradigmatic reference of a community of practice within the framework of the management of social complexity, it leads not only to the gains in performance described above, but also asks far-reaching questions of how different communities of practice behave towards each other. Certain paradigmatic sets of models, methods and instruments justify a specific practice or discipline. Other paradigmatic sets devise other practices. One may, in considering the coexistence of different paradigms and practices, and this is a suggestion for further research, perceive that ecological perspectives are at the basis of this notion. Ecology should describe, in this relation, that the coexistence of different paradigms and practices could be mappable on a far-reaching scale that goes from competition as an extreme at one end of the spectrum, through to ignorance and up to symbiosis at the other extreme of the spectrum. It is interesting here to look at the terms and conditions of possibilities of different forms of coexistence with regard to the paradigms and practices whereby, and this is the special bon mot of evolution research, symbiosis and collaboration or co-operation are the drivers for development and not competition (Allen & Wyleto 1983; Hoekstra, Allen & Flather 1991).

(b) Social innovation

In these contexts, social innovation, the further social systemic development of diverse social settings, increases prospectively in significance. The majority of social systemic performance gains can be achieved by making perspectives in social and cultural complexity clear and more manageable, in order to facilitate further negotiation and development. However, over the course of time, performance gains in processes of continual improvement become marginalised. Then, it becomes essential to shift the focus to innovation and not just to improve what one does or that which is accorded as practice, but to also achieve further gains in performance by beginning to do things differently and further developing practice. This relationship between continual improvement and innovation is not new. What is new is applying this in social systemic contexts (Mulej 2006).

(c) Competitive social design

Competitive social design refers to two things. First, to the idea of social design, which allows the understanding that different social systemic settings can be more or less functional, more or less capable of performance. Along with this idea, there is the idea of evaluation, which social systemic settings seem more or less worthwhile. This links the idea of social design to a perspective of advantage within a competitive environment. Whoever succeeds in translating and managing social and cultural complexity into a capable social design receives performance gains and a clear advantage in competition (Klein & Tang 2008; Klein 2009b). It is not yet foreseeable how intense or conscious this competition will be in scope, but one can already assert and observe that those who do not succeed in managing social and cultural complexity will not only fail in competition, but will also inflict failure on themselves.

Conclusion

Besides the above summary, it is remarkable how difficult it is for the professional community of project managers to expose their practices to include social sciences insights (Flyvbjerg 2008). Scientists and project managers face difficulties in terms of formats and language to embrace and incorporate social knowledge. This is not only about the difficulties academics face understanding projects managers and vice versa but also about the difficulties academics and project managers meet amongst themselves within their own communities. It may be frustrating to see this entire knowledge sitting around without application, yet this was the challenge that comes with the territory. It is all about balancing social and cultural complexity.

References

Allen, T F H; Wyleto, E Paul. 1983. 'A hierarchical model for the complexity of plant communities'. *Journal of Theoretical Biology*, 101 (4): 529–540.

Ashby, W Ross. 1956. *An Introduction to Cybernetics*. New York: Wiley.

Baecker, Dirk. 1994. *Postheroisches Management*. Berlin: Merve.

Beneke, Jürgen, ed. 1998. *Thriving on Diversity. Cultural Differences in the Workplace*. Bonn: Dümmler Verlag.

Bourdieu, Pierre. 1998. *Praktische Vernunft. Zur Theorie des Handelns*. Frankfurt: Suhrkamp.

Breidenbach, Joana; Nyíri, Pál. 2008. *Maxikulti*. Frankfurt: Campus.

Flyvbjerg, Bent. 2008. *Making Social Science Matter. Why Social Inquiry Fails and How it can Succeed Again*. New York: Cambridge University Press.

Foerster, Heinz von. 1996. *Wissen und Gewissen. Versuch einer Brücke*. Frankfurt: Suhrkamp.

Nonaka, I; Takeuchi, H. 1995. *The Knowledge-Creating Company. How Japanese Companies Create the Dynamics of Innovation*. Oxford: Oxford University Press.

Hoekstra, T W; Allen, T F H; Flather, C H. 1991. 'The implicit scaling in ecological research. On when to make studies of mice and men'. *Bioscience* 41(3): 148–154.

Klein, Louis. 2005. 'Systemic inquiry – exploring organisations'. *Kybernetes* 34 (3/4): 439–447.

Klein, Louis. 2006.'Kultur, führung und kontingenz: Von der primären kontingenzerfahrung zur cultural mastery.' In *Interkulturelle Kooperation, Wirtschaftskybernetik und Systemanalyse*, edited by Bouncken, Ricarda B. Berlin: Duncker & Humblot.

Klein, Louis. 2009a. 'Organisational excellence: Die kompetenz zur selbst-innovation.' In *Unternehmenskybernetik 2020 – betriebswirtschaftliche und technische Aspekte von Geschäftsprozessen*, edited by GWS Berlin: Duncker & Humblot.

Klein, Louis. 2009b. 'Competitive social design. Die nächste soziale frage'. In *Minima*

Moralia der nächsten Gesellschaft, edited by Dettling, Daniel; Schüle, Christian. Wiesbaden: VS Verlag.

Klein, L. 2009c. Alpha Change – Den Kulturwandel wagen. *Wirtschaftspsychologie aktuell, voraus* 2. Halbjahr.

Klein, Louis; Tang, Suk-Han. 2008. 'Social design: Exploring the systemic conditions of sustainable change'. Paper presented at Changing the Change Conference, Turin.

Luhmann, Niklas. 1984. *Soziale Systeme*. Frankfurt: Suhrkamp.

Luhmann, Niklas. 2000. *Organisation und Entscheidung*. Köln: Westdeutsche Verlagsanstalt.

McGregor, Douglas. 2006. *The Human Side of Enterprise*. Columbus OH: McGraw-Hill.

Maturana, H; Varela, F. 1980. *Autopoiesis and Cognition*. Dortrecht and Boston: Reidel.

Mulej, Matjaž, ed. 2006. 'Systems, cybernetics and innovations'. *Kybernetes* 35 (7/8). Emerald, Bradford, UK: MCB University Press.

Shirky, Clay. 2008. *Here Comes Everybody*. New York: Penguin Books.

Surowiecki, James. 2004. *The Wisdom of Crowds. Why the Many are Smarter than the Few and How Collective Wisdom Shapes Business, Economies, Societies and Nations*. New York: Doubleday.

Wenger, Etienne. 1998. *Communities of Practice: Learning, Meaning and Identity*. Cambridge: Cambridge University Press.

Willke, Helmut. 1998. *Systemisches Wissensmanagement*. Stuttgart: UTB.

Chapter 3

The project as a socio-cultural system

Investigating humanitarian projects managed by volunteers in not-for-profit organisations

Shankar Sankaran

University of Technology, Sydney, Australia

Non-profit organisations – also known as the third sector or non-government organisations – are playing an increasing role in the political, social and economic spheres of many countries around the world including Australia. This paper will use the acronym NGO to refer to such organisations. Over the last two decades NGOs have become an object of considerable research interest. NGOs are responsible for several projects managed by volunteers, who may not be trained in project management methodologies. Efforts are now being made to help NGOs manage their projects more effectively. Some organisations have been set up in developing countries to help NGOs to be more effective in managing their affairs as they contribute significantly to the social capital of these countries. A joint project to educate project managers in NGOs has been recently created as a collaborative effort between the Project Management Institute, Learning for International NGOs and several prominent NGOs who are concerned about the effectiveness of projects managed by volunteers in their organisations. However, academic research in the area has been scarce. This paper describes a study being undertaken by an Australian academic on the complexities of projects managed by a voluntary organisation called Rotary Medical Aid for Children.

Prologue

I was sitting in a coffee house in Canberra next to the Canberra Convention Centre watching the joy of Yang Shi Yan and Lin Zhi Ying, two children from China, running around, taking photos using a mobile phone and chatting happily as the adults around the table sipped their coffee. Rob Wilkinson and I had just finished our presentation at the PMOz conference about a humanitarian project which had helped these children to live with dignity and hope for the future. Lin Zhi was born in China with Hirschsprung disease, and Yang Shi, also from a small Chinese village, had suffered from severe burns when she was four after an accident. As I watched the children play, the Chinese translator who had helped us during our presentations at the conference walked up to me and said: 'The children look really happy. But I am really concerned for Yang Shi as she is going back next week to live in a remote village in China with her family, where she has to cook for the whole family. She will not have a mobile phone to play with or be able watch the cars going by, as there are very few cars in her village'. This left me thinking about the socially complex issues faced by the volunteers who enthusiastically worked on saving these children's lives.

Introduction

The humanitarian project that helped Lin Zhi and Yang Shi is part of a program called Rotary Medical Aid for Children (ROMAC) managed by the Rotary clubs in Australia and New Zealand. The mission statement of ROMAC (2007/8) is 'to provide medical treatment for children from developing countries in the form of life- saving or dignity restoring surgery'.

The objectives of ROMAC are:

1. To provide hope where there is no hope.
2. To restore dignity to human life.
3. To transform a child's life.
4. To provide the best medical and surgical expertise (ROMAC 2007/8).

The ROMAC story started with the dream of a dedicated volunteer, Barrie Cooper, from Bendigo in Victoria, Australia, who was distressed by the sight of a child in Fiji who was too sick to be treated locally. The child was brought to Australia for treatment and the idea of ROMAC was born. Since its inception twenty years ago more than 400 children have been given a new lease of life. From a project management perspective each child treated by ROMAC can be considered a project as each case is unique. On talking to people involved in ROMAC projects it becomes clear that a ROMAC project is a complex undertaking managed by dedicated volunteers, Rotarians, caring families, doctors and surgeons supported by well-meaning stakeholders. The ROMAC program is governed by a board which has representatives in each state of Australia and New Zealand. The projects carried out by ROMAC volunteers have had higher rates of success than what is reported in the literature generally about project success (Turner 2009). Investigating the project management and decision-making processes used in these complex projects can be beneficial to the project management community to gain an appreciation of how humanitarian projects are managed by volunteer organisations in the not-for-profit sector. This paper describes a study being undertaken by the author to investigate such projects.

Why are we interested in project management practices in the not-for-profit sector?

Not-for-profit organisations or non-government organisations (NGOs) are often referred to as the third sector. Government and its agencies are normally considered the first sector while commercial organisations that operate for profit are considered the second sector.

According to Aneiher (2005, 4, 10) the third sector has gained more prominence and attention from educators and researchers over the past two decades due to the prominent part played by them in welfare provision, education, community development, international relations, environment, arts and culture. One reason why NGOs have become an emerging field of study is due to their impact on the daily life of people at the local, national and international levels. At the local level these organisation build communities and empower people. At the national level they are involved in the provision of welfare, healthcare and education, and form partnerships with private organisations to provide essential services. At the international level there are a number of international NGOs that participate in an international system of governance. NGOs play an important role in the welfare systems of our societies and take an active part in the social, economic and political aspects of many countries.

Both internationally and in Australia, NGOs have grown rapidly in terms of assets and complexity and have become major service providers. This is mainly because governments and government agencies are unable to provide these services efficiently and the private sector is not interested if there is no money to be made. NGOs are increasingly operating in areas where government and for-profit sectors also operate, and with significant financial and human resources at their disposal, are expected to achieve similar outcomes (Lyons 2001; Salamon 1994).

According to Lyons (2009), there are around 700,000 NGOs in Australia employing around 890,000 people (8.6 per cent of Australians employed), and they contribute A\$34 billion (or 3.4 per cent) to the gross domestic product. NGOs make a noticeable contribution to the national economy as well as employment.

There is an increasing interest from project management bodies such as the Project Management Institute (PMI) to help NGOs to manage their projects better. PM4NGOs is a joint effort between Learning for International NGOs or LINGOS (www.lingos.org) and the PMI (www.pmi.org), set up in 2007 due to a concern that 'NGO project managers often have significant responsibility for life-affecting (sometimes life-saving) projects, large financial budgets and even larger opportunity costs, yet very few of them have been trained in, or are certified in, the project management practices employed in other sectors' (Cattaway 2008, 1). An online community has also been created (www.pm4ngos.org) to create a community of practice for project managers in the NGO sector to share experiences. PM4NGOs also recognises that NGOs have a great deal of useful experience to share and vice versa. This has also been the findings of the author of this paper.

The founding members of PM4NGOs are Accion International, CARE, Catholic Relief Services, Habitat for Humanity International, Mercy Corps, The Nature Conservancy, Oxfam, Plan International, Save the C US and UK, World Vision US and International, LINGOs and the PMI Educational Foundation. According to Cattaway (2008, 2) these 12 NGOs employ around 15,000 project managers with annual project budgets of US\$ 4.7 billion.

Other organisations across the world working in the voluntary sector are also interested in improving the project management skills of their volunteers. The Directory of Social Change was set up in 1975 in the United Kingdom to help volunteer organisations become more effective. It has published *The Complete Guide to Creating and Managing New Projects* (Lawrie 2002) which is in its second edition. Rotary International (2009) has also produced a comprehensive guide to planning, executing and evaluating effective service projects.

Large organisations involved in international aid projects have provided guidelines for carrying out and evaluating projects that could be useful to voluntary organisations. Aid agencies such as USAID, AusAID and the UNDP are some of the agencies which advocate the use of the logical framework approach, which was developed in the 1970s and is based on management by objectives (MBO) (http://www.ausaid.gov.au/ausguide/pdf/ausguideline3.3.pdf).

The author feels that a dialogue between project managers in the commercial and public sector and project managers in the third sector would help the former to understand the intricacies and complexities of managing projects where traditional ways of evaluating projects using time, cost and scope may not be that important whereas realised benefits are. The project managers in NGOs could also benefit from this dialogue and enhance their project management practices to deliver better outcomes.

ROMAC projects

A typical ROMAC project follows the following steps:

1. The project starts when a child is referred to ROMAC from a developing country. The call usually comes from a local Rotary club, charitable organisation, church or an individual who is concerned about a child in distress.

2. An assessment is made by the ROMAC medical board about the possibility of treating the child and if it considers this feasible, the project is initiated.

3. Volunteer surgeons and a caring hospital are then identified including a date for further diagnosis and treatment.

4. Passports and visas are organised for the child and carer.

5. Transport is organised to bring the child and carer to Australia or New Zealand. In an emergency, such as a burn victim, it has to be arranged speedily.

6. A host Rotary club and local families (where possible, of the same ethnic background as the child), or volunteer Rotarians, are located in Australia or New Zealand to provide accommodation and care for the child and an accompanying carer.

7. A translator for the child and accompanying carer is found.

8. Sometimes a doctor from the country where the child comes from accompanies the child as well to witness or participate in the treatment to gain experience.

9. The major expenses are for travel, hospital and, in some cases, doctors' fees (although many doctors and nurses also provide their services free or at greatly reduced costs).

To accomplish all these activities ROMAC had to develop excellent relations with the Immigration Department to process visas, airlines (Qantas) and even the United Nations to obtain aircraft in an emergency.

The complexities of a ROMAC project

When the author started studying how ROMAC projects were carried out, he was amazed by how the volunteers managed to achieve significant outcomes with minimum resources. He found that they had to deal with many aspects of projects that are not encountered in commercial projects. Following is a list of such issues.

- *Scope* is often fuzzy and ambiguous: When a child is referred to ROMAC the decision is made to take the child on with minimum details. It is not clear how long it will take to treat the child and how many operations need to be performed, or whether the child can be treated at all.

- *Timeline* is uncertain: It is difficult to estimate how long the treatment would take as a child usually has to come for multiple visits.

- *Cost* is difficult to estimate: Due to the uncertainty surrounding the intensity of treatment costs can escalate and additional funds may have to be obtained for more treatment.

- *Risk* could be high: Often the surgery is life-saving surgery and the safety of the child is a big concern.

- *Human relations* are complex: People from several national cultures, ethnic backgrounds and professions come together to carry out these projects making it socially and culturally complex. Uncertainty surrounding the number of visits may also put a strain on caring families in the host country.

Yet 400 such children have been successfully treated over the past twenty years with the efforts of volunteers who may not be trained in project management methodologies or certified or accredited as project managers.

An analysis of ROMAC as a project using the nine knowledge areas of project management reveals that:

1. Scope is often determined at evaluation, acceptance and initial diagnosis, but could change as the treatment progresses.

2. Time is dependent on the length of treatment and availability of hospital, surgeons and appropriate support structure. Availability of medical support is uncertain, as it is imperative that no local child is disadvantaged in the host country as a consequence of a ROMAC project.

3. Cost can vary depending on length of treatment and number of visits. There is an initial allocation of costs but this can vary.

4. Quality is based on restoring basic functionality to the child.

5. Risks are primarily related to safety as well as success of the treatment. Safety is paramount. One of the unanticipated risks is what happens when the child goes back after treatment. This is a complex issue as the child is often given a great deal of care and attention in the host country and can enjoy many privileges which may not be available when the child returns home.

6. Human resource management issues are associated with looking after the child in the host country, finding a cultural match between the child and the host family.

7. Communication has to deal with two aspects. One is the reporting of progress to the stakeholders and the child's family. The verbal communication needs of the child and the carer also are to be taken care of.

8. Procurement issues are associated with travel, accommodation and the logistics of organising hospitals.

9. Integration is usually carried out by a group of volunteers and often rests with the local Rotary club which agrees to take on the project. (Not all Rotary clubs are involved in ROMAC projects.)

How is project success defined? It is gauged by whether the project has been able to give hope and dignity to the child for a better future.

An idea for conducting research

The author's interest in working with NGOs started when he was invited by the CEO of a church-based organisation offering health and community care services to help their operational managers learn strategic and project management skills. He conducted a workshop about project management using conventional methodologies based on PMBOK but the managers did not succeed in implementing their projects. The main reasons were the lack of organisational support and lack of confidence in carrying out projects. The organisation did not have a system to initiate and implement projects. The author realised that project managers in NGOs faced different challenges.

The author joined a Rotary club in 1996 and has undertaken some projects for them. He observed that some Rotarians had a knack for identifying and implementing projects with bare minimum resources and without having to use standard project management tools such as Gantt charts. In most Rotary projects it was the passion of the project champion combined with an ability to influence other volunteers to assist, as well as the ability to find funding as and when required, that contributed to its success.

When the author joined the Rotary Club of North Ryde in 2006 he came into contact with two Rotarians, Phil Isaacs and Rob Wilkinson, who were actively involved in ROMAC projects. He also met Ramesh Chand, from Fiji, and Wang Zhei Mei, from China, two children who came under the care of this Rotary club through ROMAC.

After a moving presentation made by Rob Wilkinson at a Rotary Conference in 2008, in Bathurst, on how Ramesh and Mei were given a new lease of life, the author became curious about finding out how such projects were managed. This was reinforced by being able to actually meet the children concerned and see for himself the difference ROMAC had made to their lives.

First phase of research

The author wanted to know more about how a ROMAC project was initiated, executed, monitored and closed but he had only a fuzzy idea from what he had heard and observed so far. He had some informal conversations with people who managed ROMAC projects in his club to find out more about how they were executed. His first opportunity to get a deeper insight into these projects came when he offered to do a presentation about the ROMAC project at the PMOz conference in Canberra in 2009 with Rob Wilkinson. The Canberra presentation was to be a trial run for a presentation he had planned at the EDEN doctoral seminar in ESC Lille in France later in the year. Presenting the project in Canberra with Rob Wilkinson gave him a clearer picture about ROMAC projects supported by several documents that Rob Wilkinson gave him about ROMAC.

The presentation at PMOz was well received although only a handful of participants attended it perhaps due to a lack of interest from commercial project managers. The few who attended it were moved by the change ROMAC had made to children's lives as the presenters were able to bring two children, Yang Shi Yan and Lin Zhi Ying, to the conference session.

The situation in France was different. There were nearly 40 academics, practitioners and doctoral students listening to the author's presentation. At the end of the presentation a prominent professor of project management,

Roland Gareis, thanked the author for reminding people about such humanitarian projects which are rarely written about. Some others felt that the project management community had much to learn from experiences of volunteers who managed projects like ROMAC. Alan Marpham from the Association of Project Managers UK provided the author with valuable information about what is being done by professional project management bodies to help NGOs improve how they conduct their projects. This has made him aware of the work done by LINGOs and PM4NGOs.

Upon his return, the author then searched for journal papers reporting research into how projects are managed in NGO's, but did not come across any papers discussing methodologies adopted by such organisations. However, there were papers that dealt with various aspects of development projects of relevance to his interest:

1. lessons learned (Youker 1999);
2. monitoring and evaluation describing an extension to the logical framework approach based on doctoral research at the Institute of Sustainable Futures at the University of Technology (Crawford & Bryce 2003; Crawford 2004);
3. analysis of performance (Ahsan & Gunawan 2008);
4. success factors (Diallo & Thillier 2005; Khang & Moe 2008);
5. approaches to project management in development projects in Africa (Muriithi & Crawford 2003).

The paper by Muriithi and Crawford (2003, 317) points out the necessity for modifications and extensions to conventional project management standards and practices to increase their applicability to cope with political and community demands, local realities, cultural and work values. Such issues could also be relevant to humanitarian projects like ROMAC.

Next phase

The next phase of the research is to interview people involved in ROMAC projects – Rotarians, ROMAC's board members, surgeons, caring families and also the initiator of the ROMAC idea Barrie Cooper to study ROMAC projects from multiple perspectives. Rob Wilkinson has agreed to provide access to these people. The author intends to also request to become a member of a ROMAC project team in the next project that his club undertakes and follow the project from conception to its implementation and closure.

In the meantime, the author intends to locate other organisations providing humanitarian services from Australian branches of organisations that funded the PM4NGOs initiative. He is also looking for collaborative researchers who are interested in this topic and intends to seek some funding.

Expected contributions from the research

The author expects that his investigation will result in a better understanding of how volunteers in NGOs carry out their projects successfully and what lessons the project management community could learn from them. He is particularly interested in the socio-cultural complex aspects of humanitarian projects and how decisions are made in such projects and how teams working on these experience emergence when faced with complex issues. The author is supervising a doctoral student who is studying the socio-cultural complexity of IT projects (Syed & Sankaran 2009) in large commercial organisations. The author would also be able to compare how commercial organisations and NGOs deal with such complexity.

Conclusions

There is increasing interest in how NGOs are managed as they have started playing major roles locally, nationally and internationally in economic, social and political spheres. Many NGOs carry out projects to implement their strategies and plans. Professional project management bodies are keen to help NGOs manage their projects better. However, the methodologies used by the commercial business world may not readily apply to NGOs due to the nature of their operations and the people who work for them, many of whom are volunteers. So there could be lessons that the project management community could learn from NGOs on how they manage their projects and how they deal with social and cultural complexities arising in these projects. Some work has already started by the author to study how one NGO manages a humanitarian project. The author also plans to compare ROMAC projects with projects carried out by other humanitarian organisations. The research described in this paper is expected to provide a clearer understanding of how NGOs manage their projects and the lessons that can be learned from these experiences. It is also likely to benefit NGOs who are interested in improving the way in which they manage their projects.

References

Ahsan, K; Gunawan, I. 2010. 'Analysis of cost and schedule performance of international development projects'. *International Journal of Project Management* 28: 68–78.

Anheier, H K. 2005. *Non-profit Organizations: Theory, Management, Policy.* Milton Park: Routledge, Milton Park.

Cattaway, C. 2008. *Introducing Project Management for NGOs.* Newtown Square: Project Management Institute.

Crawford, P; Bryce, P. 2003. 'Project monitoring and evaluation: A method for enhancing the efficiency and effectiveness of aid project implementation'. *International Journal of Project Management* 21: 363–373.

Crawford, P. 2004. 'Aiding aid: A monitoring and evaluating framework to enhance international aid effectiveness'. Ph.D. Thesis, Sydney: Institute of Sustainable Futures: University of Technology.

Diallo, A; Thuillier, D. 2005. 'The success of international development projects, trust and communication: An African perspective'. *International Journal of Project Management.* 23: 237–252.

Khang, D B; Moe, T L. 2008 'Success criteria and factors for international development projects: A life-cycle based framework'. *Project Management Journal* 39 (1): 72–84.

Lawrie, A. 2002. *The Complete Guide to Creating and Managing New Projects for Voluntary Organisations.* 2nd edn. London: Directory of Social Change.

Lyons, M. 2001. *Third Sector: The Contribution of Non-profit and Cooperative Enterprises in Australia.* Crows Nest: Allen and Unwin.

Lyons, M. 2009. *Non-Profit Fact Sheet.* Accessed 22 October 2009. Available from: http://www.mdsi.org.au/pub/Non_Profit_Fact_Sheet.pdf

Muriithi, N; Crawford, L. (2003). 'Approaches to project management in Africa: Implications for international development projects, '*International Journal of Project Management* 21: 309–319.

Rotary International. (2009). *Communities in Action: Guide to Effective Projects.* Rotary International. Accessed 22 October 2009. Available from: http://www.rotary.org/RIdocuments/en_pdf/605a_en.pdf

ROMAC (2007/8). *2007–8 Annual Review: Celebrating 20 Years of Changing and Saving the Lives of Underprivileged and Deserving Children,* Parramatta: ROMAC.

ROMAC 2007/8. *2007–8 Annual Review: Celebrating 20 Years of Changing and Saving the Lives of Underprivileged and Deserving Children.* Parramatta: ROMAC.

Salamon, L. 1994. 'The rise of the non-profit sector'. *Foreign Affairs* 73 (4): 109–122.

Syed, G; Sankaran, S. 2009. 'Investigating an interpretive framework to manage complex information technology projects'. Paper presented at the IRNOP IX Conference, Berlin, 11 October 2009.

Turner, R. 2009. 'Modelling success on complex projects: Multiple perspectives over multiple time frames'. Paper presented at the IRNOP IX Conference, Berlin, 11 October 2009.

Youker, R. 1999. 'Managing international projects: Lessons learned.' *Project Management Journal* 30 (2): 6–7.

Chapter 4

Information systems project management mentoring practices in multi-national corporations

Paul TM Leong

Auckland University of Technology, New Zealand

Felix B Tan

Auckland University of Technology, New Zealand

Mentoring is well documented in the research literatures of management, academia and counselling. Many notable professionals have testified to the effectiveness of mentoring. As an organisational support mechanism, mentoring generally enhances the likelihood of success for the mentee. There is anecdotal and practice-related evidence that suggests mentoring is effective in and within the information system (IS) project management process, but rigorous evidence of this fact remains absent. This state of play survey suggests that IS project management mentoring practice resonates with Mumford's (2002) general definition of mentoring as a trusted, confidential and protected relationship. Mentoring facilitates skills development through an active process of learning and exchange. The respondents in this qualitative web-based survey are IS project management practitioners (n=46) in multi-national corporations. The respondents generally perceived mentoring as positive as it produces tangible benefits of learning from someone more experienced. It is hoped that the IS project managers' insights on mentoring and experience as mentees will enrich the body of IS project management knowledge. The results of this state of play survey provide a theoretical foundation for future research related to the systematic adoption and application of mentoring, and potentially contribute to the promotion and enhancement of greater IS project success.

Introduction

Mentoring is generally well documented in the research literature from the fields of psychology, management, academia, counselling, social work and sociology (Tashakkori, Wilkes, & Pekarek 2005). The mentee generally learns from a more experienced person (or a group of people) by means of reflecting on past experiences. This intentional learning and exchange process of engaging with one another results in transformation and improvement (Brockbank, McGill & Beech 2002). The mentoring model of Wanberg, Welsh and Hezlett (2003) affirms that being mentored provides favorable career outcomes to the mentee as it brings about improvements in cognitive and skill-based learning. The experiential reflective learning that underpins the mentoring process is a valid and relevant approach to learning and development (Brockbank & McGill 2006; Brockbank et al. 2002). Jarvis (1987) appropriately sums it up as: 'all learning begins with experience'. There are many definitions of mentoring. According to Mumford's (2002) definition, mentoring is a relationship that is protected, where 'experimentation, exchange and learning can occur and skills, knowledge and insight can be developed'.

Individuals have benefited from and testified to the relevance of experiencing a mentoring relationship (Ensher & Murphy 2006; Gabbaro 1987; Thomas & Kram 1987). *The Blackwell Handbook of Mentoring* (Allen & Eby 2007) documents many innovative and multi-disciplinary approaches to the practice of mentoring. In general, mentoring is an organisation supporting mechanism but little research on the benefits to the organisation has been reported (Singh, Bains & Vinnicombe 2002). Similarly, in project management related studies, 'little systematic empirical research had been done to test the growing body of anecdotal evidence' on the benefits of mentoring (Dai & Wells 2004).

In a complex and fluid business environment, the management of potential success and business continuity is a necessity (Doughty 2002; Heracleous 2000). In this respect, business organisations are increasingly dependent on effective information systems (Raggad 1997). Successful, experienced and skilful IS project managers are in great demand. Effective IS project management that ensures IS project success is not only highly desirable but has become a priority for most businesses (Klein & Jiang 2001). The IS project manager as the single point of accountability/responsibility must learn not only to get ahead, but to deliver services and products that meet the needs of the business (Association for Project Management 1995; Heerkens 2001).

The IS project management process is a critical organisational/management challenge (Benko & McFarlan 2003; Xia & Lee 2004). It is an integral part of the implementation and deployment cycle of information systems. It is challenging, especially in managing the tight integration between the variety of business processes, priorities and information technologies (Benko & McFarlan 2003). The complexity of the project management process is further compounded in a more globalised business as IS projects are being increasingly implemented across multiple geographies (Powell, Piccoli & Ives 2004). The element of increased business sophistication with respect to organisational and business functions has also added to the complexity of the project management process (Rodriguez-Repisoa, Setchib & Salmeronc 2007). The high investment cost of information technologies and human capital (Johnson 1995) also accentuate the criticality of effectiveness in the IS project management process.

IS projects have had high failure rates (Johnson 1995). There are many documented IS projects that were not completed on time or within budget (Pinkerton 2003). On average, IS projects are more than a year late and cost twice their initial estimate (Moller & Paulish 1993). Studies indicate an alarmingly high failure rate of approximately 85 per cent (Klein & Jiang 2001). Only 20 per cent of large software systems are successfully implemented within the scheduled time and about two thirds of those experience cost overruns by almost 100 per cent (Jones 1995). These phenomena are widespread (Keil 1995; Tiwana, Keil & Fichman 2006). Notwithstanding these many failed IS project statistics (Lam & Chua 2005), there are also numerous IS projects implemented successfully (Fitzgerald & Russo 2005).

IS project failure has been attributed to many factors including unrealistic user expectations, lack of competent resources, project size, weak management, political rivalry and technical aspects of the system (Brown & Jones 1998; Drummond 1996; Markus & Keil 1994). Plant and Willcocks (2007) highlighted the significance of the project management process and it has been being cited as the reason for substantial project cancellation, significant cost over-runs and serious schedule slippage. The lack of project management skills has strongly contributed to IS project failure, in particular the lack of soft skills (Du, Johnson & Keil 2004; El-Sabaa 2001). Generally, this soft skill aspect has the greatest influence on the practice of project management. It is often described as an art and many include communication management, conflict management, vendors and suppliers management, human resource management and motivation and team building (Du et al. 2004; El-Sahaa 2001; Pant & Baroudi 2008).

Mentoring plays an important role in IS projects. In practice, the 'been there and done that' approach of mentoring in project management practice is exemplified in the government of New York State (OFT 2008) and in the Project Management Institute (www.pmi.org.nz). These two organisations have encouraged the practice of IS project management mentoring through purposeful adoption and application. The mentoring relationships provide a platform where limited resources are being utilised productively and facilitates the up-skilling process of project team members in the IS projects through experiential-based learning (Kolb, Boyatzis & Mainemelis 1999).

Despite the importance of mentoring in IS projects, little is known about the nature of IS project management mentoring in practice. This paper seeks to document the mentoring characteristics, relationships, patterns and trends within the boundary of the IS project life cycle. The objective is to provide some insights into the adoption and application mentoring in IS project management processes.

Research approach

This paper aims to further understand the phenomenon of mentoring as perceived by the IS project manager. A web-based survey approach was adopted based on the inherent advantages of cost benefit (Schmidt 1997), time efficiency (McCoy & Marks Jr 2001), quality of responses (Kiesler & Sproull 1986), human error reduction (McCoy & Marks Jr 2001) and broader distribution (Schmidt 1997).

The survey instrument was designed as an exploratory tool with the intention of gathering the data relevant to project management mentoring adoption and application within the IS project management life cycle. That is, the five project management process groups (Project Management Institute 2004). The survey questionnaires were framed along the following dimensions: rationale of adoption and application of mentoring; characteristics of adoption and application of mentoring; perceived benefits; barriers/obstacles; and the IS project managers' recommendation to fellow IS project managers. The questionnaires consist of a mix of open and closed questions together with ranking questions and multiple choices. That is, the questions include simple branching type of questions with a 'yes' or 'no' answer, multiple choice type questions with one or many mandatory selection(s), multiple choice type questions with an option for the respondents to insert personalised inputs and multi-point scales (i.e. Likert) type of questions where the respondents were asked to select a preferred option based on scale of 'Strongly Agree', 'Agree', 'Neither', 'Disagree' or 'Strongly Disagree'. The survey questionnaire was developed using the web survey tools of www.questionpro.com (under Student Research Sponsorship support).

A survey URL was created for the respondents to access the web-based questionnaires and provide survey feedback and comments. The survey was conducted during the period of 28 June 2009 to 6 September 2009. On average, the respondents took about 19 minutes to complete the questionnaire. A total number of 46 respondents completed the questionnaire. These respondents were from 26 of the 87 multinational corporations (MNCs). These MNCs are the World Class MSC (Multimedia Super Corridor) status companies (MSC 2009) and are based in Malaysia. They operate as local regional subsidiaries and as global offices. The respondents are IS professionals who generally are involved in IS project implementations with responsibilities of IS project management in one form or another.

The communication process with the selected participants was done via email where a unique URL was hyperlinked from the email message with an access password provided. This process ensured that only the selected participants who were assigned from the participating MNCs responded to the questionnaires. This research study took many other proactive steps to handle potential problems as the web-based survey data gathering approach is not without its limitations and concerns. These steps are to address the potential lack of security in the World Wide Web space and its inherently unrestricted access (Crawford, Couper & Lamias 2001). Additionally, an audit trial of the completed survey responses was printed and tallied against the respondents by way of email addresses.

To overcome a potentially low response (Witmer, Colman & Katzman 1999), this research study conducted pre-survey notifications and reminder email follow-ups during the data gathering time-window (Fox, Crask & Kim 1988). Concerns related to usage of and familiarity with the World Wide Web (Crawford et al. 2001) were not considered significant because the targeted respondents were IS professionals and they have a high affinity and natural inclination towards the World Wide Web.

At the completion of the data gathering stage, the data was analysed and presented in an aggregated format. The collected data was analysed and categorised along the afore-mentioned dimensions.

Results and analysis

A very low number of the respondents (slightly over 10 per cent) considered themselves as having no knowledge or a poor level of knowledge of mentoring. A substantial majority of the respondents (i.e. more than 80 per cent) ranked themselves as having a positive and a very positive attitude towards mentoring. While their level of knowledge is high and their general attitude is positive, 62 per cent of the respondents expressed a preference to be assigned an IS project mentor.

With regard to the involvement of a project mentor, slightly over 28 per cent of the respondents preferred a more experienced mentor, slightly over 24 per cent of respondents preferred an informal mentoring relationship and just over 18 per cent preferred an internal mentor.

Respondents were asked to rank benefits that are perceived to have been accrued in a mentoring relationship in IS project. Each of the top three reasons received more than 92 per cent of the agreement votes. The respondents' choices are in the order of:

1. accessibility to the wealth of professional expertise and experience of the project mentor;
2. knowledge gain from another perspective and learning new ideas;
3. enable and provide feedback, reflection and introspection of the project.

As for the rationale of mentoring adoption, each of the top three reasons received more than 94 per cent of the agreement votes. The respondents' choices are in the order of:

1. availability of a free and open exchange of knowledge and experience;
2. needs the guidance, support and encouragement of a more experienced IS project manager;
3. promotes learning on the job.

Figure 4.1 listed the top three general perceptions concerning mentoring in IS projects. Slightly more that 45 per cent of all the votes cast for this category considered mentoring an effective method for the development of potential and 33 per cent voted that it is best adopted in a spontaneous manner. The distant third-ranked perception (i.e. at a slightly over 7 per cent of the total votes) is that mentoring is only effective when the mentee's superior is involved. One of the respondents suggested the importance and necessity of soft skills mentoring in 'complicated and high-end' IS project.

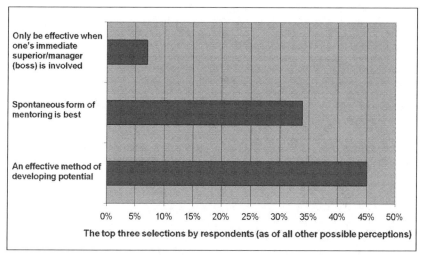

Figure 4.1. Perceptions concerning mentoring in IS project management

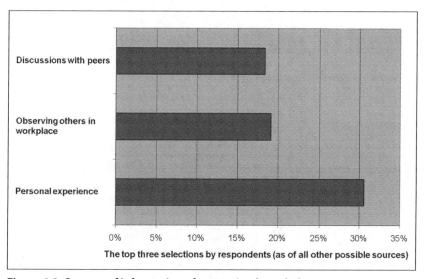

Figure 4.2. Sources of information of mentoring knowledge

As to the sources of mentoring knowledge, the top three sources considered by the respondents are summarised in Figure 4.2. The choices of 'observing others in workplace' and 'discussions with peers' received a slight over 19 per cent and 18 per cent of total votes respectively. The choice of 'personal experience' as a source of information about mentoring received the highest number of the total votes with slightly over 30 per cent. One of the respondents considered 'in-house training courses and materials' as a possible source of information.

Respondents were asked to rank the potential and perceived barriers that confront an IS project manager in the adoption of a mentoring relationship during an IS project. They are ranked in the order of:

1. non-availability of suitable mentors/experienced project managers (received slight more than 75 per cent of the respondents' agreement);

2. lack of available time within the project schedule (received slight more than 72 per cent of the respondents' agreement);

3. other project responsibilities interfering with mentoring (received slight more than 62 per cent of the respondents' agreement).

The preference for a trusted and confidential mentoring relationship received an almost unanimous vote of agreement. The top five rankings are displayed in Figure 4.3.

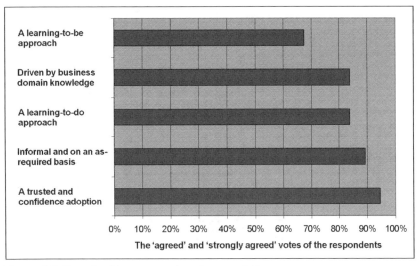

Figure 4.3. Perceived key mentoring characteristics

Lastly, the respondents were asked for their recommendations and advice to other IS project managers with respect to the adoption and application of a mentoring relationship in their respective projects. The advice of 'a need basis adoption' was ranked with an almost unanimous vote of agreement. Figure 4.4 summarises the recommendations.

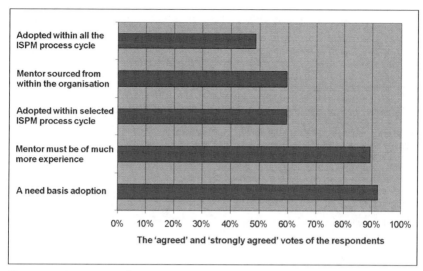

Figure 4.4. Recommendations to other IS project managers
Note: ISPM means IS project management

Conclusion

Not surprisingly, the survey results were consistent with Mumford's (2002) general definition of mentoring. Hence, IS project management mentoring is no exception. In this respect, the respondents indicated their almost unanimous agreement for the need for a trusted and confidential relationship. The preference is that mentoring should be adopted on a needs basis. The respondents cited the perceived benefit of being able to access the wealth of professional expertise and experience of an IS project mentor. An IS project mentor is generally someone who has much more experience as compared to the IS project manager. The main reason of adopting mentoring is the availability of a free and open exchange of knowledge and experience that much can be derived from such a relationship.

Broadly, the level of mentoring-related knowledge is considered to be high. One of the main sources of information about mentoring is personal knowledge. Generally, the attitude towards the adoption of mentoring within the IS project is positive. The non-availability of suitable mentors in the form of experienced project managers (that is, with more experience than the IS project manager) is generally perceived as a major barrier in the consideration of mentoring adoption. A large majority of the respondents expressed the preference to be assigned a IS project mentor.

It is hoped that these results will provide a foundation for future research to enrich the body of IS project management knowledge related to the systematic adoption and application of mentoring in the promotion and enhancement of greater IS project success. For example, it may lead to refinement of the IS project management process framework and better definitions of boundary issues vis-à-vis project management mentoring practice. It is also hoped that it can provide pragmatic recommendations and suggestions to the key stakeholders such as IS project manager practitioners and professionals, decision makers and owners of businesses.

References

Allen, T D; Eby, L T. 2007. *The Blackwell Handbook of Mentoring: A Multiple Perspectives Approach.* Oxford: Blackwell Publishing.

Association for Project Management. 1995. *APM Body of Knowledge (BoK).* 2nd edn. Buckinghamshire, UK: Association of Project Management.

Benko, C; McFarlan, F W. 2003. *Connecting the Dots: Aligning Projects with Objectives in Unpredictable Times.* Boston, MA: Harvard Business School Press.

Brockbank, A; McGill, I. 2006. *Facilitating Reflective Learning through Mentoring & Coaching.* Philadelphia, PA: Kogan Page Publishers.

Brockbank, A; McGill, I; Beech, N. 2002. *Reflective Learning in Practice.* Aldershot, UK: Gower.

Brown, A; Jones, M. 1998. 'Doomed to failure: Narratives of inevitability and conspiracy in a failed IS project'. *Organization Studies* 19 (1): 73–89.

Crawford, S D; Couper, M P; Lamias, M J. 2001. 'Web surveys: Perceptions of burden'. *Social Science Computer Review* 19 (2): 146.

Dai, C X; Wells, W G. 2004. 'An exploration of project management office features and their relationship to project performance'. *International Journal of Project Management* 22 (7): 523–532.

Doughty, K. 2002. 'Business continuity: A business survival strategy'. *Information Systems Control Journal* 1: 28–36.

Drummond, H. 1996. *Escalation in decision-making: The tragedy of Taurus.* Oxford: Oxford University Press.

Du, S M; Johnson, R D; Keil, M. 2004. 'Project management courses in IS graduate programs: What is being taught?' *Journal of Information Systems Education* 15 (2): 181–188.

El-Sabaa, S. 2001. 'The skills and career path of an effective project manager'. *International Journal of Project Management* 19 (1): 1–7.

Ensher, E E; Murphy, S E. 2006. *Power Mentoring.* San Francisco: John Wiley & Sons, Inc.

Fitzgerald, G; Russo, N L. 2005. 'The turnaround of the London ambulance service computer-aided despatch system (LASCAD)'. *European Journal of Information Systems* 14(3): 244–257.

Fox, R; Crask, M; Kim, J. 1988. 'Mail survey response rate: A meta-analysis of selected techniques for inducing response'. *Public Opinion Quarterly* 52 (4): 467–491.

Gabbaro, J J. 1987. 'The development of working relationships'. In *Handbook of Organizational Behaviour,* edited by Lorsch, J. Englewood Cliffs, New Jersey: Prentice Hall: 172–189.

Heerkens, G. 2001 *Project Management*. New York: McGraw-Hill Professional.

Heracleous, L. 2000. 'The role of strategy implementation in organization development'. *Organization Development Journal* 18 (3): 75–86.

Jarvis, P. 1987. *Adult Learning in the Social Context*. New York: Croom Helm.

Johnson, J. 1995. 'Chaos: The dollar drain of IT project failures'. *Application Development Trends* 2 (1): 41– 47.

Jones, C. 1995. 'Patterns of large software systems: Failure and success'. *IEEE Computer* 28 (3): 86–87.

Keil, M. 1995. 'Pulling the plug: Software project management and the problem of project escalation'. *MIS Quarterly* 19 (4): 421–447.

Kiesler, S; Sproull, L S. 1986. 'Responses effects in the electronic survey'. *Public Opinion Quarterly* 50: 402–413.

Klein, G; Jiang, J J. 2001. 'Seeking consonance in information systems'. *Journal of Systems and Software* 56 (2): 195–202.

Kolb, D A; Boyatzis, R E; Mainemelis, C. 1999. 'Experiential learning theory: Previous research and new directions'. In *Perspectives on Cognitive, Learning, and Thinking Style*, edited by Sternberg, R J; Zhang, L F. NJ: Lawrence Erlbaum.

Lam, W; Chua, A. 2005. 'Knowledge management project abandonment: An exploratory examination of root causes'. *Communications of the AIS* 16 (35): 723–743.

Markus, L; Keil, M. 1994. 'If we build it, they will come: Designing information systems that people want to use'. *Sloan Management Review* 35 (4): 11–25.

McCoy, S; Marks Jr, P V. 2001. 'Using electronic surveys to collect data: Experiences from the field'. Paper presented at the Americas Conference on Information Systems (AMCIS). Boston, August 3–5.

Moller, K H; Paulish, D J. 1993. *Software Metrics*. London, UK: Chapman & Hall.

MSC. 2009. *MSC Malaysia Company Directory*. Accessed 2 July 2009. Available from: http://www.mscmalaysia.my/topic/Company+Directory

Mumford, A. 2002. 'Choosing a development method'. In *Individual Differences and Development in Organizations*, edited by Pearn, M. England: Wiley.

OFT. 2008. *A State Agency that Provides Centralised Technology Policies and Services to Other New York State Government Entities*. Accessed 9 October 2008. Available from: http://www.oft.state.ny.us/Services/training/SrvTRPMMP.htm

Pant, I; Baroudi, B. 2008. 'Project management education: The human skills imperative'. *International Journal of Project Management* 26 (2): 124–128.

Pinkerton, W. 2003. *Project Management: Achieving Project Bottom-line Success*. New York: McGraw-Hill.

Project Management Institute. 2004. *A Guide to the Project Management Body of Knowledge (PMBOK)*. 3rd edn. Newtown Square, PA: Project Management Institute Inc.

Powell, A; Piccoli, G; Ives, B. 2004. 'Virtual teams: A review of current literature and directions for future research'. *The Data Base for Advances in Information Systems* 35 (1): 6–36.

Raggad, B. 1997. 'Information systems concepts: A guide for executives'. *Logistics Information Management* 10 (4): 146–153.

Rodriguez-Repisoa, L; Setchib, R; Salmeronc, J L. 2007. 'Modeling IT projects success: Emerging methodologies reviewed'. *Technovation* 27 (10): 582–594.

Schmidt, W C. 1997. 'World-wide web survey research: Benefits, potential problems, and solutions'. *Behavior Research Methods, Instruments, & Computers* 29 (2): 274–279.

Singh, V; Bains, D; Vinnicombe, S. 2002. 'Informal mentoring as an organisational resource'. *Long Range Planning* 35 (4): 389–405.

Tashakkori, R; Wilkes, J T; Pekarek, E G. 2005. 'A systemic mentoring model in computer science'. Paper presented at the ACM-SE 43: Proceedings of the 43rd annual Southeast regional conference.

Thomas, D; Kram, K. 1987. 'Promoting career-enhancing relationships: The role of the human resource professional'. In *Employee Career Development and the Human Resource Professional*, edited by M. a. M. London, Greenwood: Praeger Press.

Tiwana, A; Keil, M; Fichman, R G. 2006. 'Information systems project continuation in escalation situations: A real options model'. *Decision Sciences* 37 (3): 357–391.

Wanberg, C R; Welsh, E T; Hezlett, S A., eds. 2003. *Mentoring Research: A Review and Dynamic Process Model*. Vol. 22. Oxford, UK: Elsevier Science.

Witmer, D F; Colman, R W; Katzman, S L. 1999. 'From paper-and-pencil to screen-and-keyboard: Toward a methodology for survey research on the internet'. In *Doing Internet Research: Critical Issues and Methods for Examining the Net*, edited by Jones, S. London: Sage Publications: 145–161.

Xia, W; Lee, G. 2004. 'Grasping the complexity of IS development projects'. *Association for Computing Machinery. Communications of the ACM* 47 (5): 68.

Chapter 5

Contingent employment in IT versus learning to enhance project management capabilities

Chui-Ha (Tracy) Ng

RMIT University, Australia

It is increasingly common that information technology (IT) workers, including project managers, are employed on contingent contract terms. This may imply that IT is not considered important. In reality, it is the opposite. There is an increasing demand for better IT project management capability to deliver mission critical projects. This paper investigates whether there are connections between the contingent employment trend in the Hong Kong IT industry and the learning required to enhance project management capabilities. This study is a pilot study to an extensive research study of the related knowledge areas. Two large Hong Kong organisations, which are typical employers of an IT workforce, were studied. The analysis is based on a three-level (individual, group and organisational) learning-at-work model. The findings support the contention that a contingent hiring policy leads to different characteristics at the individual, group and organisational level learning of IT project management capabilities. At the same time, however, a lot of learning characteristics are equally evident across permanently and contingently employed IT professionals. In addition to identifying specific learning practices, this paper raises new questions and recommendations for further studies into IT project management learning and contingent employment policy.

Introduction

The role of the IT (information technology) professional is becoming strategic for organisations, and it is becoming more common-place for IT project managers to have seats in board-room meetings (McLean 2006, 36).

What McLean (2006) highlights above indicates that IT plays an increasing strategic role in today's business world. Literature reviews show that there is a clear demand for IT project management capabilities (Perelman 2007; Project Management Institute 2005).

A recent Australia case study (Ng 2008) found that many existing IT project managers learn their project management capabilities through on-the-job experiential learning. Learning at the individual, group and organisational levels was concluded to be essential for building and enhancing IT project management capabilities in a large organisation. An additional finding from the research was that contingent employment of IT professionals is increasingly common. However, individuals, groups and organisations lack the incentives to share knowledge and invest in project management capabilities enhancement. This phenomenon does not seem to align with the increasingly strategic roles of IT which leads to the demand for the continuous enhancing of IT project management capabilities. The same issue is observed in the Hong Kong IT industry. There, it is not unusual to find an IT project has over 50 per cent of the staff employed under contingent employment contract terms. The project manager may be one of them. The knowledge drain and lack of organisational learning observed in Ng's (2008) case study can also be observed in some large Hong Kong organisations that hire large pools of contingent IT professionals to deliver projects.

For the most part, contemporary studies on contingent employment practices have focused on human resource aspects (Anonymous 2006; Redpath et al. 2007) or on non-IT industries (Wong 2001). In relation to Hong Kong's IT industry and project management capabilities development, there are no published studies on how individuals, groups or organisations have prepared to acquire better project management capabilities in the context of an increasing number of IT professionals (including project managers) working under contingent employment contracts. Organisations employing IT staff do not consider that they have a responsibility to enhance practitioners' capabilities, especially when the employment is contingent. This employment trend will continue in the Hong Kong IT industry but the impacts on individual, group and organisational learning are unknown. This paper attempts to explore if there are connections between contingent employment in the Hong Kong IT industry and the learning required to enhance project management capabilities. It is a pilot study to an extensive research study of the related knowledge areas.

Contingent employment and IT

New organisations and contingent employment

In the twenty-first century, the rapid pace of change presents a range of challenges to organisations. In the workplace, computer technology has changed the nature of work (Hodson et al. 2008; Matusik et al. 1998). It increases productivity, creates new jobs, increases the pace of change and gives rise to faster economic growth. Technology also deskills some workers, displaces others and creates globalisation (Hodson et al. 2008; McMorrow 1999; Nesbit 2005) and increased competition in the world economy (Fuchs 2002; Hodson et al. 2008). These worldwide pressures force organisational restructuring, downsizing and contracting out (Peel et al. 2004; Webster 2005).

Organisations have employed various solutions to tackle these challenges such as flexible employment (Fuchs 2002), innovation and marginal employment (Hodson et al. 2008), core and non-standard dual employment (Nesbit 2005), and outsourcing (McMorrow 1999. Contingent employment is a common element in all of these organisational strategies. As Peel and Inkson (2004, 542) conclude: 'the growth in contingent employment arrangements has been one of the most significant human resource trends in recent times' (Belous 1989; Marler et al. 2002).

The workforce category of contingent employment includes those who do not have explicit or implicit contracts to stay with an organisation for an indefinite period of time (Redpath et al. 2007). The contingent workforce may consist of independent contractors, temporary workers, part-time workers, leased workers, self-employed individuals, home-based workers, individuals brought in through employment agencies, on-call or day labour and on-site workers whose services are provided by contract firms (Anonymous 2006; Gregory 2001; Matusik et al. 1998).

Recent trends show that new organisations may adopt multiple forms of employment at the same time such as standard versus non-standard (Kallenberg 2001), or core versus periphery (Atkinson 1984). According to Lepak, Takeuchi and Snell (2003), an organisation may simultaneously have four types of employment – knowledge-based employment (an internal employment arrangement; employees possess specialised skills that are critical), job-based employment (employees are acquired from labour market; skills are not specific; they meet clear performance objectives for a well-defined range of tasks), contract work (external individuals are contracted to perform tasks with limited scope, purpose and/or duration), and alliances/partnership (independent/autonomous external parties that have established ongoing partnership; applying specialised knowledge to perform tasks in some customised capacity).

Advantages versus disadvantages of contingent employment

New organisations have various rationales for creating different forms of contingent employment. The ultimate goal is to survive in a dynamic and competitive economy. From an organisational or employers' perspective, contingent employment brings in numerous benefits. Cost and flexibility is one of the key incentives (Allan & Sienko 1998; Gregory 2001; MacDougall et al. 2005; Matusik et al. 1998; Redpath et al. 2007). Employing contingent workers drives down labour costs (Gregory 2001; Matusik et al. 1998), cuts benefit and training expenditure (Allan & Sienko 1998) and reduces the cost of laying-off employees (Matusik et al. 1998). Hiring contingent workers is a temporary arrangement. This strategy enables organisations to have flexibility in managing fluctuations of demand by reducing or expanding their workforce (Matusik et al. 1998). It also enables organisations to avoid tackling the rigid hiring and firing rules of permanent employees and minimises the impact on downsizing (Allan & Sienko 1998). Lower costs and higher flexibility help organisations to respond speedily to changing market conditions and to achieve better returns on investments (Matusik et al. 1998; Redpath et al. 2007). The second benefit of contingent employment for organisations, mentioned mostly by scholars, is the acquiring of public knowledge (Allan & Sienko 1998; Gregory 2001; MacDougall et al. 2005; Matusik et al. 1998). 'Public knowledge' consists of knowledge not unique to any one firm, but that which resides in the external environment. It includes industry and occupational best practices. 'Private knowledge' is unique to the firm and a source of competitive advantage (Matusik et al. 1998, p. 683). Contingent workers are hired because they possess the expertise that the employers require. Valuable performance-enhancing or specialised knowledge and skills are imported (Gregory 2001; MacDougall et al. 2005; Matusik et al. 1998). Some employers utilise this as part of their hiring strategy in order to get a chance to preview a worker's ability and work habits before committing to a regular position (Allan & Sienko. 1998; Gregory 2001). Another advantage is the development of private knowledge. Contingent employment helps organisations to focus the company on core competences (Gregory 2001). Their knowledge-based employees (Lepak et al. 2003) can utilise firm-specific private knowledge to gain an advantage in the market. Simultaneously, contingent workers bring in public knowledge that provides a stimulus to internal employees. The cross-fertilisation of existing private knowledge with fresh public knowledge produces new private knowledge (MacDougall et al. 2005).

Employers are not the only beneficiaries of contingent employment. Contingent workers may also benefit from such arrangements. They experience career and personal development by accumulating diverse competencies through variety of work and assignments. They have opportunities to work in different organisations, industries and projects. Contingent work can be rewarding and enjoyable (Peel et al. 2004). In addition, contingent employment provides flexibility to individuals. Contingent workers have boundaryless careers and freedom of choice. They have higher autonomy and flexibility, higher mobility and better control over their own activity. They can adjust work commitments to fit their personal circumstances. They also have advantages over permanent employees in terms of remaining separate from company politics and having less commitment (Allan & Sienko 1998; Peel et al. 2004; Redpath et al. 2007). The opportunity of having higher wages due to their specialised skills (Redpath et al. 2007) is also attractive to contingent knowledge workers.

Nevertheless, contingent employment also has drawbacks that organisations need to balance against its advantages. Organisations obtain public knowledge from contingent workers. By the same token, there is the chance of leaking private knowledge to the public domain or competitors. Private knowledge leakage may lead to imitation by competitors and a loss in differential advantage and cost advantage (Matusik et al. 1998). Cost is major incentive to hire contingent workers, however, organisations may pay higher hourly rates or more money to contingent workers when they do not pay for additional employment-related benefits (Matusik et al. 1998); they also have to pay a premium to acquire the right expertise (Redpath et al. 2007). The attitude and quality of work of contingent workers may also be hidden costs. Contingent workers may be less devoted to the company and to productivity. There is a potential production and management efficiency issue (Anonymous 2006; Gregory 2001; Matusik et al. 1998). The performance of contingent workers may decline as their termination day approaches. Loss of skills, knowledge and experience (Hall et al. 2008), loss in continuity and quality, and difficulty in implementing process improvement are common issues. The management of contingent workers is also problematic. The on-and-off nature of a contingent workforce makes the associated hiring and retention tasks difficult. Human resources personnel may not manage all contingent workers. Organisations must also deal with the management issue of how to blend contingent workers with the core workers to avoid overt mistrust, poor working relationships, or conflict (Allan & Sienko 1998).

From an employee's perspective, there are numerous disadvantages to being a contingent worker. The first concern is the lack of career development. Organisations do not look after the career of contingent workers (Peel et al. 2004). There is no opportunity to get the experience or training to progress to the next level of proficiency. Moreover, workers are normally contracted to work on the same job. There is no opportunity to develop management skills. Career plateau is a common phenomenon (Peel et al. 2004; Redpath et al. 2007). Contingent employment is a fit-for-now; it is not a good long-term career fit. Contingent work is not a preferred working condition to certain contingent workers (Redpath et al. 2007). The second disadvantage is the absence of training and development provided by organisations. Contingent workers are hired for their specialised skills and knowledge. Employers do not provide training/development funding nor longer-view investment in these workers. This leads to the absence of formal training and qualification opportunities. On the other hand, contingent workers are expected to maintain and enhance their skills to secure employment (Peel et al. 2004; Redpath et al. 2007). This brings the third disadvantage – job security and stability. Contingent work by nature contains the risk of unemployment, job insecurity and employment uncertainty (Allan & Sienko 1998; Gregory 2001; Peel et al. 2004; Redpath et al. 2007). Contingent workers have little control over the length of contracts (Redpath et al. 2007). They always have to deliver high performance to ensure future employability and to overcome fear of job insecurity (Redpath et al. 2007). They have to keep changing jobs and workplaces (Peel et al. 2004). Some contingent workers find this costly and tiring. They may be unable to balance work and family or personal life because they have to move to follow job opportunities. Some are frustrated at having no paid vacations and have little time off (Redpath et al. 2007). Contingent employment also makes it difficult to take on long-term financial commitments or to secure access to credit (Gregory 2001; Redpath et al. 2007). Life is less predictable and workers experience lower stability and more changes (Peel et al. 2004). The fourth disadvantage is the lack of a sense of inclusion. Contingent workers may feel their status is lower than that of regular employees (Gregory 2001) and that they are not a full member of the social and operational fabric of the organisation. They are excluded from organisational events and are not part of the employer family (Allan & Sienko 1998; Peel et al. 2004). Last but not least, contingent workers may have lower pay, less benefits and poorer working conditions than permanent employees (Gregory 2001).

Table 5.1 below summarises the advantages and disadvantages of contingent employment as discussed above.

	Organisation perspective	Contingent worker perspective
Advantages	Cost and flexibility Acquiring public knowledge Developing private knowledge	Career development through variety of work Flexibility and autonomy Higher wages for specialised skills
Disadvantages	Leakage of private knowledge Higher pay to acquire right expertise Potential attitude and work quality issues Contingent workforce management issues	Career plateau Absence of training / development Lack of job security Lower sense of inclusion Lower pay and benefits

Table 5.1. Advantages and disadvantages of contingent employment

Contingent IT professionals and project managers

New organisations include those in the IT sector. Strategies employed by new organisations are also applicable to the IT sector. The IT industry is among the most fast-paced industries and 'changes in the IT sector were most frequently related to the unpredictable nature of the work due to technological developments ... no firm can actually promise that the work you are doing today will remain the same tomorrow' (Loogma et al. 2004, 336). In the IT industry, even large corporations like IBM, HP and AT&T are 'making continued employment explicitly contingent' (Rousseau et al. 1996, 247). Recent reports reveal that the demand for IT temporary workers is expected to outpace permanent employment (Anonymous 2007a) and temporary employment may grow three times as fast as total employment over next decade (Anonymous 2007b). According to the US Newswire (Anonymous 2007b), there is 'Strong demand for IT workers to continue with no end in sight. The top five occupations expected to experience the largest annual growth in temporary employment in the coming decade are all information-technology related'.

IT skill shortage is not news (Hall et al. 2008; Holland et al. 2002). IT workers are known as 'gold-collar workers' (Holland et al. 2002). They have highly paid but challenging jobs. Holland et al. (2002) see the shortage of IT skills combined with the trend of contingent employment as a major concern for organisations in developed economies. Sullivan (2008) has similar concerns over the situation of project managers. Sullivan (2008) sees the competition for project managers as similar to that for IT workers. Organisations are head-hunting project managers from one another. Sullivan (2008) empathises that you may 'call it sharing, stealing, enticing [but] we all have to go to the same pool to get people. You have to raid your competition and they do the same' (p. 54). There is only one pool of project managers in any economy; the trend of having project managers employed on contract terms may be risky. He sees 'more companies ... contracting project managers for the duration of a project instead of making them part of the staff ... along with all this new-found popularity comes the danger of project management becoming a victim of its own success'(p. 58).

Characteristics of contingent IT professionals

The advantages and disadvantages for new organisations utilising contingent employment as a strategy are applicable to the IT sector. However, from the findings of Gregory (2001), some characteristics of contingent employment in IT sector are different from other industrial sectors. The characteristics specific to the IT sector are summarised as follows:

1. Different pay rates: Contingent IT employees receive more than regular IT employees, but less benefits. This is not a major concern for contingent IT workers.

2. Focus on core competencies: IT services are not directly related to the main processes of the company. Contracting in IT saves money.

3. Acquiring specialised skills: IT skills are complex and change rapidly. It is advantageous to contract out IT functions to avoid the need for extensive, on-going training of IT workers. IT skills are non-firm specific making them easily transferable.

4. As part of hiring strategy: The IT sector experiences high demand for and a low supply of workers with complex IT skills. Organisations see that IT professionals are less likely to be interested in regular employment without some other non-pecuniary inducements.

Gregory (2001) believes that IT professionals' loyalty is owed less to their employer than it is to their career. They are highly mobile and lured by new jobs, which offer technical challenges or opportunities for self-development. Holland et al. (2002) express a similar view. They see that 'gold-collar' employees will manage their own careers and direct their own training and development for a broader range of skills and accept greater role ambiguity and responsibility.

From the above discussion, it may be concluded that the twin phenomena of strong demand for IT talents (including project managers) and the growth in temporary employment co-exist and impact upon each other in the IT sector. The advantages and disadvantages imposed by contingent employment consistently include two elements: finance and knowledge. Cost and wages are the basic financial considerations of employers and employees respectively on contingent employment. In a knowledge-intensive industry such as IT, knowledge plays an ever important role. Organisations demand a skilful workforce (including project managers) and individuals seek to enhance their employability.

Learning to enhance IT project management capabilities

IT is a 'learning-intensive' industry. According to the Hong Kong Computer Society (HKCS 2007, 4):

> People generally agree that IT is a knowledge-intensive industry. It means professionals practicing in IT industry are well trained in a variety of disciplines. At the same time, IT is by far one of the most learning-intensive industries of today. Its practitioners are required to continuously upgrade their skills throughout the career life. This constant requirement of new skills in the IT industry has resulted in the regular displacement of old job categories and the creation of new ones.

In this paper, the term 'IT project management capabilities' is loosely defined. The online Compact Oxford English Dictionary (2007) defines 'capability' as simply 'the power or ability to do something'. Various project management methodologies have defined their own terminologies on the body of knowledge and competencies or skills related to project management (Bentley 1997; Project Management Institute 2004). The IT industry is highly dynamic, the content of IT project management 'capabilities' is also continuously changing. The focus of this paper is how to enhance IT project management capabilities. It will not focus on specific capabilities. Thus, the simple definition of 'IT project management capabilities' is the 'ability to perform IT project management actions'. This section surveys the literature on IT project management learning and capability enhancement practices. Common practices in IT groups/departments and among individuals in large Hong Kong organisations are also discussed.

Informal learning

According to Day (1998, 31) 'researchers discovered that up to 70 per cent of learning actually takes place informally'. In fact, many project managers began their career as an 'accidental project manager' (Baccarini et al. 2006; Ensworth 2001; Graham 1992; Pinto et al. 1995). Informal learning is essential to most IT project managers.

Challenging work and on-the-job learning

Similar to Silicon Valley engineers, IT people 'seek challenge, variety and change in the contracts undertaken, enabling not just personal stimulation but the development of new career-relevant skills' (Peel et al. 2004, 554). Webster (2005, 5) also notes that 'on-the-job learning and skills maintenance are considered critical in the IT professions'. IT contractors look for jobs where they have the opportunity to learn from colleagues and engage in problem solving (Loogma et al. 2004, 336) in order to enhance their marketable skills.

Marketable skill learning

In contingent employment conditions, occupational commitment is likely to replace organisational commitment (Loogma et al. 2004, 325). Individuals assess their career opportunities and may change occupation and jobs in order to remain competitive in the labour market (p. 325). Contingently employed IT workers are keen on learning marketable skills in their professional.

Communication networks

With frequent change of jobs, contingent employees have a network of colleagues, customers and employment agencies. Such channels provide them with information about the labour market and the skills that are in demand. Moreover, 'the IT sector informal communication networks such as virtual and web-based communities play a significant role in creating professional belonging and enhancing self-development. These kinds of informal communities give a sense of togetherness as "IT people" and provide a platform for problem solving and learning' (Loogma et al. 2004, 332). The contingent IT workforce acquires information on what to learn and actually learns from these communication networks.

E-learning

Regardless of whether IT people are contingent contractors or permanently employed by organisations, they all rely on the Internet to learn informally. According to Sauve (2007), research into the impact of e-learning shows 'more than 80 per cent of adult learning takes place outside the classroom' (p. 22).

Formal learning

Formal qualifications cannot guarantee employability, but are important. Nerland & Jensen (2007) agree that 'strategies for securing employability may take the form of a more formal approach to learning' (p. 267).

Certifications

Multinational companies and providers of new technologies offer certifications for working with their technologies. These emerge as important requisites for obtaining external work contracts (Nerland et al. 2007, 265, 267). Contingently employed contractors may self-study or attend formal classes (including e-learning mode classes) to take examinations and obtain professional certifications.

For project management certification, the most popular programs are PMP (project management professional) (Project Management Institute 2004) and PRINCE2 (Project IN Controlled Environments) (Bentley 1997). These certification programs are not IT-specific. In 2006, Hong Kong has 1100 certified PMP (Cheung 2006, 6). For an IT-specific project management certification scheme, the HKITPC (Hong Kong Institute for IT Professional Certification) pioneered the first IT professional certification scheme in 2007. Project Director – CPIT (PD) was launched in 2007 and Associate Project Manager – CPIT (APM) was launched in 2009 (HKITPC 2009).

Formal education

Loogma et al. (2004) see 'formal education is still very much appreciated … although it is not necessarily a precondition for a future career in the [IT] sector' (p. 333). Unfortunately, Perelman (2007) finds that 'CIOs argue, and complain that educational institutions are not putting adequate focus on these skills through coursework' (p. 1). Most undergraduate programs are not designed to educate undergraduates to be project managers (Dulaimi 2005). In a study on how university professors teach project management for information systems (IS), Reif and Mitri (2005) find that 'over 200 faculty members … reported they are teaching PM (project management) components in various (undergraduate) courses, with just 25 per cent teaching an entire course dedicated to PM' (p. 134).

Hong Kong's situation resembles the descriptions above. By searching the curricula of six major Hong Kong universities that offer IT-related bachelor degree programs (computer science, information systems, information engineering, etc.) in 2008, it found that IT/software project management was consistently excluded from the core course lists. About 50 per cent of these undergraduate programs had IT/software project management as one of the elective courses. For post-graduate programs, only three universities offered project management master programs. Two of them were on construction/real estate project management and the other was a generic project management program. None of them were IT-specific. Similar to the undergraduate programs, IT/software project management was usually taught as one of the elective courses in IT-related master programs. Only two universities had project management as a core course in their Master of Information Systems programs. As a whole, there was no degree program focused on IT project management.

Nevertheless, there is an abundant supply of short courses on project management from industrial bodies or training institutes in Hong Kong. Most of these courses are tailored for industrial project management certification programs like PMP (Project Management Institute 2004) and PRINCE2 (Bentley 1997). With the popularity of such training programs and the push for IT professional credentials (e.g. Certified IT Project Director of HKITPC) in the industry, more Hong Kong employers are searching for IT project managers with formal qualifications.

Project management capabilities learning at work

> The increasing competitive nature of the economy, and demographic, occupational and workplace change, have had a significant impact on the nature of the workplace ... The skill mix required by organisations is changing ... As such, workplace learning ... is taking on an increasingly important role in the education and training of the workforce (Johnston, Hawke, McGregor, & Johnson, 2002, 50 cited in NCVER, 2003, 1).

Learning from experience in the workplace is crucial to IT project managers and research shows that project managers generally have limited formal training on project management (Crawford et al. 1999; Dulaimi 2005; Turner 2003). Learning at work is not a new educational concept. Many scholars have offered models of learning at work (Billett 2001; Boud et al. 1999; Burns 2002). Among the many different models, at least three learning models propose that learning happens at individual, group and organisational levels. Figure 5.1 illustrates how Turner (2003, 42) sees the relationships between individual, team and organisation learning.

Crossan, Lane and White's (1999) three-level (individual, group and organisational), four-process (four-Is – intuiting, interpreting, integrating and institutionalising) learning model (see Figure 5.2) is a popular organisational learning approach.

Similarly, the process model of learning at work from Jarvinene and Poikela (2006, 182) that integrates Kolb's (1984) experiential learning model, Nonaka and Takeuchi's (1995) knowledge creation model and

Crossan et al.'s (1999) organisational learning approach, emphasises there are three contexts of learning. They are individual learning, shared learning and organisational learning (see Figure 5.3).

In this paper, the analysis of two case study organisations is based on a generic three-level learning model where learning happens collaboratively at individual, group and organisational levels.

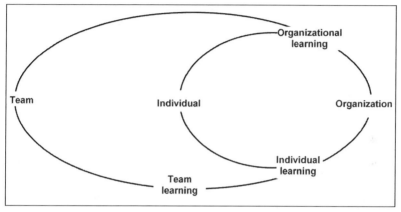

Figure 5.1. Relationships between individual, team and organisation learning (Turner 2003, 42)

Learning/Renewal in Organizations: Four Processes Through Three Levels		
Level	**Process**	**Input/Outcomes**
Individual	Intuiting	Experiences
		Images
		Metaphors
	Interpreting	Language
		Cognitive map
		Conversation/dialogue
Group	Integrating	Shared understandings
		Mutual adjustments
		Interactive systems
Organization	Institutionalizing	Routines
		Diagnostic systems
		Rules and procedures

Figure 5.2. Crossan, Lane and White's (1999) organisational learning approach

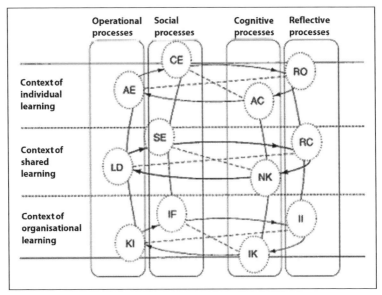

Figure 5.3. The process model of learning at work (Jarvinen et al. 2006, 182)

Research method

This is a pilot study for an extensive research study of the related knowledge areas of IT project management learning and contingent employment policy. The objective of the study is to identify findings that will be utilised to refine further research studies.

Based on the survey of the literature on the contingent workforce in Hong Kong (HKCS 2004; OGCIO 2008a; 2008b; 2008c), IT departments of government bureaus/departments and IT service providers are the two major categories of employers of contingent IT workers. One representative large organisation from each of the two categories of employers was selected for this study. The first is a large Hong Kong public organisation (hereafter referred to in this paper as 'IT-PUB'). It utilises a high percentage of contract IT staff with some of them coming from the Office of the Government Chief Information Officer (OGCIO), which coordinates IT contract staff services in the Government through the establishment and administration of 'body-shopping' contracts (i.e. T-Contracts) (OGCIO 2008a). The other organisation is a large IT service provider (hereafter referred to in this paper as 'IT-SVR') that also employs a high percentage of contingent IT professionals including project managers.

The pilot study was carried out as a case study (Yin 2003). Table 5.2 summarises the demographic data of the two organisations considered in the case study. In each organisation, one participant is in a managerial role in the group under study and the other is employed (or has been employed) as a contingent project manager in that group. Open-ended interviews were conducted with each participant.

The case studies

IT service providers and IT departments of government bureaus/departments are among the major employers of contingent IT workforce in Hong Kong. An organisation from each of these two categories of organisation is studied in this exploratory study.

IT-SVR (see Table 5.2) is a multi-national IT service provider. The Hong Kong branch is a sales office delivering various IT services to the Hong Kong community. The group under study is the IT service delivery business unit that specialises in systems integration and IT project delivery. The organisation has over 800 permanent employees in Hong Kong. There are more than 200 staff in the group under study, but only 20–30 per cent are permanently employed (Type 0). All others are under different employment contract terms. A small percentage of contract employees have a direct contract (Type 1) (see Table 5.2) with IT-SVR and while the majority of the contract employees are hired under agency contracts (Type 2) (see Table 5.2). IT-SVR procures IT services from these contingent workers' employers that play the role as agency and provide human resources services to their employees. IT-SVR utilises its own permanent staff, direct contract staff and agency staff to deliver projects and IT services to its customers. In addition, IT-SVR uses sub-contractors and off-shore development centres in mainland China to partially fulfil the contractual obligations to its customers. In theory and in practice, some projects' team members may include permanent staff, direct contract staff, agency staff, sub-contractor(s)' staff and off-shore development centre(s)' staff.

IT-PUB is an executive arm under a government statutory body that delivers public services to the general public of Hong Kong. It serves more than one third of the population of 7 million. It employs over 2000 staff including both permanent and contract employees. The group under study is the internal IT department of IT-PUB. It is a typical end-user organisation (VTC 2006). There are more than 150 IT employees in the group under study, with 40–50 per cent of these staff permanently employed as civil servants (Type 0). Similarly to IT-SVR, IT-PUB also has a small percentage of contract employees (Type 1) who have direct contracts with the statutory body. A substantial number of contract employees are hired through T-contracts (Type 2) or skill bulk contracts (Type 3). These contract types are both agency contracts; the major difference is that the T-contract vendors are sourced by the OGCIO and the skill bulk contracts are procured by IT-PUB. The IT department of IT-PUB utilises its own permanent staff, direct contract staff, T-contract staff and skill bulk contract staff to deliver IT services to various departments of IT-PUB. In addition, IT-PUB outsources IT projects through different procurement methods, like tender and standing contracts, to IT service providers such as IT-SVR. These project teams may work on-site at IT-PUB's venues (Type 4) or at the IT service providers' own venues. Therefore, at IT-PUB's IT department, Type 0 to Type 4 staff may exist and work together as a team.

	IT-SVR	IT-PUB
Industry	Information technology	Public services
Business nature	Multi-national IT service provider	Local public services provider serving one third of the Hong Kong population.
Organisation	Local office delivering software and hardware products, systems integration services and IT projects to customers in various business and public sectors	Executive arm of the related public services under a government statutory body
IT group under study	IT service delivery business unit specialised in systems integration and IT project delivery	Internal IT department of the organisation
Total no. of local staff	800 + (permanent staff)	2000+ (permanent + contract staff)
Total no. of staff in the IT group	200+ (permanent + contract staff)	150+ (permanent + contract staff)
Permanent staff % in the IT group	20–30%	40–50%
Contingent workforce % in the IT group	70–80%	50–60%
Outsourced IT projects	Subcontracting to local vendors and off-shore development centres are common	Approx. 50%
Types of IT workforce in the IT group	Type 0: Permanent staff Type 1: Direct contract staff Type 2: Contingent agency contract staff	Type 0: Civil servants Type 1: Staff signing direct contract with statutory body Type 2: Body shopping T-contractors Type 3: Body shopping – skill bulk contractors Type 4: Total outsourced project staff

Table 5.2. Demographics of case study organisations

Learning IT project management capabilities

The four participants of the two organisations expressed their views on enhancing project management capabilities in their roles as management and contingent project manager. Their first response was that there is little or no difference between permanently employed or contingently employed project managers. Following further discussion, however, they identified a number of distinctive differences in certain aspects of learning at individual, group and organisational levels. In fact, both IT-SVR and IT-PUB's participants expressed concern over the future of the Hong Kong IT industry given the increasing trend of using contingent workers.

> Today's IT labour market direction is not healthy from my view (Participant A).

> Today IT services are purchased. There is no investment on the resources, and a lack of home-grown experts. IT practitioners (especially contractors) look for well-being of self. They don't spend time/energy to invest on learning. Contract term employment normally has less salary, less benefits, no training or development, no career advancement path, etc. (Participant C).

In the following sections, the views of the four participants are analysed regarding learning and enhancing IT project management capabilities at individual, group and organisational levels in large organisations. At each level, the learning characteristics that are common to both permanent and contingent project managers are considered and this is then followed by a discussion of the learning characteristics that are specific to contingent project managers.

Enhancement of project management capabilities at the individual level

Learning opportunities and practices shared by both permanent and contingent employees

> By nature, project management job is contingent. There is start day and end day. Such a job can be outsourced by its nature (Participant B).

> There is no difference between permanent or contingent project managers. The role of the organisation in project management skill advancement is minimal. Most learning is from on-the-job experience.

Moreover, training programs from professional bodies are open to all. There is no need to rely on organisational support (Participant D).

As project management is contingent by nature, the role of a project manager on a project is also contingent. The views of the contingent project manager participants from both case study organisations were similar. IT project managers rely a lot on experiential learning at the work place. Project managers can always gain and enhance their project management capabilities from their project experience. Both contingent project manager participants agreed that the project manager's role is critical to project success. However, they felt that there was nothing wrong for a project manager to be contingently employed if the tenure of employment is long term (e.g. two years or more) and the project manager has job security. With longer periods of tenure, the project managers' status and authority in the organisations closely resembles that of permanent employees.

Individuals learning to be project managers normally take a bottom-up approach. They start from some hands-on technical positions in IT projects. With time, they start to lead small teams on simple tasks and gradually move on to lead larger teams on more complex tasks. Nowadays employers prefer project managers to have formal qualifications; and to advance their careers, it is helpful for IT practitioners to acquire some form of qualification like project manager certification. Nevertheless, on-the-job learning is essential to be a good project manager. Some form of mentoring and apprenticeship from senior project managers is very useful. Both contingent project manager participants consider that this is difficult to achieve regardless of the individual's employment terms. It is not easy to identify good mentors with the right skills and characters. Furthermore, both project manager participants felt that project managers need to have some characteristics that cannot to be taught in the form of project management skills.

> Project managers need to have the right characteristics like being mission-oriented, understanding project objectives and being able to manage people and tasks. Not everybody can be a project manager (Participant B).

> Project manager's capabilities determine project success, but this is not the only factor. Project manager's characteristics determine the way they solve problems, face challenges, make decisions and use power ... Project managers may apply skills and adhere to project management

processes ... but more importantly, they needs to have the spirit to apply the processes and skills (Participant D).

Learning opportunities and practices specific to contingent employment

In fact, each project needs to 'find the right person to do the right things' (Participant B). Organisations need to employ appropriate project managers with the necessary domain knowledge and experience. It may not be easy to find such skills internally. The dynamic and rapidly changing nature of IT technologies make this even more difficult. Contingent employment brings in the right skills and the necessary diversity.

As an individual, a contingent project manager moves from one job to another so as to expand their scope and exposure. According to Day (2008), 'contracting is excellent for broadening your own skill set. Most contract positions will enrich your resume, be it a new skill or experience. You could probably build a completely different area of strength.'

In both case study organisations, there is a practice of offering permanent positions to well-performing contingent staff. However, this is not an easy process for IT-PUB.

The chance to advance to project manager position as a non-permanent staff member is low. Internal promotion is always preferred unless there is no internal candidate (Participant D).

Furthermore, being a contingent project manager has some limitations that cannot be resolved regardless of how long the tenure is, or for how long they have been contracted to the organisations (e.g. Type 2 or Type 3 staff in Table 5.2). These contingent project managers are prohibited from accessing or exercising authority on financial matters, contractual matters, hiring/firing of project team members and the latest management decisions. Contingent project managers are handicapped in these aspects. These limitations prevent a contingent project manager from learning certain project management skills on-the-job.

Providing funding to contingent project managers for formal learning or certification activities is not officially offered in the case study organisations. IT-SVR management, however, do not consider it impossible. For those contingent workers with a long work history with IT-SVR, special arrangements can be made. IT-PUB also has some administrative 'workarounds' to allow contingent workers to join some training programs that are not counted by seats. In terms of company policy, however, the time and budget allocation for training and development activities for permanent and contingent staff are substantially different. It may be a 10·1 ratio as quoted by one of the participants.

Lack of job security is a major concern for contingent workers. One management-level participant observed that because of the lack of job security, contingent project managers see themselves as dispensable. They may not exercise the best project management practices like controlling cost. Contingent project managers, especially experienced ones (aged late 30s to early 40s), may have all the right skills, knowledge and experience, but may not exercise such capabilities for the good of the project or the organisations. Project delay may mean the contingent project manager's employment contract will be extended; late release of resources may mean he/she has less pressure on committing to project timelines. Contingent employment contracts may cause some project managers to learn new 'survival' skills.

Although there are many similarities between the groups studied in IT-PUB and IT-SVR, there is one major difference. The contingent workforce at IT-PUB, especially at the level of project managers and systems analysts, has a relatively low attrition rate compared to that of IT-SVR. According to a participant from IT-PUB, one of the reasons for this may be related to the marketability of their skills. Type 2 and Type 3 contingent project managers have very little chance to advance to next level or to be promoted to Type 1 project managers. The most valuable knowledge accumulated at IT-PUB as project managers is probably the people network with the end-users, internal departments and organisational knowledge. Although there is a lack of career advancement and development in IT-PUB, the rate of pay is comparable to that in the private sector and job security is relatively high as many contingent project managers can renew their contracts year after year.

These findings are summarised under the 'individual level' section of Table 5.3.

Project management capabilities advancement at the group level

Learning opportunities and practices shared by both permanent and contingent employees

Here, 'group' refers to the department or business unit where project managers reside and that hires project managers to deliver projects to its internal or external customers. The two project manager participants in this study agreed that project management methods or processes have to be applied appropriately based on experience and by utilising appropriate soft skills. In most cases, challenges faced by permanent or contingent project managers are the same. No two projects are the same. Every project manager needs to adapt to a new project environment.

The group under study in IT-SVR is the IT service delivery business unit that specialises in systems integration and IT project delivery. All the projects are delivered on a contract basis to external customers. There is a vast diversity of projects as the customers are from different industries like finance, telecommunication, government and logistics among others. It is common that IT-SVR's staff work on-site at customers' venues for long periods of time. It is not easy for staff working on different projects to meet one another on a day-to-day basis. There are regular meetings that involve management of the IT group. Formal project progress reports, especially in relation to project payment milestones, are discussed in such meetings. Project managers, regardless of the terms of their employment, rarely join these managerial level meetings. They are only involved in project meetings related to their own projects. IT-SVR has a project management office (PMO) that serves multiple business units. PMO plays a key role in promoting organisation-wide project management methodology and provides governance support. PMO reviews all large projects in pre-sales and delivery stages and monitors the progress of projects experiencing problems (essentially, financial problems). It also plays a role in diffusing lessons learnt from different projects when PMO conducts reviews with project managers on a monthly basis. PMO brings in questions and knowledge from other projects to ensure the same mistakes will not be repeated and some good practices are leveraged. With the constraints of project managers and leaders working across different locations, some informal workgroups are established to encourage cross-sharing on learning from projects. Some high-performing contingent project managers who have a long-term relationship with IT-SVR are also involved in such workgroups. Study participants from IT-SVR had not observed any formal mentoring/coaching programs. However, there are some gradual changes in the group structure such that experienced project managers/project directors are assigned people management responsibilities to take care of the training and development needs of all staff, including contingent workers. This is happening in the group under study, but not across the whole organisation. In practice, IT-SVR project managers may learn more from people at the customer site than from those working in other IT-SVR projects. However, being a vendor project manager at a customer's site is like the situation of Type 4 staff in IT-PUB; formal learning and sharing are unlikely to happen.

For IT-PUB, the nature of business is very different from IT-SVR. The group under study in IT-PUB is its end-user IT department. The customers are all internal customers. The majority of the IT project staff work in a single venue, but are distributed over a few floors of the building. There are regular meetings that involve the head of IT, senior IT managers, permanent project managers (Type 0) and direct contract project managers (Type 1) to report progress of various projects of the group. Similarly, each senior IT manager calls upon their project managers (Type 0, 1, 2 and 3) to provide progress reports on projects. These meetings are described as 'formal' and 'factual'. The opportunity for interactive sharing on problems or lessons learnt is limited. The group has a formal PMO that plays a key role as the centre of project management knowledge. With the leadership of PMO, by mid-2008, the group successfully obtained CMMI (Capability Maturity Model Integration) certification. The project management methodology, processes and tools are made available on the organisation's internal portal. All project managers (Type 0, 1, 2 and 3) have access to the majority of the group's project information, except sensitive data like financial data. With the implementation of CMMI, project management process training is provided to all levels of IT staff. A team of CMMI auditors is established to audit all IT projects on a random basis. This encourages an overall advancement in project management capabilities within the IT department. Tools like project repository, lessons-learnt database and others are made available to project managers to capture, share and leverage project management knowledge at the group level. It is yet to observe the outcomes. Participants of IT-PUB see there is a need to motivate project managers to leverage these facilities to obtain the ultimate benefits. On people-to-people sharing, there are no formal mentoring/coaching programs. Recently, a new initiative – newcomers' orientation – was introduced. Experienced staff introduce organisational and group levels' knowledge to new comers including project managers with different employment terms. Nevertheless, participants commented that to be a successful project manager in IT-PUB essentially relies on informal knowledge sharing.

Learning opportunities and practices specific to contingent employment

A few participants mentioned that the way contingent project managers are treated has a lot to do with the culture of the group. Even within the same organisation, different groups may employ contingent workers for different reasons and thus manage them differently. Some participants believed that the way that contingent staff were treated ranged along a spectrum with one extreme being permanent-staff-like and the other being project-material-like. One participant mentioned that he had worked in multiple organisations as a contingent IT project manager and had experienced the differences across the spectrum. If the group's culture is closer to the 'project-material-like' end of the spectrum, then the contingent project manager's relationship with the hiring organisation is a transactional one. Both parties aim at fulfilling the contractual obligation and are not looking for a long-term relationship. At the other end of the spectrum, the group wants to maintain a good relationship with the contingent staff member and may potentially hire them permanently. The tenure of contracts is related to the group culture. Most participants agreed that if the group offers long tenure contracts to contingent project managers (like two years or more) it is more likely to have the participation of contingent project managers in group level knowledge management activities. When the employee enjoys job security, they will demonstrate greater loyalty and commitment to the job. In fact, many contingent project managers are highly knowledgeable and have brought in specific skills demanded by the employers. Their willingness to share knowledge is beneficial to group level capability enhancement.

In order to advance project management capabilities at the group level, the two case study groups focused on the project management processes that include knowledge management components. As discussed above, IT-PUB has CMMI certification and has set up the necessary tools to facilitate knowledge management. Similarly, in IT-SVR, the group under study has obtained ISO (International Organisation for Standardisation) certification on their project processes for over five years. The methodology and tools are all available on the internal portal of IT-SVR. Type 0 and Type 1 staff have full access to this information, but not others.

Nevertheless, in most aspects, the case study groups did not distinguish between the way they treated contingent or permanent project managers. Only within some sensitive areas such as financial management, people hiring/firing and contractual liabilities were contingent project managers constrained. In the case study groups some bridges have been built to manage these gaps. In the group of IT-SVR, some permanent employees play the role of project director (PD) and take care of the organisational process requirements and represent contingent project managers as internal liaison officers. Contractual matters related to the projects are also handled by the PD. In IT-PUB, Type 2 and 3 contingent project managers have free access to most information on the corporate portal. However, when it comes to confidential data, they are prohibited from accessing it; they need the support of Type 0 or Type 1 staff. Type 4 project managers are basically outsiders in IT-PUB; they do not have access to any internal systems. They normally have a counter-part in IT-PUB to provide any necessary liaison within IT-PUB.

These findings are summarised in the 'group level' section of Table 5.3.

Organisational level learning

Learning opportunities and practices shared by both permanent and contingent employees

Learning at organisational level has a lot to do with whether the corporate culture supports organisational learning or knowledge management. Regarding organisational level facilitation of IT project management capabilities enhancement, Ng (2008) concludes that it depends on whether the organisation sees IT project management capabilities as a core competence of the organisation and whether it considers knowledge and information as capital that is worth investing in.

In Hong Kong, IT is playing a more important role in organisations (Ma 1999). In the case study organisations, the ability to deliver high quality IT projects was crucial to the organisation's success, not just to the groups. For IT-SVR, the capabilities of the group under study to deliver profitable projects was the most essential measurement. IT-SVR has a keen interest in investing in organisational learning in terms of IT project management capabilities and in retaining the capabilities in-house. The group under study retains experienced project managers/project directors as permanent staff. They need to lead contingent project managers and contingent IT workers to deliver profitable and high quality projects to external customers. For IT-PUB, the IT department accounts for almost 10 per cent of the total workforce of IT-PUB. It is one of the largest IT groups among Hong Kong government bureaux/departments. All key user departments within IT-PUB have mission critical IT projects under implementation or that have been implemented during the past few years. In summary, IT plays an essential role in the two case study organisations. IT project management capabilities are considered as one of the core competences of both organisations.

Nevertheless, the investment in advancing project management capabilities is essentially confined to processes and tools such as CMMI and ISO qualifications. Both organisations prefer to employ experienced project managers who have the necessary skills and qualifications to fulfil specific projects' requirements. Like many other organisations, '[the] hiring managers ... have assumptions that the contractors are experts and should be able to perform' (Ng 2008, 61). With the dynamic nature of their business, IT-SVR prefers to identify the project manager when it plans to bid on certain projects which normally have specifications for the project manager role. For IT-PUB, the government has frozen the headcount of civil servant hiring for over five years. They have no choice but to employ contingent project managers when the permanent project managers are unavailable. In reality, even the most senior level staff in the IT department of IT-PUB consists of a considerable percentage of direct contract staff (Type 1). Employing project managers on a contingent contract basis is the normal practice in IT-PUB.

With the trend of outsourcing and contingent employment, organisations are paying less attention to IT professional development (Ma 1999). The management participants of the two case study organisations pointed out that the IT labour market in Hong Kong is unhealthy. They concurred that Hong Kong's IT market is small and that the pool of IT project managers is a very small one. When organisations are seeking good project managers, they go to the same pool. IT project management capabilities, like other core competencies, need on-going investment. One participant believed that business owners of IT projects should take responsibility for developing IT project management capabilities.

The trend to integrate mainland China (VTC 2006) has been observed in both case study organisations. In IT-SVR, multiple business units, including the group under study, have projects partially delivered by mainland China workers. It is expected that the percentage of project work delivered by mainland China workers will expand in the coming years. In most cases, the Hong Kong side employs front-end staff like project managers and systems analysts, and the mainland China side provides back-end staff like coding and testing resources. Both IT-SVR and IT-PUB have piloted importing labour from mainland China to work on-site at Hong Kong project venues. Most of these workers are hired as Type 3 staff. Currently, this kind of hiring does not include project managers. With the recent economic downturn, there may be increasing demand for the relatively low-cost labour from mainland China. In IT-SVR, they are facing keener price competition and driving the cost down is mandatory for their survival. Not collaborating with mainland China's IT industry is not a choice. Project managers need to acquire the capabilities to manage cross-culture and multi-location project implementation issues. The group under study in IT-SVR has a specific workgroup to identify critical success factors on cross-border projects.

Learning opportunities and practices specific to contingent employment

In the discussion above about the advancement of project management capabilities at the group level, it was noted that group culture affects the way contingent workers are treated. This also applies at the organisational level. In some human resource matters, some organisations may have policies that make contingent workers easily identifiable. They may have different job titles, name badges, different name cards (or no name cards at all), smaller office space or specific email accounts. In both IT-SVR and IT-PUB, these kinds of external differences are quite apparent.

The two case study organisations have policies that well-performed contingent workers can be converted to permanent staff. In IT-SVR, when permanent positions are available, opportunities are normally given to existing contingent workers. In IT-PUB, as a government organisation, hiring for every position has to go through proper open and fair processes. Realistically, there is no opening for Type 0 employment and almost no opening for Type 1 contract project managers. Even when there is an opening, existing contingent workers only have a slight advantage over competitors without IT-PUB's organisational knowledge. According to participants of IT-PUB, it is difficult to gain 'promotion' through this channel. Some successful cases have been where the staff member left IT-PUB to obtain external advancement in job level elsewhere prior to applying for the same job level in IT-PUB. The participants from IT-PUB joked that it is an IT school that develops IT professionals for the community.

The four participants agreed that the training and development budgets for short-term staff are significantly less than for permanent staff. Contingent workers are hired because their expertise and skills meet the task requirement. In principle, no investment should be provided by the hiring organisations. The group under study in IT-PUB has allowed contract staff to sit in on training classes without specific limits on head counts. For IT-SVR, not much facilitation has been done for contingent workers in this regard. However, in some long-term contractors' cases, training or professional certification sponsorships are arranged on a case-by-case basis.

The management participants of both organisations agreed that it is not costly to sponsor contingent project managers on training or certification programs, it is a matter of policies and measurements. Contingent workers are essentially measured by their utilisation. At the point of hiring, they are expected to be fully utilised on the assigned project or task. There is no time allocated for training and development. Moreover, contingent workers prefer to spend time on fulfilling the job requirements so as to increase the chance of contract renewals. This also leads to the low incentive for contingent workers, including project managers, to contribute to knowledge-sharing activities. The weak sense of job security also hindered contingent employees from sharing their knowledge and experience. In practice, there is no reward or measurement to encourage such behaviours in the contingent workforce pools.

In both case study organisations, the investment in organisational learning activities seems to concentrate on permanent staff only. Some informal practices are observed at the group level, but not at organisational level.

The above findings are summarised in the 'organisational level' section of Table 5.3.

The findings related to learning facilitation across the individual, group and organisational levels indicate that there are challenges at all three levels. In the context of contingent employment, the findings clearly reveal that employment terms (permanent or contingent) impose a different set of challenges and opportunities in advancing IT project management capabilities.

Permanent and contingent employment: Common characteristics	Characteristics specific to contingent employment
Individual Level	
• Acquiring project management skills is more an individual's work. • Both formal learning and on-the-job learning can be self-managed, not relying on organisations. • Under long tenure contract terms, there is no obvious difference as a contingent project manager. • Difficulties on finding the right mentor are the same for all project managers. • The key success for a project manager is on the characters, not just on capabilities or employment terms.	• Contingent employment helps individual project manager to enrich skills and experience. • Key issues on contingent employment regarding advancing project management capabilities include: • career path; • limitation on learning critical project management skills (e.g. project finance); • low training opportunities; • accumulating bad project management practices; • and skill marketability maintenance.

Group Level	
• Project challenges are the same for different project managers. • Project managers need to adapt to project environment. • Project management methodology is developed in large IT departments or groups as the basis to guide project management. • Industrial certification programs at group level (e.g. ISO, CMMI) boost the project management maturity at group level. • PMO exists in large organisations as a component of knowledge management and centre of expert on project management. • Mentoring is mostly informal; there is difficulty to identify the right mentor. • Formal knowledge sharing is less effective than informal knowledge sharing.	• The treatment of contingent project manager depends if the group views contingent project manager as a permanent-staff-like or as project-material-like identity. • The tenure of contract affects the behaviour of contingent project manager on knowledge activities. • Contingent project managers may be excluded from some information access or knowledge activities. • Groups hiring contingent project managers establish bridging roles to complete tasks that contingent project managers cannot fulfil due to their identity.
Organisational Level	
• IT is gaining strategic position in organisations. • Investment on organisational learning is dependent on the how the organisation sees IT project management capabilities as a core competence or knowledge as capital. • Hong Kong's IT talent pool is small; IT project management capabilities need investment from business owners. • IT labour industry is going to unhealthy direction in Hong Kong. • More collaboration with the mainland China IT industry is happening in both ways.	• Company culture and HR policy may make contingent employment explicit in organisations. • Contingent workforce' career advancement within the hiring organisations depends on organisational policies, but generally more difficult than permanent staff. • The investment on training and development of contingent workforce are significantly less. • Contingent workforce is more aware of measurements like utilisation that affect their contract renewals. • Incentives are not provided to contingent workers on contributing to organisational learning.

Table 5.3 Summary of case study findings

Conclusion

This paper explored the connections between the contingent employment trend in the Hong Kong IT industry and enhancement of project management capabilities.

For an individual project manager or to-be-project-manager, the chance of falling into contingent employment is increasing. With the recent financial crisis, more IT staff will involuntarily depend upon contingent employment.

Not everyone can be self-driven and capable of managing their own career and development. In such work environments, young people will find it difficult to find the good mentors/coaches to provide the necessary guidance for the development and enhancement of project manager capabilities. Older workers may be frustrated by such employment arrangements and lose the passion to be good project managers. Nevertheless, as they may have greater exposure to different project environments, this may assist in advancing their capabilities of adaptation.

At the group level, CIOs are definitely experiencing continuous financial pressure. With the recent economic downturn, the tension will be higher than ever. The increase in knowledge complexity of the IT industry and organisations' intense dependence on IT for strategic competitiveness further drives CIOs to seek cost effective solutions. However, the solutions impose new questions regarding what competences or knowledge are core to the groups and how to bring them in-house. Some previously non-existent skills such as vendor management, contract management, contingent workforce management, distributed project team management and others may now be in demand (Ma 1999). The groups in the case study organisations have provided 'workarounds' and 'bridging roles' to fix some of the problems of contingent workforce management. However, these may not be long-term solutions to the problems.

The recent financial crisis has led to organisations being more cost conscious, but it has also motivated management to look for IT solutions to drive operational efficiency, manage risks and improve competitiveness. Good knowledge management practices may be a solution (Handzic 2004). From the findings of the two case studies, the organisations have an investment in retaining the knowledge of permanent staff and maintain a knowledge management system for IT project management processes (e.g. CMMI, ISO). There is little evidence that the case study organisations have policies to help contingent employees or outsourcing partners' staff in terms of organisational learning. They do not have any incentive for contingent project managers to learn the organisation's processes nor do they encourage contingent project managers to share their knowledge and experience. Organisations employing IT staff may not see they have a legitimate responsibility to enhance practitioners' capabilities, especially when their employment is contingent. However, some participants felt that organisations hiring contingent staff should take an active role in enhancing practitioners' capabilities for the good of the whole industry.

The number of project managers in the workforce [in Hong Kong] is small and this is the only available pool of talent. They either work for organisation X or organisation Y … Any program to help contingent project managers is for the whole IT project manager pool in the labour market (Participant A).

Limitations of research

The conclusions drawn from these case studies are limited by the scope of the study. The data collected was from a small number of participants in two large organisations. Moreover, the organisations selected hire a considerable percentage of contingent IT workers. In reality, there are organisations that employ a low percentage of IT workers, or that do not have contingent employment for IT project manager positions which are normally classified as key positions in IT groups of organisations. The findings are therefore likely to be biased and cannot be generalised to represent the situation of typical large organisations in Hong Kong.

Further studies

The purpose of this paper has been to identify findings that may be utilised to refine further research studies. The open questions left behind the conclusions above provide a basis for further exploration of the issues related to IT project management learning and contingent employment policy.

References

Abraham, T; Beath, C; Bullen, C; Gallagher, K; Goles, T; Kaiser, K; Simon, J. 2006. 'IT workforce trends: Implications for IS programs', *Communications of AIS* 2006: 2–43.

Allan, P; Sienko, S. 1998. 'Job motivations of professional and technical contingent workers: Are they different from permanent workers?' *Journal of Employment Counselling* 35 (4): 169–78.

Anonymous. 2006. 'More contingent workers are a blessing and sometimes a challenge for HR'. *HR Focus* 83 (1): S1–S4.

Anonymous. 2007a. 'Demand for IT temp workers expected to outpace permanent', *eWeek*.

Anonymous. 2007b. 'Temporary employment to grow three times as fast as total employment over next'. *US Newswire*.

Atkinson, J. 1984. 'Manpower strategies for flexible organisations'. *Personnel Management*: 28–31.

Baccarini, D; Darrell, V. 2006. 'Experiences of accidental project managers – An Australian survey'. A paper presented to PMOZ – 3rd Annual Project Management Australia Conference, Melbourne, 8–11 August.

Belous, R S. 1989. *The Contingent Economy: The Growth of the Temporary, Part-time, and Subcontracted Workforce*. Washington, DC: National Planning Association.

Bentley, C. 1997. *PRINCE 2. A Practical Handbook*. Oxford, UK: Butterworth-Heinemann.

Billett, S. 2001. *Learning in the Workplace: Strategies for Effective Practice.* Crows Nest, NSW: Allen & Unwin.

Boud, D; Garrick, J. 1999. *Understanding Learning at Work.* New York: Routledge.

Burns, R. 2002. *The Adult Learner at Work: The Challenges of Lifelong Education in the New Millennium.* 2nd edn. Crows Nest, NSW: Allen & Unwin.

Cheung, D. 2006. 'Hong Kong IT Professional Certification Introduction'. Dissemination Seminar for IT Project Director and IT Systems Architect. Hong Kong Institute for IT Professional Certification, 2 December 2006. Accessed on 5 October 2008. Available from: http://www.hkcs.org.hk/itpcrs/files/seminar/20061202/HKITPC_DS_ProfDCheung.pdf.

Crawford, L; Gaynor, F; 1999. 'Assessing and developing project management competence'. Proceedings of the Learning, Knowledge, Wisdom: 30th Annual PMI Seminars and Symposium, 10–16 October 1999, Philadelphia.

Crossan, M M; Lane, H W; White, R E. 1999. 'An organizational learning framework: From intuition to institution'. *The Academy of Management Review* 24 (3): 522.

Day, G. 2008. 'Contracting can open new doors'. *South China Morning Post* 11 October 2008: 26.

Day, N. 1998. 'Informal learning'. *Workforce* 77 (6): 30–6.

Dulaimi, M F. 2005. 'The influence of academic education and formal training on the project manager's behavior'. *Journal of Construction Research* 6: 179.

Ensworth, P. 2001. *The Accidental Project Manager: Surviving the Transition from Techie to Manager.* New York: John Wiley & Sons.

Fuchs, M 2002. 'Changing employment relations, new organizational models and the capability to use idiosyncratic knowledge'. *Journal of European Industrial Training* 26 (2–4): 154–64.

Graham, R J. 1992. 'A survival guide for the accidental project manager'. A paper presented to Annual Project Management Institute Symposium, Drexel Hill, PA.

Gregory, J L. 2001. 'Contingent workers' impact on the pay and promotions of traditional employees in the information technology profession'. Ph.D. thesis. Michigan: Michigan State University.

Hall, T; Beecham, S; Verner, J; Wilson, D. 2008. 'The impact of staff turnover on software projects: the importance of understanding what makes software practitioners tick'. A paper presented to Special Interest Group on Computer Personnel Research Annual Conference Charlottesville, VA, USA.

Handzic, M. 2004. *Knowledge Management: Through the Technology Glass.* Series on innovation and knowledge management; Vol. 2. New Jersey: World Scientific Publishing Co.

HKCS. 2004. *IT Matters for Hong Kong Survey Result.* Hong Kong Computer Society. Accessed on 3 October 2008. Available from: http://www.hkcs.org.hk/doc_journal/survey_results.pdf.

HKCS. 2007. *IT Professional Roster System Feasibility Study Report.* Hong Kong Computer Society. Accessed on 5 October 2008. Available from: http://www.hkcs.org.hk/itpcrs/files/Roster_FSR.pdf.

HKITPC. 2009. *Press Update Briefing Lunch – HKITPC Announces Endorsement of Course Providers for its CPIT Scheme (2009-02-03).* Hong Kong Institute for IT Professional Certification. Accessed on 10 May 2009. Available from: http://www.hkitpc.org/filemanager/en/content_16/press_briefing020309v1Eng.pdf

Hodson, R; Sullivan, T A. 2008. *The Social Organization of Work.* 4th edn. Belmont, CA: Wadsworth.

Holland, P J; Hecker, R; Steen, J. 2002. 'Human resource strategies and organisational structures for managing gold-collar workers'. *Journal of European Industrial Training* 26 (2–4): 72–80.

Jarvinen, A; Poikela, E. 2006. 'The learning processes in the work organization: From theory to design'. In *Learning, Working and Living: Mapping the Terrain of Working Life Learning*, edited by Antonacopoulou, E P. Houndmills, Basingstoke, Hampshire: Palgrave Macmillan: 170–87.

Johnston, R; Hawke, G; McGregor, C; Johnson, G. 2002. 'Changing models for changing times: Learning and assessment practices in the workplace'. RCVET working paper RP112 02-02. Accessed in June 2003. Available at: http:// www.rcvet.uts.edu.au

Kallenberg, A L. 2001. 'Organizing flexibility: The flexible firm in the new century'. *British Journal of Industrial Relations* 39 (4): 479–505.

Lepak, D P; Takeuchi, R; Snell, S A. 2003. 'Employment flexibility and firm performance: Examining the interaction effects of employment mode, environmental dynamism, and technological intensity'. *Journal of Management* 29 (5): 681–703.

Loogma, K; Ümarik, M; Vilu, R. 2004. 'Identification-flexibility dilemma of IT specialists'. *Career Development International* 9 (3): 323–48.

Ma, L C K. 1999. 'Critical issues of information systems management in Hong Kong'. Hong Kong Computer Society. Accessed on 5 October 2008. Available from: http://www.hkcs.org.hk/doc_journal/lm02.htm

MacDougall, S L; Hurst, D. 2005. 'Identifying tangible costs, benefits and risks of an investment in intellectual capital: Contracting contingent knowledge workers'. *Journal of Intellectual Capital* 6 (1): 53–71.

Marler, J H; Barringer, M W; Milkovich, G T. 2002. 'Boundaryless and traditional contingent employees: Worlds apart'. *Journal of Organizational Behavior* 23 (4): 425.

Matusik, S F; Hill, C W L. 1998. 'The utilization of contingent work, knowledge creation, and competitive advantage'. *The Academy of Management Review* 23 (4): 680–97.

McLean, C. 2006. '21st century IT: What does outsourcing mean for you?' *Certification Magazine* 8 (2): 36–8.

McMorrow, J. 1999. 'Future trends in human resources'. *HR Focus* 76 (9): 7–9.

NCVER. 2003. *What Makes for Good Workplace Learning? At a Glance.* The National Centre for Vocational Education Research Australia.

Nerland, M; Jensen, K. 2007. 'Insourcing the management of knowledge and occupational control: An analysis of computer engineers in Norway'. *International Journal of Lifelong Education* 26 (3): 263 – 78.

Nesbit, P L. 2005. 'HRM and the flexible firm: Do firms with "high performance" work cultures utilise peripheral work arrangements?' *International Journal of Employment Studies* 13 (2): 1–17.

Ng, C H. 2008. 'The place of experiential learning in developing information technology project management capabilities in a large organisation'. MA thesis. Melbourne: RMIT University.

Nonaka, I; Takeuchi, H. 1995. *The Knowledge-Creating Company: How Japanese Companies Create the Dynamics of Innovation.* New York: Oxford University Press.

OGCIO. 2008a. *Government IT Sourcing and Contracting.* The Office of the Government Chief Information Officer (OGCIO) – The Government of the HK SAR. Accessed on 5 October 2008. Available from: http://www.ogcio.gov.hk/eng/itbusiness/econtract.html

OGCIO. 2008b. *Government IT Staff.* The Office of the Government Chief Information

Officer (OGCIO) – The Government of the HK SAR. Accessed on 5 October 2008. Available from: http://www.ogcio.gov.hk/eng/about/eitstaff.htm

OGCIO. 2008c. *OGCIO IT Contract Staff Services – Body-shopping Contracts.* The Office of the Government Chief Information Officer (OGCIO) – The Government of the HK SAR. Accessed on 5 October 2008. Available from: http://www.ogcio.gov.hk/eng/about/econstaff.htm

Oxford Dictionary. 2007. 'Capability'. Oxford. Accessed on 19 October 2007.Available from: http://www.askoxford.com/concise_oed/capability?view=uk

Peel, S; Inkson, K. 2004. 'Contracting and careers: Choosing between self and organizational employment'. *Career Development International* 9 (6): 542–58.

Perelman, D. 2007. 'Survey: Project managers in high demand, short supply; A new Forrester study puts project management, security, architecture and change management skills at the top of CIOs priorities in 2007, with training programs in vendor, sourcing and service management not far behind'. *eWeek*: 1.

Pinto, J K; Kharbanda, O P. 1995. 'Lessons for an accidental profession'. *Business Horizons* 38 (2): 41–50.

Project Management Institute. 2004. *A Guide to the Project Management Body of Knowledge.* 3rd edn. Sylva, NC, USA: Project Management Institute.

Project Management Institute. 2005. 'Demand for IT project managers rises down under'. *PM Network* 19 (5): 12.

Redpath, L; Hurst, D; Devine, K. 2007. 'Contingent knowledge worker challenges'. *Human Resource Planning* 30 (3): 33–8.

Reif, H L; Mitri, M. 2005. 'How university professors teach project management for information systems'. *Communications of the ACM* 48: 134.

Rousseau, D M; Arthur, M B. 1996. *The Boundaryless Career: A New Employment Principle for a New Organizational Era.* New York: Oxford University Press.

Sauve, E. 2007. 'Informal knowledge transfer'. *T+D* 61 (3): 22–4.

Sullivan, T. 2008. 'The great talent shortage'. *PM Network* 22 (1): 52–8.

Turner, R. 2003. *People in Project Management.* Hants, England; Burlington, VT: Gower, Aldershot.

VTC. 2006. *Manpower Survey Report: Information Technology Sector.* Committee on Information Technology Training and Development, Vocational Training Council, Hong Kong.

Webster, J. 2005. 'Women in IT professions: Corporate structures, masculine cultures'. A paper presented to Third European symposium on gender & ICT: Working for change. Manchester, UK, 1 February 2005. Available from: http://ict.open.ac.uk/gender/papers/webster.doc

Wong, M M L. 2001. 'The strategic use of contingent workers in Hong Kong's economic upheaval'. *Human Resource Management Journal* 11 (4): 22.

Yin, R K. 2003. *Case Study Research: Design and Methods.* 3rd edn. Thousand Oaks, CA: Sage Publications.

Section 2
Strategic Aspects of Project Management

Chapter 6

Whole of enterprise portfolio management

An integrated approach to managing projects as a social system

Michael Young

University of New South Wales at the Australian Defence Force
Academy, Australia

Jill Owen

University of New South Wales at the Australian Defence Force
Academy, Australia

James Connor

University of New South Wales at the Australian Defence Force
Academy, Australia

Project portfolio management is an emerging phenomenon that has its original theoretical grounding in business finance. Due to the relatively recent identification of the project portfolio management phenomenon and the lack of empirical research in the application of these techniques used in organisations, a proliferation of definitions and conceptual frameworks has occurred, resulting in confusion. This paper provides a review of the current literature and seeks to demonstrate the differences between each type of portfolio, highlight the specific nature of project portfolio management and how it differs from other enterprise-wide project management functions. The terms 'portfolio management', 'program management', 'enterprise project management' and 'multi-project management' have been used interchangeably (Larsson 2007; Sanchez Robert & Pellerin 2008; Thiry 2004). In addition, there are divergent views as to whether project portfolios should be managed with reference to other portfolios operating within the enterprise, or whether they should be viewed in isolation. We offer a definition of 'Whole of Enterprise Portfolio Management' and suggest that this conceptual tool will allow an organisation to control programs and portfolios, particularly where organisations adapt to emergent situations.

Introduction

Project management has a relatively well conceptualised Body of Knowledge (BoK), underpinning tools and approaches (Owen et al. 2009; Project Management Institute 2008a). However, somewhat curiously, when projects are aggregated into programs and portfolios the literature on how to manage a collection of projects or programs is relatively sparse, divergent and poorly integrated. Projects very rarely operate in isolation within an organisation and are usually delivered to satisfy broader strategic priorities, thus it is essential to develop both the theory and praxis of how projects are selected, prioritised, integrated, managed and controlled in the multi-project context that exists in modern organisations.

Project portfolio management is an emerging aspect of business management that has its theoretical underpinnings in business finance to control financial investments (Markowitz 1952; McFarlan 1981; Kendall & Rollins 2003). However, as an emerging practice that has extended beyond its original sector, there is considerable argument as to what portfolio management is in a project context. This has resulted in some confusion amongst both the academic and practitioner communities (Thiry 2004). The terms 'portfolio management', 'program management', 'enterprise project management' and 'multi-project management' have been used interchangeably in the literature (Buttrick 2000; Center for Business Practices 2005; Dye & Pennypacker 2000; Kendall & Rollins 2003; Morris & Jamieson 2004; Office of Government Commerce 2009). Terms such as 'program', 'portfolio' and even 'group of projects' have been used to describe such an environment (Patanakul & Milosevic 2005; Platje & Seidel 1994). Others such as Gareis (2006) have instead examined the social (network of projects) and temporal (chain of projects) relationships between individual projects, creating another set of definitions.

Each of these seeks to address a particular business occurrence and attempts to describe the nature of a particular problem; that is, coherently selecting, controlling and managing multiple projects. Gareis (1989) notes that organisations are grappling to find solutions and strategies that help manage multiple concurrent projects and make decisions in relation to investments and strategic initiatives in a rapidly changing and increasingly competitive environment (Kendall & Rollins 2003) or determine strategies to optimise the use of resources (Engwall & Jerbrandt 2002).

The use of portfolio management concepts and techniques is seen as a potential solution in a multi-project context (Dye & Pennypacker 2000) and, as such, there has been a proliferation of different types of portfolios. In effect, systems employed in the management of individual projects are 'up-scaled' to manage programs and adapted for the management of project portfolios. The literature identifies investment portfolios, project portfolios, asset portfolios, resource portfolios, product portfolios and agile portfolios (see for example: Buttrick 2000; Cooper 2005; Krebs 2009; Larsson 2007; Center for Business Practices 2005).

This paper demonstrates the differences between each type of portfolio, highlights the specific nature of project portfolio management and how it differs from other enterprise project management functions and argues why the current views of project portfolio management are insufficient. It concludes by establishing a definition of 'Whole of Enterprise Portfolio Management', introducing a conceptual framework that integrates the various portfolio concepts occurring in the organisation, highlighting the need to manage a project portfolio in conjunction with these other organisational portfolios, and making explicit a number of the key directions identified as part of the Rethinking Project Management research agenda (Winter et al. 2006).

The conceptual underpinnings of portfolio approaches

The traditional focus of project management research has been on tools and techniques to develop a tangible output for a single project (Morris 2002). The Rethinking Project Management research agenda found this body of research is limited and developed a new framework complementing and extending this existing BoK (Winter et al. 2006). The first research direction recognises the complexity of projects and that there are a number of ways to manage them, thereby leading to numerous models and theories. The second direction recognises the social nature of projects involving human interactions, multiple stakeholders and power relations. The third direction shifts the focuses to value creation in projects thereby highlighting emergence, sense-making and multiple expectations/meanings (Winter et al. 2006; Sauer et al. 2009). The fourth direction concerning broader conceptualisations of projects acknowledges the multidisciplinary, emergent and negotiable concepts and approaches that can be pursued. The fifth direction involves a movement of practitioners from trained technicians to that of becoming reflective practitioners who can learn, adapt and apply theory effectively in their practice domains (Winter et al. 2006).

The concept of project portfolio management has emerged from two complimentary, yet independent drivers, these being the need to make rational investment decisions that result in the delivery of organisational benefits (Markowitz 1952); and the need to optimise the use of resources to ensure the delivery of such benefits occurs in an effective and efficient manner (Dye & Pennypacker 2000). In 1952, Markowitz first introduced the concept of the portfolio to the financial sector. He proposed the Modern Portfolio Theory and suggested that rational investors use diversification to optimise their portfolios: the portfolio in this case being a collection of financial assets and investments. His theory also suggested that investors can reduce their exposure to individual asset risk by holding a diversified portfolio of assets with the portfolio allowing a higher return with reduced risk, compared to the inherent risk and return ratios of the individual investments that comprise the portfolio. Whilst applicable to a project portfolio, the diversification advice offered by Markowitz does not necessarily take into account resource constraints and the interactions between various portfolios across the organisation.

McFarlan (1981) introduced the use of the portfolio management approach to the field of information technology (IT), suggesting that projects, rather than assets or investments, are the components of the portfolio and that the collective management of these unrelated projects could occur in a manner that optimises the organisation's desired business outcome whilst minimising the organisations overall level of risk. The desired business outcomes McFarlan refers to are not static, but instead, change over time as a result of shifts in the various legislative, political, economic, social and technological drivers. Whilst individual projects represent specific risks to the organisation, they also provide particular opportunities. Achieving an optimal balance between risk and reward across the diversified set of projects was seen as the key to success in the business environment (Hubbard 2007).

Jensen and Meckling (1976), in the Theory of the Firm, suggest that organisations seek to create wealth or maximise profit through the allocation of resources to a particular strategy. By extension, Jacob's (1999) hypothesis that organisations use portfolio models and portfolio management approaches as a means to evaluate markets and to strategically allocate resources amongst business units. These resource allocations need to be sufficiently dynamic to take into account adjustments to the organisation's priorities that occur as a result of environmental changes. This shift in focus towards a 'management by project' approach (Gareis 1989) means that organisations allocate resources to projects and use these projects as vehicles to deliver strategic outcomes or to implement innovative business strategies that help them maintain their competitive advantage (Milosevic & Srivannaboon 2006). The tools and techniques used are based on deterministic scientific management approaches and organisational theories that were developed as a means to manage and control individual projects. However, as Dye and Pennypacker (2000) suggest, tools and techniques that have been developed for individual projects do not work in the dynamic environment of multiple projects that exists in the modern organisation, as these rational tools that have been developed to deal with single projects are unable to deal with the complexity of managing multiple projects with different objectives, emerging and unstable project objectives.

In this multi-project context, individual project managers attempt to resource their project from a common pool of resources that exist within the organisation. Project team members perform work and consume financial resources and in turn generate deliverables, implement solutions and achieve business outcomes. Each project may be selected due to its strategic importance to the organisation and, as such, incorporated into a portfolio on the basis of providing an optimal balance between risk and reward. However, if this is done without consideration for the capacity of organisation's current resource pool, the resource allocation syndrome occurs (Engwall & Jerbrandt 2002). Traditional mechanistic tools and techniques used in singular projects do not support intra-project decision making or resolve issues of intra-project resource contention that exist in the multi-project context (Nash 2002). In addition, these mechanistic tools do not allow for changes in strategy that occur to shifts in the environment. What is needed is a new set to tools to dynamically identify, select and balance the projects being undertaken in the organisation whilst also providing a clear priority for the allocation of the limited pool of available resources.

The multi-project management literature is an attempt to address these concerns, and has been written with a focus on the tools, techniques and strategies to manage and prioritise individual projects where such multiple projects exist. This line of thinking has been driven by the need for appropriate resource allocation across multiple concurrent projects (Dye & Pennypacker 2000), particularly where multiple projects are grouped for management efficiency (Milosevic & Patanakul 2002) and where projects are drawing on scarce and limited resources (Zika-Viktorsson, Sundstrom & Engwall 2006). In such a scenario, project human resources work across more than one project and actively switch focus between projects on a time share basis, or alternatively they are time-sliced across projects (Engwall & Jerbrandt

2002). In switching their focus from project to project, the work performed by members of the project team is fragmented, with such fragmentation resulting in a cost to efficiency. While multi-project management techniques provide a useful way to understand a complicated environment, these techniques do little to address the underlying resource management and strategic alignment issues organisations face.

Another approach is enterprise project management which seeks to adopt a common, systematic, organisational-wide approach to project management in a multi-project context, enterprise or organisational project management space. Aimed at establishing and applying individual project management principles across the enterprise in a drive to systematise and standardise project activities, the focus has been: the implementation and management of standards, tools and templates; individual project manager competency assessment and development; or project approvals and review mechanisms (Kendall & Rollins 2003; Hill 2008). It is through the application of such quality management and quality control techniques that the organisation improves its overall project management maturity. However, the increase in maturity does not necessarily resolve issues of resource allocation and priorities, as organisations still have to ensure that resources are effectively allocated to projects based on organisational priorities. Nor does an increase in an organisation's project delivery capability ensure that individual projects meet the organisations investment criteria or deliver strategic outcomes for the organisation as this focus may be on single project delivery capability rather than at an organisational level.

Whilst traditional portfolio management, multi-project management and enterprise project management approaches serve a useful purpose, they fail to take into account the cross-organisational dependencies between various portfolios in the dynamic manner that is required to deal with the regular and ongoing shifts in organisational priorities. What is needed is a conceptual framework that not only addresses their resource, strategic and multi-project coordination needs, but also addresses how changes in resource levels and the organisation's priorities in a way that can be adjusted dynamically.

Defining project portfolios

Recognising the shortcomings of traditional portfolio management, multi-project management and enterprise project management approaches, the portfolio concept has been adopted across discrete functions within the organisation as a means to address such shortcomings in a holistic manner.

The project portfolio has been defined as 'a collection of projects or programs and other work that are grouped together to facilitate effective management of that work to meet strategic business needs' (Project Management Institute 2008a). Project portfolio management involves identifying, prioritising, authorising, managing and controlling the component projects and programs and the associated risks, resources and priorities. The International Project Management Association (2008) in their Competence Baseline support this definition but highlight the focus being a common and shared pool of scarce resources. The Association for Project Management (2006) focuses on the projects and programs being carried out under sponsorship of an organisation. The UK Office of Government Commerce (OGC) (2009) defines a portfolio as 'the totality of an organisation's investment in the changes [projects and programs] required to achieve its strategic objectives'. The portfolio may be implemented in part of the organisation, such as a Division, or may be enterprise-wide, or they may be nested, in that there may be both a divisional and enterprise-wide portfolio. However, as Foti (2002) suggests, regardless of the scale and scope of the portfolio and the location in which it occurs within the organisation, the use of project portfolios allows organisations to make the most of their resources allowing the organisation to achieve its strategic purpose.

The disciplines of program and portfolio management are often confused due to their emerging nature (Larsson 2007; Sanchez Robert, & Pellerin 2008; Thiry 2004). The Office of Government Commerce (2009) defines a program as 'a temporary, flexible organisation created to coordinate, direct and oversee the implementation of a set of relate projects and activities in order to deliver outcomes and benefits related to the organisations strategic objectives'. The focus, in this instance, is the implementation of the identified change (project or program) in a strategic context. Whereas Turner (1999) suggests that a program is a portfolio of small to medium-sized projects. The Association for Project Management (2006) appears to confuse matters by stating that portfolios can be managed at the program level. Buttrick (2000) also adds to this confusion stating that 'a portfolio is a range of investments held by an organisation' and that 'a business program is a special type of portfolio.' He defines a business program as a series of 'current benefit generating business activities together with a loosely coupled but tightly aligned portfolio of project and programs, aimed at delivering the benefits of part of a business plan or strategy' (Buttrick 2000).

Whilst these definitions attempt to establish the link between the projects selected and the organisation's priorities and go some way towards examining the interdependencies between projects, there is limited recognition of the importance of the organisations pool of resources, assets and ideas and the criticality of the inter-relatedness between these portfolios and the project portfolio.

Resource-based portfolio

The Resource-Based View (RBV) of the firm has emerged as a way of explaining how organisations create competitive advantage through the use of rare, valuable, non-immutable and non-substitutable resources (Penrose 1959). The RBV literature offers a number of alternative definitions for 'resources', however in the context of project portfolios and their management, Barney's (1991) definition seems most appropriate. He suggests that the organisation's resources include all assets, capabilities, organisational process, firm attributes, information and knowledge controlled by an organisation to conceive and implement strategies that improve its efficiency and effectiveness. Krebs (2009) identifies the concept of a resource portfolio, drawing the link between resource management across the organisation and the benefits offered by taking a portfolio management approach. He suggests resource portfolio management is focused on managing the common pool of 'talent' in the organisation ensuring there is an available pool of resources to work on both current and future projects. Traditional approaches to managing resource supply do not operate in a sufficiently dynamic manner and do not take into account the differences between the workload as it appears on a plan and the workload is it is executed (Krebs 2009; Engwall & Jerbrandt 2002; Kendall & Rollins 2003).

Traditionally, through the normal course of business, both functional managers and project managers forecast and define their resource requirements for individual projects (Project Management Institute 2008a). Collectively these forecasts and requirements are used to formulate an organisational-wide resource demand profile which changes as projects move through their life cycle from inception to closure, and as new projects are created. These resource demands are fulfilled through the allocation of individuals from the organisation-wide resource pool to both projects and other operational activities, based on their mechanistic and logical forecasts and plans (Kendall & Rollins 2003).

Many organisations focus their priorities and effort on the management of resources across large projects, high-risk projects or the 'top ten' projects in the project portfolio. Whilst this may seem a logical and rational choice, when examining the entire resource portfolio, it can commonly be the large number of small, low profile projects or low priority operational activities that utilise the largest pool of resources and as such, the high-profile and priority projects and operational activities may lose access to their critical resources (Engwall & Jerbrandt 2002).

Through a resource portfolio, short-term, mid-term and long-term resource forecasts are used to determine the optimal future level of staffing, across the organisation not only for periods of normal operations but also for peak periods of demand, based on project and operational work that has been prioritised, strategically-linked. This in turn can allow resource managers to put in place plans to acquire the required types and level of resources needed to satisfy both the planned and latent demand. Utilising this approach, resource demand and resource supply can be compared and balanced (Turner and Cochrane 1993), not only in terms of quantitatively (numerical totals), but also qualitatively (skill sets). A similar situation may also occur with an organisation's assets.

Asset portfolio

Traditionally, assets have been reviewed as systems, buildings, equipment or other physical assets, practices and processes that an enterprise uses to manage the total life cycle cost investment in its portfolio of strategic assets (American Association of Cost Engineers 2006). A common asset-based portfolio is the IT or applications portfolio, the focus being the planned and operating IT systems in the organisation.

Modern Portfolio Theory has been applied across some IT Portfolios as a risk-based approach to the selection and management of component projects (McFarlan 1981; Weill & Broadbent 1998). Forrester Research (2004) suggests that the IT Portfolio is comprised of the IT Project Portfolio and the Applications Portfolio. Whilst Krebs (2009) suggests a linear single interaction between a Project Portfolio and an Asset Portfolio it could be argued that the interaction is two-way. Based on our observations, not only do projects produce physical assets (as deliverables or capabilities delivered by the project), but assets in their own right also generate a series of projects, by way of maintenance and enhancement activities required to ensure the asset continues to function and performs as designed.

Whilst these maintenance and enhancements activities may be rationally planned through the development of an Asset Maintenance Plan, assets, such as a building plant or system, malfunction from time to time and require unplanned, emergency maintenance to be performed. These unplanned activities draw on a pool of organisations resources and may draw resources away from other priority activities, thus impacting the ability of the organisation to achieve their strategic objectives (Engwall & Jerbrandt 2002).

Therefore, whilst deterministic, scientific and rational planning techniques are used to formulate priorities for the isolated portfolio assets, unplanned events not only impact the Asset Portfolio, but also dynamically impact both the Project Portfolio (through the creation of unplanned projects) and the Resource Portfolio (through the unplanned request for critical resources). Whilst these newly identified and emergent asset, project and resource priorities may be seen to be critical, they do not necessarily align with the organisation's priorities and, as such, undermine progress towards achievement of overarching organisational priorities and strategies.

A more dynamic approach is needed to establish a consistent and common set of priorities across resources, assets and projects that recognises the cross-organisational impacts of unplanned projects and activities taking into account the organisation's priorities at any given time and the manner in which the organisation's priorities shift in relation to environmental influences.

Ideas portfolio

The existence of an Idea Portfolio draws on the concept of ideation and the fuzzy-front end (Larsson 2007). The Idea Portfolio is a systematic approach to transforming ideas into a business opportunity by focusing on enriching the right ideas to maturation from the multitude of initial concepts identified. This approach helps individuals in an organisation to choose which products to fund, given limited investment availability and limited resources (Kendall & Rollins 2003). The ideas feed the new product development portfolio after screening and initial investigation (Larsson 2007). This has been adopted by the Boeing Company as part of their Ideas to Innovation (I2I) program (Lacontora & Mathews 2009). A direct connection exists between product portfolio management and project portfolio management as shown in Figure 6.1); however, most organisations make the mistake of viewing both functions independently of each other (Kendall & Rollins 2003), and in a linear normative manner.

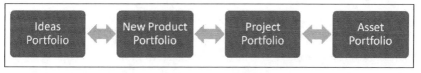

Figure 6.1. Interaction between portfolios (adapted from Larsson 2007)

Within the New Product Portfolio, projects are identified, planned and managed throughout the product development life cycle. Using traditional project portfolio management techniques, individual projects within the New Product Portfolio will be prioritised in isolation, without necessarily considering the priorities of the resources situated in the Resource Portfolio, the priority of other projects in the Project Portfolio or the unplanned and emergency maintenance projects occurring in the Asset Portfolio.

The inter-relatedness of portfolios

Despite their definition, the UK Office of Government Commerce point out that the Project Portfolio is not the total investment portfolio and such portfolios should not be confused with more general Investment Portfolios or Product Portfolios (Office of Government Commerce, 2009; Morris & Jamieson, 2004). It is a mistake for organisations to conduct product portfolio management without including activities such as asset maintenance and new product development projects in the Project Portfolio due to the use of an inter-related pool of resources (Rollins & Kendall, 2003). Through their Project Portfolio Management Maturity Benchmarking survey, the Center for Business Practices (2005) discovered that more than one third of respondents also practiced product portfolio management, asset portfolio management and application portfolio management, with the prevalence increasing as the organisation's project portfolio management maturity increases.

Definitions and findings of this nature suggest that a degree of inter-relatedness exists between varying types of portfolios that occur in the organisation. Given this interaction between projects and the various types of portfolios, it is essential that we examine portfolios in a more holistic sense. Not only must we examine life span from project inception to project closure, but also examine the interaction a project across the various types of portfolio due to the linkages and interdependencies of the Project, Asset, Resource, Idea and other portfolios that occur across the organisation.

A conceptual framework is needed to demonstrate and to help make sense of these linkages and interdependencies and integrated the various portfolio approaches to cater for the emergent and dynamic nature of projects, rather than the singular, mechanistic approaches used to date.

Conceptual framework

Project portfolio management is predominantly focused on ensuring an organisation works on the right projects (Archer & Ghasemzadeh 1999; Morris & Jamieson 2004). Cleland and Ireland (2007) suggest a balancing of risk and strategic fit is of importance, extending on Markowitz's original construct. The UK Office of Government Commerce (2009) makes the point that the focus in a portfolio is the portfolio of organisational change. Miller (2002) simply indicates that project portfolio management focuses the organisation on achieving what is needed, rather than on merely doing their best. Foti (2002) suggests that the portfolio approach puts a lens of the question of what is strategically important to an organisation.

Whilst these definitions all appear to make sense, a gap still exists between current tools and the needs of the modern project-based organisation. Longman et al. (1999) advocates that the issue has also been due to the lack of sufficient management tools to establish and maintain priorities among projects. (Krebs 2009) suggests that current portfolio management tools and techniques are not enabling organisations to effectively deal with the emergent and dynamic nature in which projects are identified, commenced, managed and cancelled. Whilst the Project Management Institute (2008) and Office of Government Commerce (2009) portfolio management frameworks imply that dynamism occurs through portfolio balancing, they are dependent upon a rational, mechanistic and linear process to determine the organisations strategy and priorities, which in turn allows the balancing function to take place.

The optimal balance is not a static situation, but instead changes according to shifts in the strategies and priorities of the organisation which change in response to market or environmental changes. A more holistic approach to project portfolio management is needed to take into account the dualism of resource management and strategic project selection and to also draw together the interactions that occur between the different portfolios. Unless all portfolios are managed in an integrated manner cross-portfolio impacts can occur, in the same way that cross-project impacts occur.

A whole of enterprise portfolio management model is required. We define 'Whole of Enterprise Portfolio Management' as:

> The management of all related organisational portfolios in an integrated, dynamic and inter-dependant manner. With consideration to the organisation's priorities, social circumstance, resource supply and strategy, whilst allowing for emergent complexity to be addressed.

The proposed conceptual model as shown in Figure 6.2 recognises both the rationally planned and emergent origin of projects whilst taking into account the complex socio-cultural elements of the organisation and the priorities set by the organisation in response to environmental shifts. It also identifies the linkages and interdependencies between all portfolios that may exist in the organisation and demonstrates how priorities are established for projects and resources in an integrated and whole-of-organisation manner.

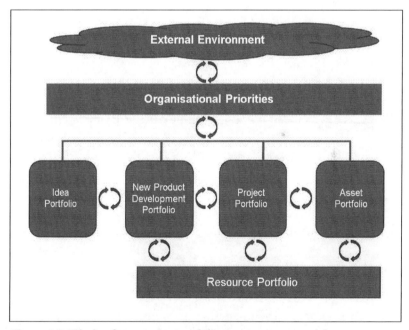

Figure 6.2. Whole of enterprise portfolio management model

The model highlights that organisational priorities are established, set and adjusted based on the interaction with the external political, socio-cultural, financial, technological and competitive environment.

These organisational priorities flow through to various portfolios, such as the Idea Portfolio, New Product Development Portfolio, Project Portfolio and Asset Portfolio. However, organisational priorities are not singular, linear or static, but are linked and dynamic in nature and change based upon not only the interaction between these portfolios but also the interaction between each portfolio and their resultant effect each interaction has on the priorities of the organisation. Dynamic interaction occurs within the context of the portfolios themselves as well as between each portfolio and the organisation and the environment in which it operates. Each individual portfolio establishes a set of priorities which interact dynamically with the priorities of each other portfolio as well with the overarching organisational priorities.

For example, for the Idea Portfolio raw ideas are conceived and pass through an idea screen (Cooper 2005) within the Idea Portfolio. Viable ideas are prioritised and flagged for development at which point the flow from the Idea Portfolio to the New Product Portfolio (after Larsson 2007 and Cooper 2005). Through the new product development process, additional ideas are conceived and may pass back into the Idea Portfolio for screening. Interactions, both within the Idea Portfolio and between the Idea Portfolio and the New Product Portfolio, generate projects (within the Project Portfolio) and consume organisational resources (in the Resource Portfolio) based on their own priorities established in the Ideas Portfolio.

The project portfolio also interacts with the Asset Portfolio (after Krebs 2009 and Larsson 2007). Projects (in the Project Portfolio) develop and create assets (in the Asset Portfolio), which over time are maintained, not only to ensure these assets continue to operate and perform as designed, but to also generate ongoing benefit to the organisation. The projects that develop, create, maintain and enhance individual assets consume resources (from the Resource Portfolio) and as such interact with the Resource Portfolio.

Conclusion

The introduction of the portfolio concept in both the finance and information technology sectors brought with it a shift in thinking. Rather than individual investments and assets being examined in isolation, the collective risk and rewards of all investments and assets are assessed to ensure the organisation achieves an optimum balance between risk and reward.

Whilst the concepts aid in sense-making in a multi-project context, and attempt to provide a framework for prioritisation, decision making and the management of competing resource priorities, a conceptual understanding of portfolio management requires a significant mental shift away from the linear and mechanistic structures used in the management of individual projects. Instead, an integrated and dynamic approach is required, given the regular and ongoing changes in the external environment and, in turn, the shifts in the organisation's strategy and priorities.

Existing project portfolio tools and techniques help the organisation to identify, select and manage an optimum selection of projects in order to achieve an organisation's strategic outcomes. However, if the asset portfolio or resource portfolio lens is used, a different set of priorities and organisational strategies may become apparent. Through this paper we have proposed an integrated portfolio model highlighting the inter-related nature of various types of portfolios in the enterprise and propose an integrated and synthesised approach to project portfolio management.

Traditional views of project portfolio management are limited. Organisational priorities are linked and dynamic in nature and change based upon not only the interaction between each portfolio, as too are the projects, assets or resources that comprise these portfolios. The inter-relatedness between each portfolio is critical and through re-balancing, impacts both the organisation's priorities as well as the priorities in each other portfolio. This approach conceptualises the research themes identified in Rethinking Project Management at the Portfolio Level.

We acknowledge that this paper provides a theoretical model that needs to be demonstrated and proven through further research, testing the theoretical boundaries of this model as well as how it fits and can be practically applied in organisations. The most obvious place to begin this research agenda is to examine the program and portfolio management in a range of government and non-government organisations, delivering varied services and products.

References

American Association of Cost Engineers. 2006. *Total Cost Management (TCM) Framework: An Integrated Approach to Portfolio, Program and Project Management.* AACE International. Morgantown: AACE International.

Archer, N; Ghasemzadeh, F. 1999. 'Project portfolio selection techniques: A review and a suggested integrated approach'. In *Project portfolio management: Selecting and prioritizing projects for competitive advantage,* edited by Dye, L D; Pennypacker, J S. West Chester, PA: Center for Business Practices: 207–238

Association for Project Management. 2006. *APM Body of Knowledge.* 5th edn. High Wycombe: Association for Project Management.

Barney, J. 1991. 'Firm resources and sustained competitive advantage'. *Journal of Management* 17 (1): 99–120.

Buttrick, R. 2000. *The Interactive Project Workout.* 2nd edn. London: Pearson Education Ltd.

Pennypacker, J S, ed. 2005. *Project Portfolio Management Maturity Model: A Benchmark of Current Business Practices.* Havertown: Center for Business Practices.

Cleland, D, Ireland, L. 2007. *Project Management: Strategic Design and Implementation.* 5th edn. New York: McGraw-Hill.

Cooper, R G. 2005. A stage-gate idea-to-launch framework for driving new products to market. In *Project Portfolio Management: A Practical Guide to Selecting Projects, Managing Portfolios and Maximising Benefits,* edited by Levine, H. San Francisco, CA: John Wiley & Sons: 285–317.

Dye, L D; Pennypacker, J S. 2000. *Project Portfolio Management and Managing Multiple Projects: Two Sides of the Same Coin?* Proceedings of the Project Management Institute Annual Seminars & Symposium. Houston, Texas: Project Management Institute.

Engwall, M; Jerbrandt, A. 2003. 'The resource allocation syndrome: The prime challenge of multi-project management'. *International Journal of Project Management* 21(6): 403–409.

Forrester Research. 2004. *Defining IT Portfolio Management.* Forrester Research.

Foti, R. 2002. 'Priority decisions'. *PM Network* April: 24–29.

Gareis, R. 1989. 'Management by project: The management approach for the future'. *International Journal of Project Management* 7 (4): 243–249.

Gareis, R. 2006. 'Program management and project portfolio management'. In *Global Project Management Handbook,* 2nd edn, edited by Cleland, D I; Gareis, R., New York: McGraw-Hill.

Hill, G M. 2008. *The Complete Project Management Office Handbook.* Boca Raton: Auerbach Publications.

Hubbard, D. 2007. *How to Measure Anything: Finding the Value of Intangibles in Business.* Hoboken: Wiley.

International Project Management Association. 2008. *IPMA Competence Baseline Version 3.0.* Nijkerk, the Netherlands: IPMA.

Jacob, K. 1999. 'Executing projects with portfolio management in large multi-business, multi-functional organisations'. In Proceedings of the 30th Annual Project Management Institute 1999 Seminars and Symposium. Pennsylvania: Project Management Institute: 1

Jensen, M.C., and W.H. Meckling (1976) 'Theory of the Firm: Managerial Behavior, Agency Costs and Ownership Structure' *Journal of Financial Economics,* October, V.3, 4, pp. 305–360.

Kendall, G. I & Rollins, S C. 2003. *Advanced Project Portfolio Management and the PMO. Multiplying ROI at Warp Speed.* Boca Raton, FL: J Ross Publishing.

Krebs, J. 2009. *Agile Portfolio Management.* Washington: Microsoft Press.

Lacontora, J; Mathews, S. 2009. 'Ideas to innovation'. Presentation to IRI New Business Development Network Meeting, Baltimore. IRI New Business Development Network. Accessed 2 November 2009. Available from:http:\\www.iriinc.org/Content/.../Idea_Portfolio_Management.ppt

Larsson, F. 2007. *Managing the New Product Portfolio: Towards and End-to-End Approach.* Technical University of Denmark.

Longman, A; Sandahl, D; Speir, W. 1999. 'Preventing project proliferation'. *PM Network* July: 39–41.

Markowitz, H. 1952. 'Portfolio selection'. *Journal of Finance* 7 (1): 77–91.

McFarlan, F. 1981. 'Portfolio approach to information systems'. *Harvard Business Review* (Sep-Oct): 142–150.

Miller, J. 2002. 'A proven project portfolio management process. In Proceedings of the Project Management Institute Annual Seminars & Symposium. San Antonio,

Texas: Project Management Institute.

Milosevic, D Z; Srivannaboon, S. 2006. 'A theoretical framework for aligning project management with business strategy'. In PMI Research Conference Proceedings. Montreal: Project Management Institute.

Milosevic, D; Patanakul, P. 2002. 'Secrets of successful multiproject managers. In Proceedings of the Project Management Institute Annual Seminars & Symposiums. San Antonio, Texas: Project Management Institute.

Morris, P. 2002. 'Science, objective knowledge, and the theory of project management.' ICE James Forrest Lecture. http://www.bartlett.ucl.ac.uk/research/management/ICEpaperFinal.pdf

Morris, P; Jamieson, A. 2004. *Translating Corporate Strategy into Project Strategy: Realising Corporate Strategy Through Project Management.* Newton Square: Project Management Institute.

Nash, T K. 2002. 'Project portfolio management – PMO application'. In Proceedings of the Project Management Institute Annual Seminars and Symposium. San Antonio, Texas: Project Management Institute.

Office of Government Commerce. (2009). *Portfolio Management Guide (Final Public Consultation Draft).* UK: Office of Government Commerce.

Owen, J. and Linger, H. (2009), Resolution of Complexity in ISD Projects. Papadopoulos, G.A.; Wojtkowski, W., Wojtkowski, G., Wrycza, S., & Zupancic, J. (eds) *Information Systems Development Towards A Service Provision Society.* Springer-Verlag: New York,

Patanakul, P; Milosevic, D. 2005. 'Multiple-project managers: What competencies do you need?' *Project Perspectives* 2005: 28–33.

Penrose, E. 1959. *Theory of the Growth of the Firm.* New York: Wiley.

Platje, A; Seidel, H. 1994. 'Project and portfolio planning cycle: Project-based management for multiproject challenge'. *International Journal of Project Management* 12: 100–106.

Project Management Institute. 2008a. *A Guide to the Project Management Body of Knowledge.* 2nd edn. Newtown Square: Project Management Institute.

Project Management Institute. 2008b. *Organisational Project Management Maturity Model* (OPM3). 2nd edn. Newtown Square, PA: Project Management Institute.

Sanchez, H; Robert; Pellerin, R. 2008. 'A project portfolio risk-opportunity identification framework'. *Project Management Journal,* 39 (3): 97–109.

Sauer, C.; Reich, B.H. 2009. 'Rethinking IT project management: Evidence of a new mindset and its implications' *International Journal of Project Management,* 27, 2: 182–193.

Thiry, M. 2004. 'Program management: A strategic decision management process'. In *The Wiley Guide to Managing Projects* edited by Morris, P. Hoboken: Wiley: 257–287.

Turner, J R. 1999. *The Handbook of Project-Based Management.* 2nd edn. Maidenhead: McGraw-Hill.

Turner, J.R; Cochrane, R.A. 1993. 'The goals and methods matrix: coping with projects for which the goals and/or methods of achieving them are ill-defined', *International Journal of Project Management,* 11, 2: 93–101.

Weill, P; Broadbent, M. 1998. *Leveraging the New Infrastructure: How Market Leaders Capitalised on Information Technology.* Boston: Harvard Business School Press.

Winter, M.; Smith, C.; Morris, P.; Cicmil, S. 2006. 'Directions for future research in project management: The main findings of a UK government-funded research network' *International Journal of Project Management,* 24:638–649.

Zika-Viktorsson, A; Sundstrom, P; Engwall, M. 2006. 'Project overload: An exploratory study of work and management and multi-project settings'. *International Journal of Project Management* 24: 385–394.

Chapter 7

Widening the perspective on organisational capabilities for project portfolio management

Catherine P Killen

University of Technology, Sydney, Australia

Robert A Hunt

Macquarie University, Australia

Project portfolio management (PPM) is increasingly recognised as a wide-ranging and valuable organisational capability. This paper is based on a study of the PPM capabilities for product and service development project portfolios in six successful and innovative Australian organisations. The findings highlight the role of wider organisational factors such as organisational structure, culture, power and politics, and organisational learning. A holistic representation of an organisation's PPM capability is presented that clusters the factors into three dimensions: processes, structures and people. An organisational learning capability is shown to support the entire PPM capability, enabling it to develop and evolve to adapt to changing environmental conditions and therefore to continue to contribute to competitive advantage in a dynamic environment.

Introduction

As many organisations shift to 'management by projects', projects are often the main vehicle for delivering organisational strategy. Project portfolio management (PPM) is an important organisational capability that enables organisations to align projects with strategy and to ensure adequate resourcing (Levine 2005; Wideman 2004). PPM is of growing importance in a dynamic environment where organisational survival and economic growth increasingly depend upon a steady stream of successful projects for the development of new products and services. Therefore the importance of maximising outcomes from new product and service development project portfolios is escalating (DITR 2003; OECD 2000).

A relatively new body of empirical research into PPM is starting to generate findings related to PPM practices and innovation outcomes. Just as project management (PM) is more than the charts and tools employed, PPM also involves a wider range of capabilities beyond the procedures and processes used. The role of wider organisational factors, such as organisational structure, culture, power, politics and organisational learning, are highlighted by recent research on the PPM capabilities for new product and service development project portfolios in a series of successful and innovative Australian organisations.

This paper presents research findings that suggest that organisations need to acknowledge and address the wide range of organisational factors that comprise a PPM capability in order to achieve the best organisational outcomes from their project portfolios. This paper first introduces PPM and its relationship to PM and then briefly summarises the literature on PPM, highlighting research on the multiple organisational factors that influence PPM capabilities. Next it outlines the methods for the research study and discusses the findings, focusing on organisational structures and responsibilities, people and organisational learning. The conclusion sums up the paper and suggests areas for future research.

Background

PPM is a management capability that aims to optimise the outcomes from project investments across a portfolio. The emergence of a distinct management capability or function for PPM is a fairly recent phenomenon compared with the related discipline of PM (Cooper, Edgett & Kleinschmidt 1997a; 1997b; Levine 2005). The past decade has seen an escalation in the amount of literature, research and practitioner activity focused on PPM, reflecting the increasing importance placed on PPM capabilities (Kwak & Anbari 2009; Levine 2005). The swell of interest in PPM can be attributed to some of the challenges presented by a globalised, information-rich, dynamic and competitive environment. One such challenge is the shift to 'management by projects' for organisational activities (Gareis 1989; Turner 1999), many of which were previously viewed as operational (Walker, Arlt & Norrie 2008). Therefore projects are often the main vehicle for delivering organisational strategy (Artto, Dietrich & Nurminen 2004; Poskela, Dietrich & Artto

2003; Turner, 1999). This 'projectisation' of organisations has many drivers, including competitive pressures, increased complexity of organisational activities and the increasing availability and success of PM tools (Cleland 1999; Webb 1994). Related to this shift is an intensified focus on improving PM capabilities and a strong trend toward a more strategic perspective for the management of projects (Cooper, Edgett & Kleinschmidt 2001; Dye & Pennypacker 1999; Levine 2005). The growing interest in PPM has led to increasing levels of research in this area aimed at understanding and improving organisational PPM capability.

One widely accepted and referenced definition views PPM as a 'dynamic decision process wherein the list of active new products and ... development projects is constantly revised. In this process, new projects are evaluated, selected and prioritised. Existing projects may be accelerated, killed, or de-prioritised and resources are allocated and reallocated to the active projects' (Cooper et al. 2001, 3). This definition focuses on PPM as a process, whereas Levine (2005, 22) takes a wider view and defines PPM as 'the management of the project portfolio so as to maximise the contribution of projects to the overall welfare and success of the enterprise'. The literature proposes that organisational capabilities often involve the exchange and development of information and supports the definition of a 'PPM capability' as an organisational capacity to deploy combinations of resources through organisational processes to produce a desired outcome (Amit & Schoemaker 1993). To emphasise a holistic organisational capability perspective, a PPM capability is defined in this paper as 'the overall organisational ability to manage the project portfolio and maximise its contribution to the success of the organisation'.

The literature regularly notes that an organisation's PPM capability includes processes such as the policies, practices, activities, procedures, methods and tools that managers use for ongoing resource allocation and reallocation among a portfolio of projects (see for example Cooper et al. 2001; Levine 2005; McDonough & Spital 2003). In addition to the process elements, the literature increasingly acknowledges that an organisation's capability to manage its project portfolio is also dependent upon a wide range of organisational factors such as culture and communication (Blomquist & Muller 2006; Yelin 2005). The PPM capability is responsible for the effective deployment of strategy through projects and it provides a holistic perspective for ongoing decision-making to maintain the most effective combination of projects. The goals of the PPM capability are: aligning projects with strategy, maintaining a balance of project types and ensuring that the project portfolio fits with resource capability so that the organisation can gain the maximum value from the investment (Cooper, Edgett & Kleinschmidt 2002; Kendall & Rollins 2003). In this way effective PPM capabilities are proposed to enhance an organisation's competitive advantage.

Relationship between PM and PPM

In recent years there has been a marked shift in PM circles to enhanced interest in multiple-project environments and the strategic impact of projects (see, for example, Artto, Martinsuo, Dietrich & Kujala 2008; Martinsuo & Ikavalko 2006; Söderlund 2004). PPM has gained recognition and attention from the PM community as a tool for maximising the organisational returns from project investments, particularly by improving the alignment of projects with strategy and ensuring resource sufficiency. Historically PM has been viewed as an operational rather than a strategic asset (Jugdev & Thomas 2002) and success has been measured in operational terms such as budget and time metrics. It is increasingly emphasised that it is not enough to perform projects really well if the wrong projects are being completed (Levine 2005; O'Connor 2004). A popular distinction between PM and PPM is that PM focuses on 'doing projects right' and PPM focuses on 'doing the right projects' (Cooper et al. 2001). The rationale is that even when on budget, in time and to scope, a project may not deliver the desired organisational benefits such as profit, market share or leadership. Furthermore, some projects that are viewed as a failure from an operational perspective (due to exceeding time or budget, for example) may actually be very successful in terms of their contribution to organisational revenue (Stander & Buys 2008).

PPM is therefore an important partner to PM for effective organisational outcomes. PPM is a more recently established discipline, but just as PM research is evolving beyond a process focus, PPM research is also starting to acknowledge the importance of factors such as learning, teamwork, leadership and human resource management. This shift is recognised by literature that emphasises the need for an integrated understanding of PM and PPM within a wider organisational context that includes social and other considerations (Winter, Smith, Morris & Cicmil 2006).

PPM and organisational capabilities, strategy and learning

PPM focuses on the decisions about how best to spend or invest resources that are central to organisational strategy. Strategic frameworks, in particular those based on the resource-based view (RBV) and dynamic capabilities help to explain how organisational capabilities for PPM can enhance competitive advantage.

A significant aspect of organisational strategy is the identification, development and maintenance of the important organisational resources that underpin competitive advantage (O'Regan & Ghobadian 2004). The RBV assumes that resources are not uniform across competing organisations and uses this heterogeneity to explain the differing organisational success rates. Resources that are valuable, rare, inimitable and non-substitutable form the best basis for sustainable competitive advantage by being difficult for other organisations to copy or acquire (Barney 1991). While some types of resources can be bought and sold, valuable resources like capabilities cannot easily be transferred from one organisation to another (Makadok 2001). Capabilities therefore need to be developed within an organisation and tailored for that organisation through organisational routines and specific investments in enhancing information exchange and learning (Ethiraj, Kale, Krishnan & Singh 2005; Zollo & Winter 2002). Therefore organisational learning plays a strong role in the development of organisational capabilities (Moingeon & Edmondson 1996).

Dynamic capabilities have been identified as a class of organisational capabilities that enable organisations to effectively respond to changes in the dynamic environments in which they compete (Eisenhardt & Martin 2000; Teece, Pisano and Shuen 1997). A behavioural orientation for understanding dynamic capabilities focuses on the learning aspects embedded in the processes (Wang & Ahmed 2007). Three component factors of dynamic capabilities that emphasise learning-based behavioural orientations are: adaptive capacity (the ability to identify and capitalise on emerging market opportunities), absorptive capacity (the ability to identify and integrate new external knowledge with existing internal knowledge for competitive gain) and innovative capacity (the ability to develop new products and/or markets) (Wang & Ahmed 2007).

Teece et al.'s (1997) 'processes, positions and paths' framework has been used to analyse existing empirical literature to illustrate mechanisms through which the PPM capability contributes to competitive advantage (Killen, Hunt & Kleinschmidt 2007). In this analysis, PPM is shown to act as a dynamic capability through processes that draw upon and contribute to the resource position and are shaped by past decisions and organisational paths as well as future options and decisions (Teece et al. 1997). PPM decisions determine which innovation activities an organisation will undertake and affect the longer term development, acquisition and retirement of organisational resources to support the strategy. In this way, the PPM capability draws on the existing resources and capabilities of an organisation while also helping to develop these resources and capabilities (Cepeda & Vera 2007; Wang & Ahmed 2007).

An organisational learning capability enables the organisation to obtain, process, interpret and respond to information and to change organisational behaviours to generate opportunities and improve organisational outcomes (Easterby-Smith & Araujo 1999; Senge 1990). Learning capabilities contribute to competitive advantage by shaping other organisational capabilities and are an essential pre-condition for the development of dynamic organisational capabilities (Zollo & Winter 2002). The literature regularly asserts that organisational capabilities that dynamically manage the use of other organisational resources must continually adapt to the environment to create a series of temporary competitive advantages (Eisenhardt & Martin 2000; Fiol 2001; Helfat & Raubitschek 2000; O'Regan & Ghobadian 2004; Teece et al. 1997). Therefore, an organisation's ability to learn and to adjust their PPM practices is an important capability for sustained innovation success.

PPM capability research

Most of the literature on PPM focuses exclusively or primarily on 'PPM processes', however a number of studies have identified and focused on various organisational factors thought to influence the PPM capability. This section highlights some of the literature on these wider organisational factors.

Some studies focus on management skills and the differences between PM and PPM environments. Different management skills are found to be required at the two levels (Frick & Shenhar 2000; Khurana & Rosenthal 1998; Pellegrinelli et al. 2006) and a recent study has helped to clarify the responsibilities of managers with respect to the PPM process, as distinct from the responsibilities of the individual project managers (Blomquist & Muller 2006). The findings suggest that roles and responsibilities will depend upon the environment and confirm that there is no standard approach to the assignment of responsibility for the PPM capability to specific departments or managerial positions (Center for Business Practices 2005). The negative influence of politics and conflicting motivations on the outcomes of PPM processes must be acknowledged and addressed by going 'beyond resource allocation and … addressing incentive structures,

accounting systems, and other deeply embedded features of the organisation'
(Engwall & Jerbrant 2003, 408).

There is no standard framework or theory behind most PPM research
other than a general proposition that some aspect of the PPM capability
will have an effect on the resulting success of the projects in the portfolio.
Organisational efforts to develop PPM capabilities are supported by research
that shows a correlation between established PPM capabilities and improved
outcomes (Cooper et al. 2001; Pennypacker 2005). Yet PPM capabilities
do not emerge fully formed and they must be established and developed
over time (Cauchick Miguel 2008; Killen, Hunt & Kleinschmidt 2008a;
O'Connor 2004). For example, the literature proposes that for a portfolio
management approach to be applied in an organisation, the organisational
structure must facilitate a portfolio-level view of the project portfolio and
enable a dynamic portfolio-level decision process (Cooper et al. 2001;
McDonough & Spital 2003). Projects must also be managed well to enable
integration with PPM processes and facilitate effective data collection for
PPM decision-making (Martinsuo & Lehtonen 2007; Wideman 2004). In
addition, the existence and communication of a strategy is an important pre-
condition for portfolio management.

The literature highlights that PPM is primarily a strategic decision-
making process that involves identifying, minimising and diversifying risk,
and understanding, accepting and making trade-offs. The bulk of the PPM
literature assumes that decisions are made on a rational basis within a PPM
process. However, some authors question this assumption and find that
other influences on PPM decisions can result in less than rational outcomes
(Christiansen & Varnes 2008; Eskerod, Blichfeldt & Toft 2004). Influences
from peers or managers, the level of complexity of the decisions and the
organisational learning processes that reinforce certain decision types all
affect decision-making and are shown to lead to PPM decisions that do not
follow the rational calculative decision-making processes often assumed for
PPM. For example, people develop an emotional attachment to a project
that can cloud their judgment and supersede rational objectives as a basis
for decision-making (Kent 2007). Humans also have a tendency for bias
towards excessive optimism. However, a PPM process can address such
human shortcomings by improving transparency in the decision-making
process (Lovallo & Sibony 2006).

To summarise, the literature on PPM reveals a strong relationship with
PM, as effective PM is required for PPM and the growth in PM interest
and research is a major driver for the increased interest in PPM. PPM

research focuses largely on processes and tools, but the literature increasingly acknowledges wider organisational factors such as culture, structure, organisational learning and human resource management. The literature suggests that these factors are important but under-researched components of an effective PPM capability; however there is a lack of research into the full scope of a PPM capability. This supports further investigation to better understand the full breadth of organisational factors that contribute to an organisation's PPM capability.

Research method

This paper reports the findings from a recent Australian research project that explored the multiple dimensions of a PPM capability as part of a wider study into the relationship between PPM capabilities and organisational outcomes. The research focused on organisations that manage a portfolio of projects for the development of new products and services. These organisations represented both manufacturing-based and service-based environments to present a wide cross section of PPM environments.

This research was conducted through a sequential two-phase mixed-method study comprised of a primarily quantitative questionnaire-based survey in the initial phase followed by a primarily qualitative multiple-case study. The initial questionnaire-based survey of 60 Australian organisations set the scene for the case studies by providing comparable PPM data for both service and manufacturing PPM capabilities, by highlighting the strategic role of PPM capabilities and by revealing significant relationships between top management support for PPM, PPM maturity and positive portfolio outcomes (Killen, Hunt & Kleinschmidt 2008a). This paper focuses on the findings from the subsequent multiple-case study that was designed to explore PPM capabilities in further detail.

The multiple-case study focused on six large Australian manufacturing and service organisations (see Table 7.1). The cases were purposefully selected to illustrate the PPM capabilities in organisations with successful new product portfolio outcomes in a wide range of industries. Research was conducted to select organisations with development project portfolios managed in Australia that were innovation leaders in their industry, with sustained (10 years or more) records of new product and service success and above average growth attributed largely to their successful product and service offerings. Each selected organisation was contacted and the reasons for selecting the organisation and the goals for the research were outlined in initial conversations and correspondence. All six of the organisations that were approached agreed to participate in the research. Annual revenues of the six organisations range from A$800 million to several billion dollars. Four of the organisations studied are independent Australian organisations and two are self-contained and locally managed entities that are part of a global group. The revenue reported for these two is for the local entity only.

	Service industries			Manufacturing industries		
Industry type	Profess-ional Services	Tele-communi-cations	Finance	Heavy Industrial Machinery	Medical Equip-ment	Building materials
Organis-ation code name	SERV	TELE	FIN	IND	MED	MAT

Table 7.1. Profile of the case study organisations

The study was designed to provide a rich picture of PPM capabilities and to explore the bounds of the PPM capability. It focused on PPM capabilities at organisations with successful project portfolios with the aim of identifying potential 'best practices' (the practices associated with improved outcomes) while recognising that correlation and causality cannot be established through such a study. The case study process included the review of public and confidential information and a total of 23 semi-structured interviews with between three and five managers at each organisation. The managers were purposely selected to represent high-level diverse perspectives including technical, marketing, operations and executive perspectives. Due to the diversity of the nature of the organisations in the study, the types of departments and titles of the managers interviewed varied; for example, partners, vice presidents (technical and marketing), product development heads and portfolio managers were included in the study. The interviews at five of the six organisations were audio recorded and all interviews were transcribed by the researcher, usually within a day of the interview. The average duration of the interviews was 109 minutes.

The interviews were constructed in a semi-structured manner to allow for stories to be told and themes to emerge. Although some themes had been previously identified in the literature, the interviews were conducted in an exploratory nature encouraging discussion and unconstrained by the pre-identified themes. Interviewees were asked about their product strategy, the nature of their products and services and any trends affecting the portfolio; the environment and culture; their processes for PM and PPM; and the portfolio outcomes. Particular attention and time was devoted to understanding the evolution of the capability and the environment, and in discussing influences, plans and expectations for future development and change. Three or four specific projects representing a range of risk, size and outcomes were analysed as embedded cases at each organisation and used to contribute to the understanding of each case environment. In addition to the interview data, four to six types of other data sources were analysed for each case including web sites and publications, internal process diagrams, procedure manuals and example templates, reports and graphs.

An iterative process of analysing the data was used to identify emerging themes during the case study process. A cross-case spreadsheet was used to identify themes and categorise information as the interviews were progressing. Information from documents and other case data was also entered into the cross-case spreadsheet. For the final analysis, all interview data was then entered into the qualitative research software NVivo™ for thorough coding and further identification and refinement of themes and sub-themes. In the findings presented below, quotations from managers are identified using the organisation code from Table 7.1 and a person code where applicable (for example, [TELEp4] indicates a comment from manager number four at TELE).

Findings

The themes identified during the cross-case analysis of the multiple case studies reveal that an organisation's capability for PPM encompasses much more than the processes and methods used. The wider organisational factors that emerged during the multiple case studies highlight the level of attention paid to establishing a suitable organisational structure, multiple people-related factors and the role of organisational learning in the case organisations' PPM capabilities. These emergent themes are categorised within 'structure and responsibility' dimensions and 'people' dimensions that interact with the 'process' dimensions in a new model of a PPM capability shown in Figure 7.1. This model also illustrates the underlying organisational learning capability that was observed in themes emerging from the case-study findings. Findings that support the identification of each of these major dimensions of the PPM capability (processes, structure and responsibility, people and organisational learning) are summarised below.

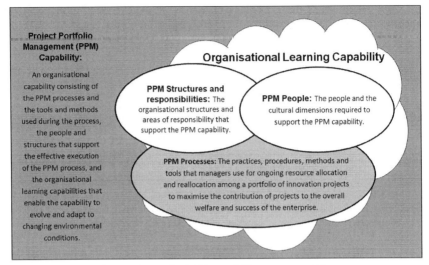

Figure 7.1. Three dimensions of a PPM capability supported by an organisational learning capability

Processes

The research findings provided detail of the process dimension of the PPM capabilities at the six case organisations. The processes were very similar across the industries and included stage gate processes, tailored to project type, with portfolio level reviews conducted by a review board at one or more of the gates. Through the organisational learning capability, processes were regularly reviewed and adjusted as the nature of the environment and the portfolio changed. These process-related findings are presented in other publications (e. g. Killen 2008); this paper focuses on the findings that relate to the wider organisational factors of structure and responsibility, people and organisational learning.

Structure and responsibility

Organisational structures vary across the six organisations studied. Nevertheless organisational structures and the assignment of PPM responsibilities are a major aspect of each organisation's PPM capabilities. In two of the cases, the responsibility for PPM is shared equally between senior managers in technical and marketing functions [SERV, IND], whereas in the remaining cases one person takes responsibility for overseeing the process. PPM roles and responsibilities are an extension of existing roles in most of the cases; however at SERV and MAT new roles and responsibilities have been created to focus specifically on the PPM capability. While there is no standard organisational structure, the prevalence of high-level reviews and changes to organisational structures and PPM responsibilities indicates their importance.

All of the organisations had experienced some changes to their organisational structure in the previous three years that were directly related to the development of their PPM capability. The changes varied between slight changes to responsibilities and emphasis on PPM [IND], elevation of the function responsible for new product projects [MAT, TELE, MED] or the creation of new departments [SERV, MAT, FIN]. The relationship between changes to a PPM capability and changes to the organisational structure is strong, although the influence was found to flow either way or both ways. In three of the cases a change to the organisational structure was the catalyst for the development or enhancement of the PPM capability [TELE, MAT, FIN], while in two of the cases the changes to the organisational structure were required as a result of the establishment of a PPM capability [SERV, MAT]. For example, in FIN the establishment of a new functional area to focus on product development was the catalyst for the development and implementation of tailored PPM processes and methods. In MAT, a major organisational restructure elevated the position and visibility of the product development project portfolio, emphasising its importance. This elevation of the strategic importance of projects led to increased efforts to establish a formal structured PPM capability. The establishment of the PPM capability at that organisation led in turn to further changes in the organisational structure and the creation of roles and responsibilities focused on PPM.

All of the organisations had created a new structure for a 'Portfolio Review Board' (PRB) as the main decision-making body for the PPM capability. The names used for the PRB differ at each organisation, but the groups have similar concepts and compositions. The members of the PRB are high-level managers in all of the organisations. PRB board members are also generally chosen to represent a diverse set of perspectives; however, the nature of the diversity varies among the organisations studied. For example, one of the manufacturers has a PRB consisting of marketing heads from diverse global regions [MED], while another has a PRB consisting of divisional heads representing different functions [MAT]. One service-based organisation selects its PRB to represent a combination of geographic regions and functional areas [SERV]. The common philosophy behind PRB member selection at each of the case organisations is that a diverse set of perspectives provided by individuals with seniority and accountability as well as broad and deep experience will lead to balanced portfolio decisions. In addition to the attention paid to the composition and structure of the PRB, the case organisations also pointed out the importance of commitment and teamwork within the PRB as outlined in the following section.

PPM as a human-centred process

The increased availability of specialised computer-based applications for the management of project portfolios was acknowledged by managers at each of the case organisations. Most of the managers are watching developments in this area, but are not convinced of the merits of extensive computerisation of the process. Managers at MAT and FIN discussed their view of PPM as a human-centred process and emphasised the value of the review board interactions in evaluating information and making decisions. They expressed concern that a computer-based method will require complex input on many factors and commented that they did not believe computers can replace the need for managerial oversight and analysis, or the role of intuition and gut feeling in decision-making. For example, one manager highlighted the importance of the communication generated by the human-centred process: 'We have looked at some [software] providers. One thing that makes me reluctant is the great thing about the [meetings] is that they generate a valuable dialogue around the process' [MATp2]. The dialogue is thought to be a major factor in the success of the PPM capability and there are concerns that any change that 'reduces the opportunities' for face-to-face dialogue may jeopardise the process [MATp1]. Another manager believes that scoring and weighting systems are 'ways to avoid accountability' and notes, 'If you had perfect knowledge you might be able to do that, but last time I looked we worked in an imperfect world ... so you've got to make calls based on your experience and your judgment' [FINp2].

None of the Australian organisations studied uses a comprehensive computer-based PPM system. While all of the managers interviewed rejected the notion that computers might become central to the PPM decision processes, some of the managers did acknowledge the potential benefits that computerising additional aspects of the process could deliver. For example, some plan to improve their ability to generate graphic displays for viewing project data and project scenarios through computerised access to project data in the future [SERV, TELE, MAT]. Portfolio maps or roadmaps are used at all but one [FIN] of the organisations in some form to help PPM teams overview the portfolio of projects and make decisions. The most common type of change planned for PPM at the case organisations will involve improved portfolio view and idea management capabilities using computers.

Organisational learning

The final theme addressed in this paper shows how organisational learning capabilities contribute to the development of PPM capabilities, and highlights the importance of learning and development in a dynamic capability like a PPM capability. One of the most notable aspects of the PPM capabilities at the six case organisations was the level of change. As highlighted earlier, the findings reveal a history of change and adjustment to the PPM capabilities. SERV and FIN had established a new PPM capability; MED, MAT and TELE introduced major re-design of their PPM capability within the previous three or four years; and IND had made ongoing incremental changes within an established PPM capability. The findings at all of the organisations provide evidence of ongoing evaluation and change to the PPM capability, and all had made changes within the previous year. All of the organisations were also planning for further changes and adjustments in the near future as they strive to increase the maturity and effectiveness of their PPM capability. Despite the evidence of regular review and change to the PPM capability, only the managers at MAT and SERV felt that their PPM capability included adequate feedback mechanisms. Managers at the other organisations recognised that their review and feedback mechanisms were ad hoc and felt that this was an area of weakness that should be addressed.

The case findings also indicate that both intentional and unintentional learning processes influence the evolution of the PPM capability. Organisations intentionally invest in learning activities that enhance both tacit and explicit learning mechanisms in order to establish and improve their PPM capabilities (Zollo & Winter 2002). The case studies show that PPM capabilities evolve through the co-evolution of tacit accumulation of experiences and explicit articulation and codification processes (Killen, Hunt & Kleinschmidt 2008b).

The research also indicates that PPM capabilities evolve organically and unintentionally through accumulated decision-making experiences. This unintentional evolution of PPM capabilities can result in undesirable changes to the PPM capability such as the 'success trap', prompting additional purposeful efforts to counteract these changes. The 'success trap' occurs when accumulated decision-making experiences create a condition that favours short-term 'exploitation' projects at the expense of long-term 'exploration' projects (Levinthal & March 1993). This is one of the primary reasons for the case organisations to make adjustments to their PPM process – to improve the balance between 'exploitation' and 'exploration'. For example, two of the organisations have included methods in their PPM process to enhance idea generation and promote exploratory projects [SERV, IND], and another is currently redesigning their PPM process because the current process has produced an imbalance of short-term incremental projects [MED].

The case findings from each organisation provide evidence of regular investments in the development of their PPM capability through activities that enhance organisational learning processes. The cases show evidence of purposeful investments in activities to enhance both tacit and explicit learning mechanisms. Three categories of learning investments were identified in the case organisations: learning activities to promote tacit learning, explicit knowledge articulation and explicit knowledge codification. Tacit learning activities are largely experiential and involve trial and error, while explicit learning activities include deliberate processes for the articulation and codification of knowledge. An example of a tacit learning investment for PPM development is a change to the organisational structure that facilitates PPM experience accumulation. An example of an investment in explicit learning for PPM is the creation of a feedback loop where the processes and outcomes are evaluated, discussed and modified (knowledge articulation) and then documented (knowledge codification) (Killen, Hunt & Kleinschmidt 2008b).

Conclusion

The cases illustrate how, while dynamically and strategically managing organisational innovation processes and resources, the PPM capabilities themselves are very dynamic, changing and adjusting regularly. The findings enhance the understanding of PPM capabilities and provide detail of the wider organisational factors that influence the PPM capability. A range of organisational factors are found to have a role in the establishment, development and evolution of the PPM capability. These findings build upon the existing literature and are presented in this paper under three main headings: 'structure and responsibility', 'people' and 'organisational learning'.

The research highlights how organisational structure and responsibilities have been adjusted in the case organisations as part of the process of establishing and improving their PPM capabilities. The findings particularly emphasise the level of investment these organisations have made in the purposeful and considered creation of a review board including a diverse set of experienced managers with portfolio responsibility.

Managers at the case organisations stressed the role of organisational culture in creating an environment that provides support for the PPM capability. PPM was thought to be a human-centred capability and people were highlighted as an important organisational resource that must be nurtured, developed and allocated effectively through the PPM capability.

Finally, organisational learning, aided by investments in learning activities, was shown to enable the PPM capabilities at the case organisations to evolve in response to their dynamic environments. This finding aligns with the literature, supporting the identification of PPM as a dynamic capability (Teece et al. 1997, Zollo & Winter 2002) and showing how, by continually adapting to the environment, PPM can help an organisation maintain competitive advantages (Eisenhardt & Martin, 2000; Fiol, 2001; Helfat & Raubitschek, 2000; O'Regan & Ghobadian, 2004).

The findings are based on a limited number of cases purposefully selected to illustrate the PPM capabilities in organisations with successful new product portfolio outcomes in a wide range of industries. However, due to the small sample size, the findings may not be representative and causality or correlation cannot be established between the observed PPM capabilities and the case organisations' successful outcomes. Future research is suggested to further investigate the relationship between the wide range of organisational factors that comprise a PPM capability and improved portfolio outcomes. Larger scale studies could be used to establish correlations or causality, and longitudinal studies are recommended to observe the ongoing evolution and change to PPM capabilities in organisations in response to dynamic environmental conditions.

References

Amit, R; Schoemaker, P J. 1993. 'Strategic assets and organizational rent'. *Strategic Management Journal (1986–1998)* 14 (1): 33–46.

Artto, K A; Dietrich, P H; Nurminen, M I. (2004). 'Strategy implementation by projects'. In *Innovations: Project management research 2004*, edited by Slevin, D P; Cleland, D I; Pinto J K. Newtown Square, PA: Project Management Institute: 103–122.

Artto, K; Martinsuo, M; Dietrich, P; Kujala, J. 2008. 'Project strategy: Strategy types and their contents in innovation projects'. *International Journal of Managing Projects in Business* 1 (1): 49–70.

Barney, J. 1991. 'Firm resources and sustained competitive advantage'. *Journal of Management* 17 (1): 99–120.

Blomquist, T; Muller, R. 2006. 'Practices, roles, and responsibilities of middle managers in program and portfolio management'. *Project Management Journal* 37 (1): 52–66.

Cauchick Miguel, P A. 2008. 'Portfolio management and new product development implementation: A case study in a manufacturing firm'. *International Journal of Quality & Reliability Management* 25 (1): 10–23.

Center for Business Practices. 2005. *Project Portfolio Management: A Benchmark of Current Practices*. Haverstown, PA: Center for Business Practices.

Cepeda, G; Vera, D. 2007. 'Dynamic capabilities and operational capabilities: A knowledge management perspective'. *Journal of Business Research* 60 (5): 426–437.

Christiansen, J K; Varnes, C. 2008. 'From models to practice: Decision making at portfolio meetings'. *International Journal of Quality and Reliability Management* 25 (1): 87–101.

Cleland, D I. 1999. 'The strategic context of projects'. In *Project Portfolio Management: Selecting and Prioritizing Projects for Competitive Advantage,* edited by Dye, L D; Pennypacker, J S. Havertown, PA: Center for Business Practices.

Cooper, R G; Edgett, S. J; Kleinschmidt, E J. 1997a. 'Portfolio management in new product development: Lessons from the leaders – I'. *Research Technology Management* 40 (5): 16–28.

Cooper, R G; Edgett, S J; Kleinschmidt, E J. 1997b. 'Portfolio management in new product development: Lessons from the leaders – II'. *Research Technology Management* 40 (6): 43–52.

Cooper, R G; Edgett, S J; Kleinschmidt, J. 2001. *Portfolio Management for New Products.* 2nd edn. Cambridge, MA: Perseus.

Cooper, R G; Edgett, S J; Kleinschmidt, E J. 2002. 'Optimizing the stage-gate process: What best-practice companies do – II'. *Research Technology Management* 45 (6): 43–49.

DITR. 2003. *Mapping Australian Science and Innovation – Main Report.* Department of Industry, Tourism and Resources, Canberra, November 2003.

Dye, L D; Pennypacker, J S, eds. 1999. *Project Portfolio Management: Selecting and Prioritising Projects for Competitive Advantage.* Havertown, PA: Center for Business Practices.

Easterby-Smith, M; Araujo, L. 1999 'Organisational learning: Current debates and opportunities'. In *Organizational learning and the learning organization: Developments in theory and practice,* edited by Easterby-Smith, M; Araujo, L; Burgoyne, J. London, Thousand Oaks, CA: SAGE Publications: 1–21.

Eisenhardt, K M; Martin, J A. 2000. 'Dynamic capabilities: What are they?' *Strategic Management Journal* 21 (10/11): 1105–1121.

Engwall, M; Jerbrant, A. 2003. 'The resource allocation syndrome: The prime challenge of multi-project management?' *International Journal of Project Management* 21 (6): 403–409.

Eskerod, P; Blichfeldt, B S; Toft, A S. 2004. 'Questioning the rational assumption underlying decision-making within project portfolio management literature'. Paper presented at PMI Research Conference, London, 11–14 July.

Ethiraj, S K; Kale, P; Krishnan, M S; Singh, J V. 2005. 'Where do capabilities come from and how do they matter? A study in the software services industry'. *Strategic Management Journal* 26 (1): 25–45.

Fiol, C M. 2001. 'Revisiting an identity-based view of sustainable competitive advantage'. *Journal of Management* 27 (6): 691–699.

Frick, S E; Shenhar, A J. 2000. 'Managing multiple projects in a manufacturing support environment'. *IEEE Transactions on Engineering Management* 47 (2): 258–268.

Gareis, R. 1989. 'Management by projects: The management approach for the future'. *International Journal of Project Management* 7 (4): 243–249.

Helfat, C E; Raubitschek, R S. 2000. 'Product sequencing: Co-evolution of knowledge, capabilities and products'. *Strategic Management Journal* 21 (10/11): 961–979.

Jugdev, K; Thomas, J. 2002. 'Project management maturity models: The silver bullets of competitive advantage?' *Project Management Journal* 33 (4): 4–14.

Kendall, G I; Rollins, S C. 2003. *Advanced Project Portfolio Management and the PMO: Multiplying ROI at Warp Speed.* Boca Raton, FL: J Ross Publishing.

Kent, S. 2007. 'Elimination plan'. *PM Network* 21 (9): 40–46.

Khurana, A; Rosenthal, S R. 1998. 'Towards holistic "front ends" in new product development'. *Journal of Product Innovation Management* 15 (1): 57–74.

Killen, C P. 2008. *Project Portfolio Management for Product Innovation in Service and Manufacturing Industries.* Ph.D. Thesis. Sydney: Macquarie Graduate School of Management. URL: http://hdl.handle.net/1959.14/44777

Killen, C P; Hunt, R A; Kleinschmidt, E J. 2007. 'Dynamic capabilities: innovation project portfolio management'. Proceedings of ANZAM 2007, Sydney, Australia, 4–7 December. Australia and New Zealand Academy of Management.

Killen, C P; Hunt, R A; Kleinschmidt, E J. 2008a. 'Project portfolio management for product innovation'. *International Journal of Quality and Reliability Management* 25 (1): 24–38.

Killen, C P; Hunt, R A; Kleinschmidt, E J. 2008b. 'Learning investments and organisational capabilities: Case studies on the development of project portfolio management capabilities'. *International Journal of Managing Projects in Business* 1 (3): 334–351.

Kwak, Y H; Anbari, F T. 2009. 'Analyzing project management research: Perspectives from top management journals'. *International Journal of Project Management* 27 (5): 435–446.

Levine, H A. 2005. *Project Portfolio Management: A Practical Guide to Selecting Projects, Managing Portfolios, and Maximizing Benefits.* San Francisco, CA, Chichester: Jossey-Bass, John Wiley distributor.

Levinthal, D A; March, J G. 1993. 'The myopia of learning'. *Strategic Management Journal (1986–1998)* 14 (Special issue): 95–112.

Lovallo, D P; Sibony, O. 2006. 'Distortions and deceptions in strategic decisions'. *McKinsey Quarterly* 1: 18–29.

Makadok, R. 2001. 'Toward a synthesis of the resource-based and dynamic-capability views of rent creation'. *Strategic Management Journal* 22 (5): 387–401.

Martinsuo, M; Ikavalko, H. 2006. 'Strategizing through projects: Practices and strategy realization in single projects and project portfolios'. *EGOS Colloquium.* Bergen, Norway.

Martinsuo, M; Lehtonen, P. 2007. 'Role of single-project management in achieving portfolio management efficiency'. *International Journal of Project Management* 25 (1): 56–65.

McDonough III, E F; Spital, F C. 2003. 'Managing project portfolios'. *Research Technology Management* 46 (3): 40–46.

Moingeon, B; Edmondson, A, eds. 1996. *Organizational Learning and Competitive Advantage.* London; Thousand Oaks, CA: SAGE Publications: 121–138.

O'Connor, P. 2004. 'Spiral-up implementation of NPD portfolio and pipeline management'. In *The PDMA Toolbook 2 for New Product Development*, edited by Belliveau, P; Griffin, A; Somermeyer, S M. Hoboken: John Wiley & Sons: 461–491.

O'Regan, N; Ghobadian, A. 2004. 'The importance of capabilities for strategic direction and performance'. *Management Decision* 42 (1/2): 292–312.

OECD. 2000. *A New Economy? The Changing Role of Innovation and Information Technology in Growth*. Paris. Organisation for Economic Co operation and Development.

Pellegrinelli, S; Stenning, V; Partington, D; Hemmingway, C; Mohdzain, Z; Shah, M. (2006). 'Helping or hindering? The effects of organisational factors on the performance of program management work'. In Proceedings of PMI Research Conference, Montreal, July 16–19.

Pennypacker, J S, ed. 2005. *Project Portfolio Management Maturity Model*. Haverstown, PA: Center for Business Practices.

Poskela, J; Dietrich, P; Artto, K A. 2003. 'Organizing for managing multiple projects – a strategic perspective'. In Proceedings of the 17th Conference on Business Studies, Reykjavik, 14–16 August.

Senge, P M. 1990 *The Fifth Discipline: The Art and Practice of the Learning Organization*. New York, Sydney: Doubleday/Currency Random House.

Söderlund, J. 2004. 'On the broadening scope of the research on projects: A review and a model for analysis'. *International Journal of Project Management* 22(8): 655–667.

Stander, M J; Buys, A J. 2008. 'Linking projects to business strategy through project portfolio management'. Paper presented at the International Association of the Management of Technology (IAMOT) Conference, Dubai, UAE, April 6–10.

Teece, D J; Pisano, G; Shuen, A. 1997. 'Dynamic capabilities and strategic management'. *Strategic Management Journal (1986–1998)* 18 (7): 509–533.

Turner, J R. 1999. *The Handbook of Project-based Management: Improving the Process for Achieving Strategic Objectives*. 2nd ed. London: McGraw-Hill.

Walker, D H T; Arlt, M; Norrie, J. 2008. 'The role of business strategy in PM procurement'. In *Procurement Systems – A Cross industry Project Management Perspective*, edited by Walker D H T; Rowlinson, S. Abingdon: Taylor & Francis: 140–176.

Wang, C L; Ahmed, P K.2007). 'Dynamic capabilities: A review and research agenda'. *International Journal of Management Reviews* 9 (1): 31–51.

Webb, A. 1994. *Managing Innovative Projects*. London, New York: Chapman & Hall.

Wideman, R. M. 2004. *A Management Framework for Project, Program and Portfolio Management*. Victoria, BC: Trafford Publishing.

Winter, M; Smith, C; Morris, P W G; Cicmil, S. 2006. 'Directions for future research in project management: The main findings of a UK government-funded research network'. *International Journal of Project Management* 24 (8): 638–649.

Yelin, K C. 2005. 'The role of executives in effective project portfolio management'. In *Project Portfolio Management: A Practical Guide to Selecting Projects, Managing Portfolios, and Maximizing Benefits*, edited by Levine, H A. San Francisco, CA, Chichester: Jossey-Bass: 217–227.

Zollo, M; Winter, S G. 2002. 'Deliberate learning and the evolution of dynamic capabilities'. *Organization Science* 13 (3): 339–351.

Chapter 8

From projects to programs to execute strategy

Bridging the top management conceptual divide

Raymond Young

University of Canberra, Australia

Simon Poon

University of Sydney, Australia

Paul O'Connor

RMIT University, Australia

Top management support is now thought to be the most important critical success factor. However a conceptual chasm has led to a lack of engagement between the top management and project management communities, high project failure rates have resulted and strategic goals have not been realised. A study of publicly-funded projects in the State of Victoria, Australia, illustrates these issues and their significance. Strategy and the realisation of strategic goals have been introduced as a unifying concept with the potential to bridge the gap. Project management, portfolio management, program management and project governance were reviewed to consider their role in strategic success and a model was developed to bridge the conceptual chasm. The highest priorities for developments in each of these fields were suggested to bridge the gap in practice. Program management was highlighted with recommendations to develop more effective frameworks to facilitate strategic conversation and adaptation to overcome uncertainty arising from incomplete information.

Introduction

This paper follows an unconventional structure to reflect the authors surprise at the initial findings and also to provide some insight into the research process which is often much messier that a traditional structure might suggest. It starts with a literature review that identifies a dysfunctional gap between the concerns of top managers and project managers. It then investigates the issue through a case study of the Victorian public sector which was expected to be at the forefront of practice. The results of the case study are then presented. However, they were not at all what were expected and the results were augmented with additional data to evaluate whether the findings might be a more widespread phenomenon. Discussion follows in two parts. First, a second literature review is conducted to try to explain the results. This review is quite wide ranging and explores portfolio management, program management and project governance. Second, a model is presented to try to make sense of both the literature and the research and the paper finishes with a discussion of what may have to be done within in the various disciplines to bridge the conceptual chasm.

Literature review – a conceptual chasm

Recent research has overturned conventional wisdom to find that Top Management Support (TMS) is not simply one of many critical success factors (CSF) but is the most important CSF (Young & Jordan 2008). This finding validates earlier speculation that TMS is a meta-factor that encompasses many of the other CSFs (Poon 2001). It also has major implications for project management practice which places more emphasis on methodology and user involvement.

The importance of TMS needs to be understood in the modern context where projects are increasingly used to implement strategy (Kwak & Anbari 2009; Crawford et al. 2006). Success in this context relates much more to the realisation of benefits than the traditional emphasis on on-time, on-budget (Baccarini 1999). The realisation of benefits is largely attributable to the efforts of operational and top management (Young & Jordan 2008; Cooke-Davies 2002) and does not relate strongly to project management effort (Thomsett 1989; Markus et al. 2000). This insight is not reflected in the highly cited Standish statistics or in the emphasis of any major project management textbook.

Project management researchers and practitioners have focused mainly on the factors they can control (Currie & Galliers 1999). They have not provided much if any guidance of relevance for top managers (Young & Jordan 2008). Instead, they have produced an enormous number of largely untested and apparently ineffective methodologies (Checkland 1981;

Strassmann 1995). Few top managers consider project management to be an issue of direct concern (Crawford 2005) and the quote below from a senior board member although extreme, is by no means an unusual perception of the profession:

> With technocrats, the only three things you can be sure of are: nothing would get finished on time, it would always cost vastly more than predicted and it would never do what it was promised to do (Young & Jordan 2002).

If project success is strongly influenced by top management and if top managers want their strategies to be implemented, then the gap between the project management and top management communities is dysfunctional. This paper seeks to explore potential conceptual bridges between the two communities and explores in particular project governance through portfolios and programs. It starts by reporting a study of the public sector to provide a context to illustrate the relative importance of the issue. It continues with a literature review of portfolio management, program management and project governance. It then introduces a framework to understand how the various domains interrelate and discusses how the domains that have the most potential may need to change to bridge the conceptual chasm between the top management and project management communities.

The case of the Victorian public sector

An opportunity to evaluate the latest developments in project management arose through a consulting assignment with the Victorian Auditor-General's Office (VAGO). One of the authors was recognised by VAGO as an authority in project governance and able to bring an independent perspective to help shape their thinking on the relative priorities for audit attention.

The VAGO consulting assignment had two objectives. The first was to evaluate the role of projects within the Victorian public sector and the second was to evaluate the appropriateness of the Victorian Investment Framework. The assignment was significant because the Victorian Government in Australia is considered to be one of the international leaders in New Public Management and frequently compared to the UK, Canada and New Zealand (Greve & Hodge 2007). Their key investment frameworks, partly based on tools developed by the UK's Office of Government Commerce, were expected to be at the forefront of practice.

Methodology

The study was performed through a methodology known within VAGO as a 'desktop study' which consists of a literature review of online public sector documents. This was supplemented by interviews with key stakeholders within the Victorian public sector. This methodology was appropriate because the public sector has high levels of transparency and information is generally readily available. The key in researching this sector, is to know what is available, where to find it and how to interpret it. This study was therefore predisposed to success because it was commissioned, guided and partly resourced by VAGO who have an intimate knowledge of the workings of government.

The study is reported in detail in papers submitted to IRWITPM a SIG held in conjunction with the 2009 International Conference for Information Systems and a workshop on top management teams to be held by the European Institute for Advanced Studies in Management (Valencia, Spain 22–23 March 2010). Only the key details will be reported in this paper but it is relevant to report that rigour was maintained through a number of mechanisms. The final consulting report was drafted with extensive consultation with VAGO performance audit managers. The final report was presented to VAGO senior managers for validation and discussion. The final report was accepted and resulted in some amendments to the portfolio of performance audits planned for 2010 and future years, published in VAGO's Annual Plan and will be tabled in Parliament (www.audit.vic.gov.au). This final output is taken very seriously because it is a key communications tool for parliamentarians and allows agencies to focus their resources to prepare for major external audits in their respective areas.

Results

The strategic objective of projects within the public sector

The Australian approach to government was found to be relatively proactive. The State of Victoria is particularly proactive and undertakes many innovative initiatives. Their broad strategic objective is to create an environment that increases the capacity of the State to compete in the context of the rapidly evolving basis for production (globalisation). In this sense they are the same as any private sector entity although broader in scope. However, the role of projects in the public sector could be more significant than in other sectors because long term economic, demographic and climate-change constraints will lead to an increase in demand for services coupled yet there is a declining capacity to fund these services. Projects are therefore essential to significantly change the underlying cost structures and maintain current levels of performance within the public service. Business-as-usual improvement efforts will simply not be enough.

Within Victoria the strategic objective is not just to maintain performance but to increase performance. Formal vision statements have guided effort since 1992 and 'Growing Victoria Together' (GVT) the most recent 10-year vision released in 2001 is expressed in terms of a number of measurable outcomes. These ambitious goals reinforce the critical role of projects within the public sector and the most tangible goals are listed below (Victorian DPC 2009):

- Reduce crime by 5 per cent and have Victorians feel safer, reduce the rate of growth of the prison population and reduce re-offending.

- Improve health services by reducing waiting times (emergency, elective and dental services).

- Improve the level of education by: increasing literacy and numeracy, have 90 per cent of young people complete Year 12 or equivalent, and increase adult participation in vocational education and training.

- Improve roads and public transport by: reducing commuting times, increasing public transport use (in Melbourne) from 11 per cent to 20 per cent by 2020, increasing the proportion of freight transported by rail from 10 per cent to 30 per cent by 2010.

- Improve the environment by: significantly improving the health of Victoria's rivers by 2010, reducing Melbourne's water usage by 15 per cent by 2010, reducing the impact of salinity and soil degradation to improve the condition of our land.

Types of projects

Three main types of projects were found to be undertaken in the Victorian public sector: Asset investments, reported non-asset initiatives and unreported non-asset initiatives.

The highest quality public information focused on asset investments and itemised specific expenditure on roads, bridges, public transport, hospitals, buildings, computer systems, etc. Figure 8.1, taken directly from Budget papers, shows that very significant amounts have been spent annually on asset investments and additional fiscal stimuli at State and Federal levels on asset investments are being made from 2008 to 2012 to overcome the global financial crisis.

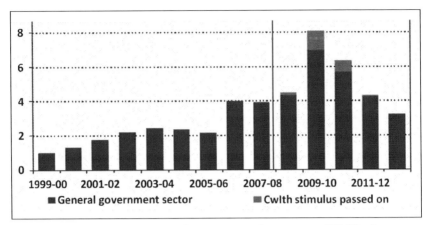

Figure 8.1. Annual project expenditure on asset investments (/$billion)

Non-asset initiatives relate to soft-projects such as organisational and business process change, staff training and public awareness campaigns to change behaviour to use new facilities, etc. Soft projects were more significant in dollar terms than the asset investments but surprisingly the information reported was not of the same quality. Interviews with key stakeholders responsible for very large project portfolios added that non-asset initiatives were outside their area of direct concern.

The soft projects can be separated into those that are specifically reported and those that are not. In Victoria the soft projects that are reported appear to be reported because specific funding was applied for and granted to undertake the project (described in Victoria as 'Output Initiatives'). Other soft-projects are not reported on specifically and are funded internally from the operational budget. The main evidence that they exist is the discrepancy between the projects reported in Budget documents and the projects listed in the strategic plans of each Agency which are quite detailed and significantly larger in scope. Interviews with managers within one of the major Agencies confirmed that many strategic projects are funded internally rather than externally and not specifically reported on. The methodology limited our capacity to report accurately on the size of the unreported projects and we have simply made an estimate based on the findings of our interviews and direct experience of several public sector agencies. This is less than ideal but the feedback from a senior manager within VAGO on our earlier academic paper suggests our estimates may be realistic:

> To be frank, the paper is so comprehensive ... and I agree with all your observations ... Your description and analysis of the investment

management guidelines is also good, although DTF [Treasury & Finance] would be a lot more circumspect – however they would admit all the issues you have raised in an off-line or informal conversation.

This finding is very significant because few if any of the strategic goals could be achieved by asset investments alone. New buildings, computer systems and roads for example are generally only enablers and are unlikely in themselves to lead directly to strategic goals such as reduced crime, increased literacy or reduced waiting times for health services.

The detailed research in the Victorian public sector was extended to an additional review of the Australian state of New South Wales (NSW) following the same methodology. This analysis has less rigour because the results have yet to be validated through interviews with key stakeholders. However, the data is included below to show the pattern that is emerging. It seems in the public sector between 25–27 per cent of the total budget is spent on projects with slightly more than half of this spent on soft-projects.

Total Budget		Asset Investments	Soft Projects	
			Reported	**Unreported**
VIC	33.5b	3.7b	2.7b	2.6b
	100%	11%	8%	8%
NSW	52.6b	5.7b	3.1b	4.2b
	100%	11%	6%	8%

Table 8.1. Estimated project expenditure in the public sector (2008)

It is very interesting to compare these findings with two of the authors' exploratory studies of the private sector. It was found that in 2008, less than 8 per cent of ASX listed companies (178 of 2224) explicitly reported their IT investment in any form at all (and IT is usually considered an asset investment). No evidence has been found of any formal reporting of soft-projects and it appears there is no requirement in the accounting Standards to report this type of project. A major vendor of portfolio management software also reported to us that across all industries, one of the major benefits from implementing portfolio software is to discover the many projects that are not currently reported.

These various considerations suggest to us that our findings on the Victorian project investment environment may be generally applicable.

The strategic impact of projects within the public sector

For this paper, the amount actually spent is less important than evaluating whether strategic objectives have been realised. However, it has been found that reporting against strategic goals is not formalised within NSW or

Victoria. Therefore there is little or no evidence to show whether strategic goals have been realised. In the case of the state of Victoria, this is surprising because as noted earlier, Victoria is considered a leader internationally in New Public Management. If the realisation of strategic goals is not systematically reported in the state of Victoria, it is likely they are not reported systematically anywhere (because the public service is generally required to have higher levels of transparency that the private sector). It is possible that strategic goals are not been systematically reported against because the results have been poor and a political liability for the government of the day.

The evidence found suggests the strategic goals are not being met despite being stable for almost two decades.

The strongest evidence is a 2009 VAGO audit of literacy and numeracy that found that 10 years of effort by the Victorian Education Department, one of the largest public sector agencies, had lifted literacy in only the early childhood years but not in the other school years. Numeracy had actually declined across all age groups. Arguably this result is influenced by changes in ministers, senior managers and their strategies over this period, by changes in the business environment caused by events such as the Global Financial Crisis and changes in the population caused by migration. However, these changes do not explain the result. It remains almost inconceivable that any of these changes would change the strategic priority for an education department to improve literacy and numeracy which must underpin almost everything they do. The sobering conclusion is that the Victorian Department of Education, one of the leaders in setting the Australian education agenda, has spent tens of billions of dollars on projects in the past decade without significantly improving two of its most significant strategic goals.

Some evidence based on the VAGO-commissioned consulting report on Health, the largest public sector agency suggests a similar pattern. Waiting times for health services, one of the most consistent strategic priorities of a health department, appears to have remained static or deteriorated over time.

The popular press suggests public sector strategic goals related to crime, traffic congestion and the environment also have not improved significantly over this time. Press reporting of course cannot be considered strong evidence. However the findings from the consulting report were considered by VAGO as sufficient evidence for them to change their audit plan to add new audits in 2010 and beyond to see if long-standing strategic goals have been impacted by projects in any of the Victorian public sector agencies.

If the investment patterns in Table 8.1 have been maintained over the past decade as suggested by Figure 8.1, the implication is that the State of Victoria, one of the better performers in the Australian public sector, has spent tens of billions on projects over the past decade with few strategic benefits being realised. As long-time residents of NSW, two of the authors believe that performance in NSW has been worse than Victoria over the same timeframe. If as suggested, the problem is also prevalent in the private sector, then the issue will be of widespread concern and the case for bridging the gap between the top management and project management communities can be justified by economic consequences as large as 1–3 per cent of GDP (Young 2006b).

Discussion

We have a high opinion of the processes used by the Victorian public service and our findings were a revelation to both us and VAGO. We believe the State of Victoria compares very favourably to the other states in Australia and internationally. It is therefore confronting to suggest that one of the best performers had spent tens of billions on projects over the past decade with few, if any, strategic benefits being realised.

After much consideration, we believe the problem is not so much a deficiency of project management but a misapplication of project management into areas it was never intend to address. Our findings correspond to a highly regarded UK study of over 14,000 organisations that found low success rates despite widespread use of project management methodologies (Clegg et al. 1997). When considered alongside Project Management Institute's large three year multinational study that found no objective evidence that project management added value (Thomas & Mullaly 2008), one is forced to conclude project management is not primarily designed to address effectiveness (e.g. deliver benefits, add value, implement strategy). Historically project management has been applied far more often to new product development than to strategy (Artto et al. 2009) and seems to be oriented along a completely different dimension: efficiency (delivering a product within quality, time and budget criteria).

The dimension of effectiveness appears to be addressed much more through program management. Program management is characterised more as a tool for strategy implementation and has different theoretical foundations to project management (Artto et al. 2009). Seminal research has shown that programs are not simply scale-ups of projects (Lycett et al. 2004) and the skills required of a program manager relate more to general management and leadership than project management (Partington et al. 2005). In our experience, the program of projects required to realise strategic benefits almost always includes the need for change, particularly behavioural change, and program management therefore needs to have strong interfaces with the disciplines of change management and operational management (or business-as-usual). This is the way program management is starting to be understood internationally with the UK's Office of Government Commerce product: Managing Successful Programs (MSP) dominating thinking and focusing on the delivery of change (Pellegrinelli et al. 2007). Some however have argued that mainstream program management is too strongly influenced by the project management tradition and that program management practices have been codified too rigidly. They are accused of being program-centric with responsibility for the realisation of benefits assigned to business managers outside a narrowly defined program (CCTA 2000). The required level of documentation works against the need to challenge and redefine the program as new information comes to hand and current guidelines underemphasise the need to adapt to the strategic context in which a program operates to ensure the strategic benefits are actually realised (Pellegrinelli et al. 2007).

Portfolio management seems to be yet another approach with a different position on the efficiency-effectiveness continuum. The conceptual foundations of portfolio management were focused on the selection of financial investments to reduce risk and increase returns (Markowitz 1952). These concepts were applied to select IT projects (McFarlan 1981) and project portfolio management (PPM) has developed and been marketed on the basis of being able to reduce risk and increase returns on a portfolio of project investments (CA 2009). However, fewer than 33 per cent of organisations using PPM report they diversify to reduce portfolio risk (Reyck et al. 2005). In our experience PPM is mainly used to manage project resource issues and is not used to inform or implement strategy. We believe the problem is that the unit of selection is the individual project rather than a program of projects. Projects as we noted earlier, seldom deliver strategic benefits in isolation, and our conclusion is that project portfolio management although more strategic than project management, is still oriented more towards efficiency (avoiding duplication) than effectiveness (delivery of value/strategic benefits). The best-practice Victorian public service investment frameworks are quite closely aligned to the concepts of project portfolio management because they emphasise selecting the right projects (Appendix A). However, the Victorian approach is less strategic than the theoretical potential of PPM because their focus is on asset investments and not on the more critical behaviour change projects that are needed to realise strategic goals.

Project governance also needs to be noted because it is an approach that provides a strong linkage between project management and top management concerns. Project governance goes beyond the concept of planning or alignment and focuses on actions needed to actually realise strategic goals. The most recent developments in this area are new project governance standards providing high level guiding principles consistent with well accepted corporate governance guidelines (AS8016, HB280 2006). Early studies have found directors respond well to the high-level approach in these standards (Young 2008) and we would argue that the concept of governing programs provides the strongest approach to bridge the conceptual divide between top management and project management. However we concede that the practice of project governance is relatively immature. The concept of active governance (i.e. governing) is often lost because practitioners influenced by project management literature and the major project/program methodologies tend to promote project governance as the establishment of organisational structures to oversee individual projects (i.e. governance) without much guidance on how they actually influence projects to succeed (Weill & Ross 2004).

This discussion of the inter-relationships between various approaches to bridge the conceptual divide is summarised as a diagram in Figure 8.2. Two axes are used to differentiate the relative emphases of the various approaches: efficiency and effectiveness. Project management is shown to focus mainly on efficiency and program management is shown to focus mainly on effectiveness. Portfolio management and the Victorian public sector investment frameworks are shown to have a similar focus on efficiency and a smaller focus on effectiveness. Governance is shown as a bridge between both portfolio and program management and the realisation of strategy.

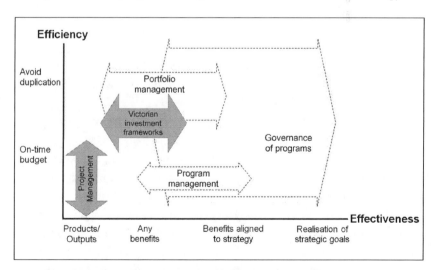

Figure 8.2. The inter-relationship between project governance and project, program and portfolio management

What more needs to be done to bridge the conceptual divide?

This paper began with the recognition that top management support is the most important factor for project success. It then highlighted a major consequence, if top managers do not consider project management to be a matter of direct concern, then project success becomes very difficult to achieve. The very high project failure rates reported through many studies over many decades and the example of projects within the Victorian public service provided compelling evidence that the gap between top management and project management has very significant negative impacts on project success rates.

The discussion leading to Figure 8.2 suggests that portfolio management, program management and governance have the potential to bridge the conceptual divide between top managers and project managers. The area of common interest seems to be strategy, specifically the successful implementation of strategy. However, it was noted that these approaches are overly influenced by project management concepts, relatively immature and not fully attuned to top management strategic agendas. We turn next to consider what more will need to be done to bridge the conceptual divide in practice.

Portfolio management

Project portfolio management (PPM) is a well-established discipline, particularly in the US. It has an extensive literature and is supported in industry by an established and growing PPM software market. However, it shares a weakness with project management and questions have been raised on whether PPM actually adds any value (Reyck et al. 2005).

The value of portfolio selection was justified in the context of selecting new product development projects (Jamieson & Morris 2004). The justification is far less convincing with the implementation of strategy. Strategic goals are rarely realised through individual projects and we feel strongly that the unit of selection generally needs to be at the program level. Others add that PPM, because it is meant to deal with fairly stable environments, can only be effective if combined with program management which is meant to deal with more turbulent environments and emergent strategies (Thiry & Deguire 2007).

Most organisations have a limited capacity to undertake major change and we question whether it is appropriate to emphasise PPM in the first instance, especially if say an organisation is only undertaking say four or five major programs. The example of the Victorian public service shows top managers are prepared to engage at the PPM level to fight for their pet projects.

However this approach does not focus on the common inter-related goals and there is a tendency to circumvent the recommended decision making criteria. PPM project selection practices tend to be based on first degree criteria identified with risk management tools and are not complementary to top managers making upper level strategic decisions through non-linear higher level considerations (Thiry & Deguire 2007).

The problem arises because there is a disconnection in the way strategy is developed and way the strategic is planned (Mintzberg 1994). Strategy development is fluid and emergent. Strategic planning, especially when following the current approaches to PPM is relatively inflexible and mechanical. In addition to this, the potential of PPM software (the focus of many PPM advocates), appears to only be justified when other aspects are in place such as top management commitment, agreed benefits measurement and a willingness to deal with project interdependencies and resource constraints (Reyck et al. 2005). These are significant obstacles and we therefore believe effort is best directed to the modest goal of moving project portfolio management to support program portfolio management. We believe PPM should not be emphasised in the first instance and that the focus should on the governance of programs with PPM enhanced to play a support role.

Program management

Program management in contrast to portfolio management is an immature discipline (Stretton 2009) and potentially easier to refocus. There are less than a dozen textbooks and almost all of them start with by commenting on the dearth of available guidance. This situation may have arisen because the origins of program management were in the US aerospace and defence industries where it was kept secret for decades. It was only in the 1980s as people moved did program management take hold in the commercial sector but even then it was sometimes only the term being misapplied to the management of large or multiple projects (Milosevic et al. 2007). A common US understanding probably exaggerates this error with the Project Management Institute's (PMI) Standard for Program Management focusing on new product development rather than strategic delivery. Realising strategic goals almost always requires behavioural change and we believe it is sub-optimal to focus only on developing new products which is only sometimes part of the overall strategy.

We believe program management needs to be revised to reflect the insights from thirty years of experience with strategic planning. It is now accepted that strategic planning is fundamentally different to strategic thinking and the level of certainty that can exist with strategy is far less than the practitioners of strategic planning and program management have traditionally assumed (Mintzberg 1994).

The World War I battle of Passchendaele is an example of how a strategy may turn out to be tactically impossible. The generals found after four months and the loss of over a quarter of a million lives, they were sending their men through a sea of impassable mud. They had never inspected the battlefield directly and feedback from the field was either not provided or not heard.

In the same way, program managers cannot assume that strategy is fixed and their only job is to implement the strategy. It is necessary for program managers to understand the context, know when to question or inform decision-makers and actively help determine alternative strategies when things do not work out as planned. They need to implement programs in ways that allows a strategy to be validated and changed if original assumptions turn out to be wrong (as they inevitably will be to varying degrees).

Successful project managers have been promoted into program roles only to flounder (Pellegrinelli et al. 2007). Program management competencies are a magnitude higher than the traditional project management competencies. Effective program managers frequently adapt formal guidelines in subtle and creative ways, or ignore or contradict them completely. They seek more to engage stakeholders than to manage them as the methodologies might suggest. It is as much about coping as it is about planning and rational decision making, as much about re-shaping the organisational landscape as it is about delivering new capabilities. Arguably many of the common guidelines have been found by them to either be not useful or not make sense. The current codification into a common set of transferable principles and processes appears to be inadequate and some even question whether it is possible (Pellegrinelli et al. 2007).

We believe what is emerging is the realisation that mainstream program management practices are not adequate to support strategic thinking and implementation. One major text provides an example of a program to develop a new product independent of another program to market the product without emphasising the need to coordinate decisions to realise the strategic goal of profitably entering a new market (Milosevic et al. 2007). When organisations view programs in this way, they tend to shoe-horn programs into project-level thinking, fail to focus adequately on building and maintaining support for the strategic goals and lose most of the benefits sought in setting up programs in the first place (Pellegrinelli 1997, Pellegrinelli et al. 2007). There is a need for program management to move away from the one size fits all approach (Lycett et al. 2004) and move away from a project management emphasis to build the flexibility to evaluate progress on an ongoing basis and the ability to rapidly adapt in order to realise strategic goals. Tools and frameworks must be developed to allow both project managers and top managers to easily transition between short term project management objectives and adaptive strategies to meet long term strategic goals. We do not believe the tools or the language currently exist to meet this demand.

Program governance

The strength of a program-governance approach aligned with corporate governance principles is that it is flexible, able to incorporate the experience of boardroom directors and top managers and be perceived at the senior levels as an extension of their job rather than another onerous burden to comply with (Young 2008). A guideline framed in this approach is exemplified by a handbook published by Standards Australia emphasising six key questions that boards and top managers need to address to influence projects to succeed (Young 2006a). The main change that needs to occur is to communicate the message that top managers need to focus on programs to achieve strategic goals and not projects to come in on-time on-budget.

Two major weaknesses of the governance approach have been revealed through this paper: The first is that there needs to be effective tools that top managers can turn to assure themselves that a key principle or question has been adequately addressed. Program and portfolio management tools appear to be major areas of deficiency because the dominant methodologies are framed too rigidly and do not seem to support the iterative, emergent nature of strategy development. The second major weakness is that the majority of advisors are grounded deeply in the project management tradition and dilute or confuse the message for top managers. They need to be exposed to the new paradigm of focusing on strategic goals, accept that strategy is realised more through programs rather than through projects, and advise accordingly. This may potentially result in a loss of expert power (Thomsett 1989) and ways need to be found for the project management profession to save face and not have their livelihood threatened.

Conclusion

In this paper we have argued that there is little in common between the interests of the top management and the project management communities: a conceptual chasm. We have suggested that the conceptual chasm has led to a dysfunctional lack of engagement between top managers and project managers resulting in high project failure rates and strategic goals not being realised. A study of the State of Victoria was described to illustrate the issue and the significance of the issue. Strategy and the realisation of strategic goals were introduced as a unifying concept with the potential to bridge the top management and project management communities. Project management, portfolio management, program management and project governance were then reviewed to consider their role in contributing to strategic success and to develop a model that bridged the conceptual chasm. Change management and operational management were considered in a limited way in the discussion of program management. We finished by considering the developments that needed to occur in each of these fields for the conceptual divide to be bridged in practice.

Our recommendation was that program management should be enhanced significantly to effectively support the emergent nature of strategic planning. We suggested tools and frameworks needed to be developed to allow rapid 2-way communication transitioning between project management and strategy issues. We recommended that portfolio management should be refined to focus on the selection of programs rather than projects. We recommended that the concept of program governance should replace project governance and that the project management community adopt the governance paradigm and focus on the delivery of strategic goals.

Acknowledgements

We thank the Victorian Auditor-General's Office for reviewing our paper and allowing us to report their study in the academic domain. We also thank the management of the School of Information Technologies at the University of Sydney for supporting our study and taking a leadership position in developing a new course to address the issues we have identified.

Appendix A. Victorian public sector investment management tools/frameworks

The tools and conceptual frameworks used in the State of Victoria to manage this investment have been developed mainly by the Victorian Department of Treasury and Finance. Their focus is mainly to support portfolio level decisions to fund projects strategically. Tools are provided to the agencies to specify the format of project proposals. The objective is to ensure proposals are aligned with strategic goals and to ensure benefits are identified. The tools and frameworks are described briefly below:

The *Investment Lifecycle Guidelines* provide a framework to help agencies understand the criteria that are used to select projects for funding. The guidelines appear to have captured many of the latest insights in the project management literature and specifically differentiate an investment from a project by defining the objective of an investment to be the realisation of benefits and the objective of a project to be the delivery of a product. The 'Investment Management Standard' operationalises the lifecycle guidelines by documenting the practices expected to be followed to define the reason for an investment, shape the solution and track the delivery of benefits through the investment lifecycle. The practices include problem definition, solution definition, benefit definition, business case development, investment reviews, benefit reporting, project management and asset management. The 'Investment Logic Map' is a specific tool mandated by Treasury requiring asset investments to specifically identify the benefits which they will enable and the additional initiatives that need to be undertaken to realise the benefits.

The 'Asset Management Framework' was developed to enable the key decision-makers to control the Victorian Government's asset base more strategically. It along with the *Gateway Review Process*, which was originally developed by Office of Government Commerce in the UK, was established to drive better government asset investment. The 'Asset Management Framework' has a service strategy, asset strategy and a multi-year strategy. The *Gateway* initiative is characterised by reviews of specific investments and a 10-year multi-year strategy to prioritise investments to help meet the service strategy.

There are also other guidelines published by Treasury. Two of the more relevant include the project alliancing *Practitioners' Guide* and project governance guidelines. The *Practitioners' Guide* provides guidelines for risk sharing when the expertise of private sector organisations is required to help deliver complex and high risk infrastructure projects. The project governance guidelines clarify, however, that departments and agencies are accountable for service delivery to achieve government outcomes even when private sector organisations assist in delivery.

We could not find any public information on the mandated project management practices in use in the Victorian public sector. The frameworks do not seem to focus on how projects are delivered. Our assessment of the project management methodology developed within the Department of Education is that it is world class. We were advised that most other agencies use either the *Project Management Body of Knowledge (PMBOK)* or PRojects IN Controlled Environments 2 (PRINCE2).

We believe the Victorian investment management frameworks only support medium levels of efficiency and effectiveness. Their strength is that they emphasise a portfolio approach to choosing projects and using benefits as the selection criteria for investment rather than simply focusing on on-time on-budget delivery. Their weakness is that they are directed at mainly at asset investments (*Investment Lifecycle Guidelines*, Overview, version 1.0, July 2008, 4) and do not focus on soft-projects even though the majority of project expenditure appears to be on soft-projects. Our consulting work within several Victorian agencies has suggested there is significant duplication of effort because the agencies were large and it was difficult for staff to know what all the different parts of an organisation were doing.

Asset investments alone are unlikely to deliver strategic benefits. An example of this weakness in the investment frameworks can be seen in the example used to illustrate the 'Investment Logic Map' tool: an investment in finger-print recognition software was justified because it led to the benefit of reducing processing time. However there was no requirement in the tool to ensure that the soft-projects were actually undertaken to reduce processing time. More significantly there was no requirement for the investment to be linked to a strategic plan of action to achieve a strategic goal such as reducing crime.

The Victorian tools and frameworks are influenced by the UK Office of Government Commerce, whose methodologies were originally focused on overcoming IT failure. There is an assertion that the tools and frameworks broadly apply to non-asset investments but there is no evidence that the assertion is justified. The majority of investments are not IT-related.

Our conclusion is that although the Victorian investment management frameworks focus on benefits, the emphasis is to ensure an asset is aligned to a benefit rather than the actual realisation of a benefit and there is no focus on realising higher order strategic goals.

References

Artto, K et al. 2009. 'Foundations of program management: A bibliometric view'. *International Journal of Project Management* 27 (1): 1–18.

Baccarini, D. 1999. 'The logical framework for defining project success'. *Project Management Journal* 30 (4): 25–32.

CA. 2009. 'Leading market research firm finds PPM software delivering over 500 percent ROI – CA.

CCTA. 2000. *Managing Successful Programs*. London: Central Computer and

Telecommunications Agency (now called OGC).

Checkland, P. 1981. *Systems Thinking, Systems Practice*. Chichester, UK: John Wiley & Sons.

Clegg, C et al. 1997. 'Information technology: A study of performance and the role of human and organizational factors'. *Ergonomics* 40 (9): 851–871.

Cooke-Davies, T. 2002. 'The "real" success factors on projects'. *International Journal of Project Management* 20: 185–190.

Crawford, L. 2005. 'Senior management perceptions of project management competence'. *International Journal of Project Management* 23 (1): 7–16.

Crawford, L; Pollack, J; England, D. 2006. 'Uncovering the trends in project management: Journal emphases over the last 10 years'. *International Journal of Project Management* 24 (2): 175–184.

Currie, W; Galliers, B. 1999. *Rethinking Management Information Systems*. New York: Oxford University Press.

Department of Treasury and Finance, 2008. *Investment Lifecycle Guidelines-Overview*. Melbourne, Australia

Greve, C; Hodge, G; 2007. 'Public-private partnerships: A comparative perspective on Victoria and Denmark'. In *Transcending New Public Management: The Transformation of Public Sector Reforms*, edited by Christensen, T; Laegreid, P. Aldershot, UK: Ashgate: 179–201.

Jamieson, A; Morris, P W. 2004. 'Moving from corporate strategy to project strategy'. In *The Wiley Guide to Project, Program, and Portfolio Management. The Wiley Guides to Project Management*, edited by Morris, PWG; Pinto, JK. Hoboken, NJ: John Wiley & Sons: 34–62.

Kwak, Y H; Anbari, F T. 2009. 'Analyzing project management research: Perspectives from top management journals'. *International Journal of Project Management* 27 (5): 435–446.

Lycett, M; Rassau, A; Danson, J. 2004. 'Program management: A critical review'. *International Journal of Project Management* 22 (4): 289–299.

Markowitz, H. 1952. 'Portfolio selection'. *Journal of Finance* 7 (1): 77–91.

Markus, M et al. 2000. 'Learning from adopters' experience with ERP: Problems encountered and success achieved'. *Journal of Information Technology* 15: 245–265.

McFarlan, F. 1981. 'Portfolio approach to information systems'. *Harvard Business Review* (Sep–Oct): 142–150.

Milosevic, D Z; Martinelli, R; Wadell, J M. 2007. *Program Management for Improved Business Results*. Hoboken, NJ: John Wiley & Sons.

Mintzberg, H. 1994. 'The fall and rise of strategic planning'. *Harvard Business Review* (Jan–Feb):107–114.

Partington, D; Pellegrinelli, S; Young, M. 2005. 'Attributes and levels of program management competence: An interpretive study'. *International Journal of Project Management* 23 (2): 87–95.

Pellegrinelli, S. 1997. 'Program management: Organising project-based change'. *International Journal of Project Management* 15 (3): 141–149.

Pellegrinelli, S. et al. 2007. 'The importance of context in program management: An empirical review of program practices'. *International Journal of Project Management*, 25 (1): 41–55.

Poon, P. 2001. 'Critical success factors revisited: Success and failure cases of information systems for senior executives'. *Decision Support Systems* 30 (4): 393.

Reyck, B D et al. 2005. 'The impact of project portfolio management on information technology projects'. *International Journal of Project Management*, 23 (7): 524–537.

Standards Australia. AS8016. *Corporate Governance of Information and Communication Technology Projects.* Sydney: Standards Australia.

Standards Australia. 2006. HB280. *How Boards and Senior Management Have Governed ICT Projects to Succeed (or Fail).* Sydney: Standards Australia.

Strassmann, P. 1995. *The Politics of Information Management.* New Canaan, Conn.: Information Economics Press.

Stretton, A. 2009. 'Program management diversity – Opportunity or problem?' *PM World Today* 11 (6).

Thiry, M; Deguire, M. 2007. 'Recent developments in project-based organisations'. *International Journal of Project Management* 25 (7): 649–658.

Thomas, J; Mullaly, M. 2008. 'Researching the Value of Project Management'. Project Management Institute. Accessed 8 October 2009. Available from: http://www.pmi.org/Marketplace/Pages/ProductDetail.aspx?GMProduct=00101065301

Thomsett, R. 1989. *Third Wave Project Management.* Englewood Cliffs: Prentice-Hall.

Victorian Department of Premier and Cabinet. 2009. 'Department of Premier and Cabinet: GVT Goals'. Accessed 4 September 2009. Available from: http://www.dpc.vic.gov.au/CA256D8000265E1A/ListMaker!ReadForm&1=30-Growing+Victoria+Together~&2=20-GVT+Goals~&3=~&V=Listing~&K=GVT+Goals~&REFUNID=E8FB5427ABB4EC7DCA2570750024A46A~c0unter

Weill, P; Ross, J. 2004. *IT Governance: How Top Performers Manage IT Decision Rights for Superior Results.* Boston: Harvard Business School Publishing.

Young, R. 2006a. *HB 280-2006 Case Studies – How Boards and Senior Management Have Governed ICT Projects to Succeed (or Fail).* Sydney: Standards Australia.

Young, R. 2006b. 'What is the ROI for IT project governance? Engaging the board and top management'. Paper presented at 2006 IT Governance International Conference. Auckland, New Zealand.

Young, R. 2008. 'Boardroom readiness for business project governance'. Accessed 4 September 2009. Available from: http://www.e8consulting.com/blog/practiceareas/governingprogramsandprojects/boardroom-readiness-for-business-project-governance

Young, R; Jordan, E. 2002. 'Lifting the game: Board views on e-commerce risk'. In Bunker, D., Wilson, D., Elliot, S, eds. *IFIP WG8.6 The Adoption and Diffusion of IT in an Environment of Critical Change.* Sydney: Pearson Publishing Service: 102–113.

Young, R; Jordan, E. 2008. 'Top management support: Mantra or necessity?' *International Journal of Project Management* 26 (7): 713–725.

Chapter 9

Who are 'they'?

Employee perceptions of organisational decision-making

Shawn D Belling

University of Wisconsin–Platteville, USA

In every organisation, there is a mysterious group of people generally referred to as 'they.' 'They' are the people who make the decisions. 'They' are the ones who, it is assumed, show up for work every day with the main goal of making life difficult for rank and file employees. 'They' are the people who set unrealistic sales and profitability objectives, who insist on project completion dates that could not possibly be met and who decide to change the food in the company cafeteria or the parking rules without notice.

This paper looks into the question 'who are "they"?' It does so by exploring employee perceptions of organisational decision-making. Do employees perceive their involvement in decision-making differently than upper management? How do attempts by management to 'empower' or involve employees actually affect employee perception of decision-making? Do these efforts actually involve employees in the decision-making that is meaningful to them?

Further discussion is given to the question of which people make up the all-powerful 'they' and why is it that employees believe this group makes all of the important decisions. And, why do employees continue to accept that 'they' will make many of these important decisions?

Introduction

The topic of this paper was inspired by a particular workplace conversation in which one of the author's direct reports attributed the setting of what this person considered unrealistic sales and profit objectives to 'they'. The author, as the manager responsible for setting these objectives, was struck by the ease with which a direct report who, upon some thought, would have realised that the author had set the objectives, instead automatically attributed this to some faceless 'they'.

Further reflection on this concept led to a realisation that many workplace decisions were unthinkingly attributed to 'they' without any further consideration of who really makes the decisions that affect people in organisations and the direction of the organisations themselves. This idea remained dormant with the author until 2006, when studies in organisational behaviour brought this concept into clearer focus and presented the opportunity for directed investigation into this topic.

The basic question this paper attempts to address is why people in organisations tend to attribute decisions to 'they' including in situations where the decision-maker is well-known. The question evolves into an exploration of employee's perceptions of decision-making within organisations and what influences these perceptions. The paper seeks first to define specifically who 'they' is – bringing clearer definition to the groups of people often collectivised into a faceless, unidentified 'they'. The paper also then studies the elements surrounding workplace decision-making that define whether people in organisations feel involved in and accountable for decisions.

The application of this concept and supporting research to project management is direct and important. As outlined in one specific example in this paper, project teams (like other members of organisations) frequently display a tendency to attribute decisions made by project managers, sponsors and stakeholders to 'they' without taking the time to consider who really made the decision or why the decision was made in the manner it was.

Project team members who engage in this behaviour may either do so out of habit or out of a lack of involvement in or understanding of the decision-making process for the project. Regardless of the reason, such behaviour can be considered a risk to the success of the project and therefore worthy of understanding its causes and implications.

The outcomes of the literature review support the concept that employee perception of decision-making in projects as well as general organisational scenarios is important to ensure the successful outcomes of projects by in turn helping project managers, sponsors and stakeholders consider the ramifications of their decision-making processes and cultures.

Research methodology

Two main methods of research were used to develop this paper. One method was the research and citations from various works in business publications and scholarly journals, which yielded supporting studies and conclusions regarding employee attitudes on decision-making and workplace relationships between employees and managers.

In addition to this research, the author developed a survey consisting of 28 questions in four sections. Although it would have been desirable to reach a larger sampling group, the survey was valuable for gaining additional insight on the perceptions and attitudes of employees regarding workplace decision-making. This survey was distributed to a group of employees at two different companies. The survey participants (totalling ten respondents) had a higher than average level of education, experience and tenure with their company.

The companies themselves had certain similarities, which might also constitute limitations of the survey in that both companies were privately held, had approximately 1000 employees and were engaged in development and manufacture of their own products as well as providing specific types of consulting services. The two firms were in completely different industries, one being in regulatory compliance products and services while the other was a bio-technology company. Employees at the bio-tech firm had terminal degrees whereas the highest attained degree at the regulatory compliance company was a master's degree.

A broader sampling would doubtless give more credibility to the survey results. It is the researcher's opinion, based on personal experience and anecdotal evidence, that the broader sampling would be unlikely to significantly alter the outcomes and conclusions developed.

Literature review and research results

One objective of the research was to identify which positions or groups of people were commonly collectivised into 'they'. Further research objectives were to determine what elements within organisational structures and behaviours determined whether people in organisations felt involved and therefore committed to decisions made on their behalf as well as decisions in which they were directly involved. The research sought to close (within the confines of the paper's topic) the gap in knowledge on how employees perceived organisational decision-making based on their involvement in decisions that directly impacted them versus these decisions being made for them with little or no input.

Another objective of the research was to ascertain the degree to which employees felt they influenced decision-making within their organisations and how this degree of influence in turn affected their commitment to organisational objectives and specific work assignments or work rules.

Research published in various scholarly journals and business articles revealed a common thread of conclusions with regard to the ways in which employees perceive their managers and organisations as well as their (employees) degree of involvement in decision-making. There are several elements that impact the perceptions that employees form about their managers as well as the degree to which employees feel that they (employees) participate in meaningful decisions about company policies, strategies and objectives as opposed to basic decisions about the way in which they perform specific parts of their work.

Employee engagement or disengagement is strongly influenced by the degree to which they 'buy in' to the company's priorities (Sull & Spinosa 2007, 79–80). The question of who actually sets a company's priorities is paramount to this level of engagement. If employees feel that 'they' set priorities with little input or influence from employees, the degree of engagement will decrease.

Related to the above, employees are more likely to carry out the commitments they make when these commitments are made voluntarily (as opposed to being coerced, or in this context, made for them) (Sull & Spinosa 2007, 84). This supports the concept that employees are less likely to support and deliver on promises or commitments made on their behalf by 'they'.

The literature provides examples as to how other factors in the workplace such as interpersonal trust, empowerment and employee perceptions influence employee perceptions of 'they'. For example, Melinda Moye and Alan Henkin (2006, 101) note that trust helps to build a positive work environment and contributes to the effectiveness of the decision-making process. Trust between employees and managers means that there is a lower likelihood that the 'they' perception will exist.

Empowerment is a widely-used term to describe many different approaches to providing employees with varying levels of autonomy in different areas of their work experience. While most researchers and practitioners agree that empowerment is generally a good thing and will create a better work experience for employees (Moye & Henkin 2006, 103, 112), other research suggests that empowerment, as generally practiced, does not facilitate employee participation in decision-making at levels that truly influence the strategy, priorities and objectives of companies (Delbridge & Whitfield 2001, 473).

Last but not least, it should come as no surprise that efforts to involve employees in decision-making are perceived quite differently by management and employees. Research supports an easily-reached assumption that while employees feel they have limited influence or chances to participate in decision-making, the employers believed that they tried to encourage greater employee involvement and participation (Scott-Ladd et al. 2006, 410). As with so many aspects of organisational behaviour, the perception is heavily influenced by one's position in the organisational structure. It is highly likely that employers are indeed seeking more employee participation, but not in the type of decision-making the employees want to influence.

Survey results

It is important to note that the survey has a weakness in that the sampling was quite small, spanning only two organisations. The participants had a high level of education (most with post-graduate degrees) and long tenures with their employers (most having ten years or more). The survey data's validity could be significantly strengthened by surveying a much larger and broader audience. However, it is the researcher's contention based on experience that the responses gained from this small audience have substantial validity on their own merits and that the larger sampling, while lending more credibility to the survey, would not substantially change the results.

The most important results from this survey support the concept that key decisions such as corporate strategies, policies and objectives are perceived as managed at higher levels of the organisation. The survey also supports that employees are less clear about who makes decisions of this nature, other than that they are made at a level above their immediate supervisor or manager. These results support the concept that the identity of key decision-makers is somewhat vague to many employees, further reinforcing the idea that 'they' decide what direction an organisation will go, what strategies will be used to achieve the objectives and how employees and resources will be allocated and compensated in the pursuit of these objectives.

The survey results supported the findings in the literature that employees are more closely involved in decision-making within their workgroups. As noted in the literature, empowerment efforts tend to focus on decisions more closely aligned with specific workgroups rather than on higher-level decisions. The survey supports the concept that as the decision moves closer to the employee's work, the probability that the employee will have some participation in the decision increases. This in turn decreases the perception that 'they' made the decision.

The survey also demonstrated that employees do sense that there are many decisions that are beyond their power to influence, with 'often' the collective response to questions such as 'Have you ever felt like there is a core group of people at your employer who make all of the decisions themselves?' and 'Do you ever feel powerless to change or influence things at your employer?' At the same time, the survey showed that there are also numerous instances in which employees feel they can influence decisions, know who makes them and have their input considered as part of the decision.

Additional research

Survey responses to questions regarding the level at which decisions are made within organisations further supports that decisions made at higher levels of the organisation are less likely to have employee participation. Research also confirmed that decisions about the performance of the work itself (as opposed to strategy, objectives, policies etc) are likely to involve employee input (Belling et al. 2007, 2). This research adds support to the theory that employees perceive that important decisions are made by people higher in the organisation – people the employees may not know and people whose roles and responsibilities may not be clearly understood by employees. This reinforces the perception that 'they' make major, influential decisions.

The results of the researcher's survey work support a theory that most employees understand, or are at least resigned, to the fact that there is a body of decisions to be made in the workplace that the average employee cannot influence – these decisions are made by 'they'. At the same time, there is enthusiastic recognition that, at some employers, decision-making about the company's core business and operations are often left to the experts: employees who know the job and share the company's values (Belling et al. 2007, 2).

Defining 'they'

The 'they' that is the subject of this paper has its roots in workplace conversations from earlier days of the researcher's career. On occasion, office conversations about sales objectives, corporate policy decisions and even operational change decisions would attribute the decisions to decision-makers collectively referred to as 'they'. 'They' (it was widely assumed) made these decisions with no knowledge of the realities of the situation, without empathy and without understanding the ramifications of these decisions. 'They', in the minds of those around the lunch table, probably made those decisions just to make life difficult for the people who actually do the hard work that made the company run. Blaming everything on 'they' is easy enough when one is working in an entry-level position, a 'doer' as opposed to a manager or other position that plans and assigns work, or sets objectives and formulates strategies.

Based on the researcher's years of business experience and many informal conversations inside and outside the workplace, 'they' are managers, supervisors, directors, executives and human resources personnel. 'They' are invisible people who may or may not be known by name or title. 'They' are most likely people who are well-known to the employees who are collectivising the complaints about a decision; however, it is easier for most employees to assign blame to 'they' than to identify single points of accountability, seek to understand the reasoning behind the decision, or perhaps accept some or all of the responsibility for decisions and objective-setting themselves.

A recent example of this phenomenon of workplace perception and casual conversation surfaced during a project discussion. This researcher, in the role of project manager, was having a discussion with a co-worker regarding some aspect of the project and related work. In the course of the conversation, the co-worker made a comment to the effect that 'they' would want to have a particular task done as soon as possible.

In the immediate context of this research paper (as well as due to the ongoing sensitivity this researcher has to the particular usage of 'they' in this context), the comment resonated. Clearly, there are one or more specific people, including perhaps the project manager, who would influence or decide when this particular task should be complete. The co-worker, if pressed for an answer, would probably be able to list at least some of these people. Yet, in the course of normal workplace conversation and backed by ongoing generalisations, this requirement was generated by 'they'

Becoming 'they'

Reaching the ranks of management means to some extent that one automatically becomes 'they'. This point was driven home for the researcher one afternoon several years ago when the team was grumbling about sales and profitability objectives. One team member was complaining about the objectives and specifically said 'they' had set them too high. This researcher turned to the team member and said 'who do you think They is? They is me!' The team member had doubtless lumped the researcher (their manager), into the all-encompassing pool of management-types known as 'they'. This exchange also heightened the fact that the team member in the example did not fully understand who was accountable for setting those particular objectives – something for which both the team member and the manager were at fault. The manager should have done a better job of clarifying how the team's input was to be used, while the team member's response was caused by years of cynicism. For the researcher, this workplace exchange sparked ongoing consideration of this topic and how the generalisation of upper management and certain areas of a company into a single entity called 'they' manifests itself in the workplace.

Various studies support the concept that movement into management automatically pushes one into the ranks of 'they'. This is partly because, despite efforts to involve employees in decision-making, these initiatives have been shown to focus on production-level decisions that have little impact on increasing employee influence within the organisation. In their paper 'Employee perceptions of job influence and organisational participation', Rick Delbridge and Keith Whitfield (2001) reference the work of George Strauss, who points out that 'only relatively unimportant decisions are made at the workplace level' and (regardless of empowerment initiatives) the really important decisions, such as those that affect things critical to workers such as job security, are still made further up the organisational structure (Delbridge & Whitfield 2001, 473). Delbridge & Whitfield (2001, 475) go on to present research that argues that those employee empowerment efforts that do not expand employee influence on decision-making to more critical decisions do not really have much positive effect on the workplace environment.

This in turn reinforces the perception on the part of employees that the concentration of decision-making on matters that truly influence the employee experience in the workplace is with upper management – 'they'. This perception, regardless of whether it is reality, reinforces on ongoing sense that becoming a manager automatically makes one a member of 'they' and therefore not interested in gaining employee participation in decision-making on important issues. Another issue to consider from a pure project management perspective is that project teams seldom request or develop the business cases for the projects that they are ultimately charged with completing, and also are seldom involved in setting the initial delivery expectations. This further reinforces a sense that 'they' request projects and then set unrealistic expectations for their completion.

Why it is easier to point fingers than take on accountability

There are many factors that lead to a culture of 'they' within organisations. One of the main contributors is the typical organisational structure within most companies which concentrates much key decision-making at upper-management levels. Despite many approaches to employee involvement in workplace process improvement and decision-making, the majority of critical decisions, those that truly affect or impact the environment in which employees work, their work structure, their compensation, their organisational structure, are still made by upper management (Delbridge & Whitfield 2001, 474).

This leads to a culture of 'they'. Because the key decisions are made by upper management with little input from rank-and-file employees, this reinforces the sense that 'they' will decide everything and that there is little an employee can do to influence their situation anyway. Why take on any accountability for change?

This is a difficult mindset to overcome. Not all employees have the combination of initiative, education and experience necessary to recognise that personal accountability for change and workplace satisfaction is a requirement to affect this change. Most efforts to involve employees in organisational decision-making, to empower them, involve limited scope, production-oriented initiatives. Studies have demonstrated that these types of initiatives to involve and empower employees are not as effective as those that attempt to involve employees in decisions that affect broader pieces of the organisation (Delbridge & Whitfield 2001, 473).

Management efforts to encourage employee participation as well as various empowerment programs focus on outcomes desired by management. That is, things 'they' perceive as effective and important to the organisation and perhaps intended to improve employee communication, commitment and efficiencies, but having nothing to do with expanding employee influence in how the organisation is run (Delbridge & Whitfield 2001, 476). Despite these efforts to involve employees, the fact that these efforts do not increase employee influence in the decision-making processes helps to reinforce the culture of 'they'. Key decisions remain in the hands of upper management, making it easier to continue to point fingers at 'they' rather than look for ways to take ownership of one's workplace situation.

Part of the issue is because of perceptions. As noted, perceptions replace objective realities (Moye & Henkin 2006, 104). This means that even though an employee may be involved or consulted on decisions close to their work, when major, strategic decisions that impact their workplace environment and their sense of security are made with no input and no understanding of why they were made, employees are likely to maintain the perception that *all* decisions are made by 'they'. This is supported by the researcher's experience with complaints regarding sales and profit objectives – objectives that the researcher's staff had participated in setting. Because so many important decisions in this particular organisation were made arbitrarily, by a single person or small group, and with little communication as to the rationale behind them, it was often assumed that *all* decisions were made by 'they', even when the employees had participated in the decision to some extent. Their perceptions caused amnesia when the decision-making outcomes were announced.

Another factor that leads to finger-pointing at 'they' as opposed to attempting to gain more influence or accountability in decision-making is education and experience. It is the researcher's experience that more experienced and educated employees tend to have a higher level of what the researcher will refer to as 'business maturity'. While there are always exceptions, the researcher's experience supports that the more time on the job, education and business maturity an employee gains, the more likely the employee is to seek influence and accountability rather than complain that 'they' make all of the decisions. This experience is supported by research that links influence with interpersonal trust and education with both interpersonal trust and perceptions of influence within departments. Less education was linked to lower levels of perceived influence as well as interpersonal trust (Moye & Henkin 2006, 110).

A final reason for finger-pointing versus accountability is employee disengagement from execution. When employees develop a perception that 'they' are making all of the decisions, there is often a degree of disengagement from their work, a decline in the sense of urgency that drives employees to complete tasks and projects on time. A root cause for this disengagement can be traced to lack of employee involvement in setting corporate objectives and strategies. This lack of involvement leads directly to a lack of connection between employee's own tasks and projects, and the execution of the company's strategies in pursuit of objectives. By clarifying the link between employee work and corporate objectives and strategies as well as empowering employees with regard to their acceptance and planning of the work and tasks in support of these objectives and strategies, employers create an environment in which accountability replaces finger-pointing (Sull & Spinosa 2007, 85).

Effects of the culture of 'they' in the workplace

What happens when employees attribute everything they disagree with or do not understand to 'they'? If the organisational structure and culture are truly the root causes of this perception, the high-level effects are doubt-less detrimental to the welfare of the organisation and its employees. This type of environment leads to higher levels of employee turnover, employee disengagement, poor project execution and, over time, poor organisational performance. Companies whose structure and culture foster the 'they' perception will perform poorly in comparison to organisations that have stronger employee involvement and transparent decision-making processes.

Change is also difficult in this environment. An organisation that seeks to execute a new strategy or other change will find it difficult to overcome the sense that 'they' are driving this change without seeking employee input or communicating as to why this change is necessary and beneficial. An organisation can become trapped in the status quo – senior executives talk about new strategies but the firm cannot execute on them (Sull & Spinosa 2007, 85).

In the culture of 'they', the reality or perception is that decisions are made by 'they' in private, without a clear sense of accountability. As noted earlier, these types of decisions do not foster employee buy-in, because the perception is that 'they' have committed the employees to achieving specific objectives without soliciting their input as to whether they can actually be achieved within the parameters promised (Sull and Spinosa, 84–85).

There is perhaps one strange benefit to the culture of 'they'. 'They' serve as a lightning rod for employee dissatisfaction while the employees themselves forge strong bonds at the workgroup, project team or department level. United in their distrust of 'they' and the decisions and objectives that 'they' set and make, project teams and departments develop trust in each other and support each other, albeit at the expense of interpersonal trust in their managers.

Conclusions and implications

The orientation of this paper and the associated research is admittedly oriented to the practitioner, and so the conclusions and implications discussed in the following section are focused on the practical application and less on the outcomes of the research efforts associated with the development of the paper.

The conclusions and implications for managers, project managers, executives and organisations that want to reduce, manage or eliminate the perception that 'they' make all workplace decisions are many. Assuming that an organisation wants to either foster more employee participation in decision-making, or increase awareness of who makes what decisions and what determines the level at which they are made as well as the degree of employee influence to these decisions, there are steps that can be taken.

A most obvious step (given the assumptions) is to provide employees with information on the types of decisions that they can be expected to participate in. Employees who understand from their date of hire (or the start of their manager's tenure) that they may (to set up an example) make most decisions on how they do their work, may provide significant input to departmental objective setting or review and hiring of peers, but little input on matters of corporate strategy and policies, are less likely to generalise that 'they' make all decisions. Clarity on the decisions employees get to participate in versus those they do not help contain or limit the formation of this perception.

As a practicing manager, this researcher has found that employees are appreciative of information and form trust relationships with managers who are willing to share information on decision-making, even when the decision is made beyond their influence or purview. Further experience is that sharing information with employees helps to create a clearer understanding of organisational decision-making processes, even when facts support that decisions were made arbitrarily by a senior executive with little or no input from subordinates.

A good example is the average driver's reaction to a traffic blockage or slowdown. Most drivers can better tolerate a traffic blockage if they know why it occurred. They do not like it any better, but they experience less frustration and confusion by knowing the cause. The same is true of organisational decision-making: An employee will not necessarily like or support a decision made without their input, but will experience less frustration and confusion by knowing why the decision was made at a particular level and why their input was not solicited or considered.

Perhaps the most important and compelling implication for organisations, managers and project managers is that elimination or at least reduction of a perception or culture of 'they' is critical to organisational and project performance. Aside from the one possible benefit noted in the previous section (the 'lightning rod effect'), all of the outcomes and influences of this culture and perception are negative. Attribution of decision-making and objective-setting to 'they' has a detrimental effect on an organisation in ways discussed previously in this paper. Controlling or eliminating the culture of 'they' will doubtless have a positive impact on an organisation's performance, long-term growth and sustainability. Controlling or eliminating this perception will also reduce employee turnover and increase employee engagement and buy-in, further contributing to organisational performance.

In conclusion, 'they' take on many forms. Usually, 'they' never meant to become 'they' – the culture forced it on them. Enlightened managers and organisations will strive to make the changes necessary to achieve a state in which 'they' means 'us,' at least to the extent practical within most organisations. By developing a more inclusive culture of decision-making and educating employees on how decisions are made within the organisation, decision-makers are no longer a faceless they to be blamed for unpopular decisions. Rather, decisions are attributed appropriately to decision-makers based on the type of the decision, the level at which it needs to be made and the extent to which it is appropriate for employees to be involved in these decisions.

Appendix A

Perceptions of Organisational Decision-Making Survey
(Averaged response selections are in bold)

Section 1

To what extent do you feel that you participate in setting goals and objectives for which you will be held accountable?

5	4	3	2	1
High	Somewhat High	**Medium**	Not Much	None

To what extent do you feel that you participate in defining your job responsibilities?

5	4	3	2	1
High	Somewhat High	**Medium**	Not Much	None

To what extent do you feel that your employer seeks your input before making changes in the workplace that will affect you and others?

5	4	3	2	1
High	Somewhat High	Medium	**Not Much**	None

To what extent do you feel that your employer values your opinion?

5	4	3	2	1
High	**Somewhat High**	Medium	Not Much	None

To what extent do you feel your manager or supervisor seeks your input on decisions that will affect you or your department?

5	4	3	2	1
High	Somewhat High	**Medium**	Not Much	None

To what extent do you feel that your manager or supervisor values your opinion?

5	4	3	2	1
High	Somewhat High	**Medium**	Not Much	None

To what extent do you feel you understand the process through which your employer develops objectives for the company's performance?

5	4	3	2	1
High	Somewhat High	**Medium**	Not Much	None

To what extent do you feel you understand and support your employer's key strategies?

5	4	3	2	1
High	Somewhat High	**Medium**	Not Much	None

Section 2

Have you ever been given a performance target (such as a sales objective, project completion date or other goal) that you felt was unattainable in the time allotted?

    Yes   No   (4 yes, 3 no)

If yes, did your manager or supervisor gather information from you or look at your or other's past performance prior to assigning the performance target?

    Yes   **No**   Of the 4, 2 y, 2 n

Does your supervisor or manager consult or discuss performance targets with you prior to setting them?

    Yes   No   4 y, 3 n

Have you ever been impacted by a policy or procedure change at your employer that you felt was unwarranted or unnecessary?

    Yes   No   6 y, 1 n

If yes, did your employer gather any information from you or co-workers prior to making the change?

    Yes   **No**   4 n, 2 y

If yes, did your employer communicate the reasons behind the change and/or any background information on how the decision was made?

    Yes   **No**   3 no, 2 y

Section 3

Who sets the performance targets for which you or your workgroup (team, dept) are held accountable?

5	4	3	2	1
Senior/ Executive Management	My Manager/ Supervisor	**My Manager/ Supv but with input from my Team/Dept/ Workgroup**	My Team/Dept/ Workgroup	Don't Know

Who makes decisions regarding your bonuses, pay increases, performance evaluations?

5	4	3	2	1
Senior/ Executive Management	**My Manager/ Supervisor**	My Manager/ Supv but with input from my Team/Dept/ Workgroup	My Team/Dept/ Workgroup	Don't Know

Who makes decisions regarding the resources that you have to use to do your job?

5	4	3	2	1
Senior/ Executive Management	**My Manager/ Supervisor**	My Manager/ Supv but with input from my Team/Dept/ Workgroup	My Team/Dept/ Workgroup	Don't Know

Who decides what training you or your workgroup has?

5	4	3	2	1
Senior/ Executive Management	My Manager/ Supervisor	**My Manager/ Supv but with input from my Team/Dept/ Workgroup**	My Team/Dept/ Workgroup	Don't Know

Who decides if the size of your workgroup is to change?

5	4	3	2	1
Senior/ Executive Management	**My Manager/ Supervisor**	My Manager/ Supv but with input from my Team/Dept/ Workgroup	My Team/Dept/ Workgroup	Don't Know

Who decides what skillsets and personality traits are desirable within your workgroup?

5	4	3	2	1
Senior/ Executive Management	**My Manager/ Supervisor**	My Manager/ Supv but with input from my Team/Dept/ Workgroup	My Team/Dept/ Workgroup	Don't Know

Section 4

Do you ever feel as though you can have an impact on the way things are done at your employer?

5	4	3	2	1
Yes	No	Often	**Sometimes**	Hardly Ever

Do you ever feel powerless to change or influence things at your employer?

5	4	3	2	1
Yes	No	**Often**	Sometimes	Hardly Ever

Have you ever felt like there is a core group of people at your employer who make all of the decisions themselves?

5	4	3	2	1
Yes	No	**Often**	Sometimes	Hardly Ever

Do you ever feel as though you don't know who sets policies and performance objectives?

5	4	3	2	1
Yes	No	Often	**Sometimes**	Hardly Ever

Do you ever feel as though you don't know how policies or performance objectives are set?

5	4	3	2	1
Yes	No	**Often**	Sometimes	Hardly Ever

Do you ever feel as though input or feedback you give is used to make decisions that affect you?

5	4	3	2	1
Yes	No	**Often**	Sometimes	Hardly Ever

Have you ever felt as though suggestions or concerns you have provided were not considered?

5	4	3	2	1
Yes	No	**Often**	Sometimes	Hardly Ever

Do you feel that you influence how performance objectives such as sales goals or project completion dates are determined?

5	4	3	2	1
Yes	No	**Often**	Sometimes	Hardly Ever

References

Belling, Shawn; Biagoni, Theodore; Butz, David; Davenport, Wendy. 2007. 'Group 1 Unit 4, University of Wisconsin – Platteville, BSAD3530/5530SU07'. *Organizational Behavior* Summer 2007.

Delbridge, Rick; Whitfield, Keith. 2001. 'Employee perceptions of job influence and organizational participation.' *Industrial Relations* 40 (3) (July): 472–489

Moye, Melinda J; Henkin, Alan B. 2006. 'Exploring associations between employee empowerment and interpersonal trust in managers.' *Journal of Management Development* 24 (2): 101–117.

Scott-Ladd, Brenda, et al. 2006. 'Causal inferences between participation in decision making, task attributes, work effort, rewards, job satisfaction and commitment'. *Leadership & Organizational Development Journal* 27 (5): 399–414.

Sull, Donald N; Spinosa, Charles. 2007. 'Promise-based management: The essence of execution.' *Harvard Business Review*: 85 (4) (Apr): 79–86.

Chapter 10

Leadership in projects and its impact on business strategy execution

An Australian case

Alan Sixsmith

University of Technology, Sydney, Australia

Ken Dovey

University of Technology, Sydney, Australia

The aim of this research in progress paper is to explore the social constructs of leadership and workplace relationships and the role they play in the execution of business strategy. A single case study based on a large Australian mobile telecommunications company, which operates a heavily outsourced IT environment is presented. Qualitative techniques were used for data collection and analysis. Data collection was undertaken using semi-structured open-ended interviews and thematic analysis was used to identify common themes in the data which were then consolidated into dominant themes. The results show that even though the formal processes were in place to plan and execute business strategy, both leadership practices and workplace relationships played a major role in ensuring that strategy was effectively executed in the case study organisation.

Introduction

Organisational projects are complicated undertakings relying on the successful utilisation of both technical and social systems (Haggerty 2000). Employees collaborate, cooperate and work effectively together in today's workplace to allow organisations to meet the demands of the marketplace (Hertel, Geisterb & Kontradtb 2005; Majchrzak, Malthora

& John 2005). Hence teams and teamwork are essential characteristics of any organisation.

However, teams need leaders and leadership. From a team perspective, leadership can pursue the traditional view of a single team leader or the more contemporary view of shared leadership. Shared leadership is a model in which the hierarchical leader is removed and power and influence is shared among a group of individuals (Pearce, Manz, & Sims 2009). Project leadership is a form of traditional leadership and is normally a role where one person assumes responsibility for the project team, sets project direction, aligns people and tasks and monitor progress to ensure project outcomes are accomplished (Cleland & Ireland 2007).

To help sustain competitiveness and address current and future opportunities organisations need leadership at all levels (Pearce et al. 2009). Effective leadership in projects is of the utmost importance to organisations to ensure strategic initiatives are successfully implemented. Many project management texts have chapters dedicated to project leadership and working in teams (e.g. Cleland & Ireland 2007; Gray & Larsson 2006; Marchewka 2009) such is the importance of projects to the functioning of an organisation.

The objective of this research in progress is to explore the social constructs of leadership and workplace relationships and the role they play in the execution of business strategy in an Australian mobile telecommunications company. The findings of this paper will be useful in adding to our knowledge of how various leadership roles in projects influence the execution of business strategy in an outsourced environment.

The paper has the following components. An overview of the teamwork, project leadership and shared leadership literature is presented. This is followed by the research methodology and the findings from the research. Finally, conclusions are drawn and future research is discussed.

Leadership and teamwork

The general management literature considers effective leadership a success factor in organisations (Turner & Müller 2003). Most people when asked their view of leadership have an image of a powerful and dominant individual (Yukl 2002). Doz & Kosonen (2007, 1) posit leadership as an organisational success factor by noting 'senior executives ... usually have a very clear idea of their roles and responsibilities and how they relate to one another and how to work together effectively, and the result is a well-oiled operation'. (Pearce et al. 2009,

235) agree noting that to sustain competitiveness organisations must leverage 'individual talent through disciplined teamwork and shared leadership'.

Lucey (2005, 118) describes leadership as 'the ability to influence the behaviour of others'. Some authors suggest leadership is specific to the situation (Marchewka 2009; Cleland & Ireland 2007) and relies on a style appropriate to the situation. Leadership styles depicted in the literature include coercive, authoritative, affiliative, democratic, pacesetting and coaching (Marchewka 2009) and dictatorial, autocratic, democratic & laissez-faire (Cleland & Ireland 2007). In order to influence behaviour in a given situation a combination of these styles may be suitable.

The traditional view of a single dominant leader may not always be the most appropriate to lead workplace teams. The notion of the hierarchical or single team leader is making way for the distributed or shared leadership model where a group of key people provide appropriate leadership at the appropriate times to steer the team toward task completion (Ancona, Bresman & Caldwell 2009). In the shared leadership model the 'individual who acts in the role of a dominant superior' is replaced by 'sharing power and influence among a set of individuals' (Pearce et al. 2009, 234). Shared leadership is an influence process among individuals which involves peer persuasion and upward or downward hierarchical influence (Pearce et al. 2009). Distributed leadership is defined by Labovitz and Rosansky (1997, 170) as 'the presence of capable leadership in different units and at different levels of an organisation, where employees are both empowered to act and knowledgeable about what must be done and aligns employee activities with the broader goals of the organisation'. The main principle of distributed or shared leadership is to empower leaders at all levels of the organisation. Empowering leadership allows followers to become leaders and participate in the management process (Manz, Pearce & Sims 2009a, 180)

Project leadership is defined as 'a presence and process carried out within an organisational role that assumes responsibility for the needs and rights of those people who choose to follow the leader in accomplishing project results' (Cleland & Ireland 2007, 381). Project leaders set direction, align people and tasks and monitor people to ensure project goals are achieved and give 'power and significance to the project effort' (Cleland & Ireland 2007, 390).

Teams are groups of individuals who have a common purpose, interact to accomplish organisational goals and share responsibility for team outcomes (O'Neill & Kline 2008). By taking on this shared responsibility all team members display leadership characteristic as part of their role in the team. Leadership is more than just a role in the team environment; it is a social process amongst team members (Pearce et al. 2009).

Organisation charts fail to portray the work processes in organisations as most work is carried out by teams that may operate across departments, product lines or geographic borders and it is these teams where strategy is put into action (Ancona et al. 2009). As a member of such a team knowing your role and responsibility to the team and the organisation is extremely important (Majchrzak et al. 2005). Employees must work effectively as part of a team and hence the ability to collaboration and cooperation among employees in today's workplace is essential to allow organisations to function in their dynamic environments and to meet the demands of both the global and local marketplaces (Forret & Love 2008; Hertel et al. 2005; Majchrzak et al. 2005).

Gray and Larsson (2006, 326) suggest that effective project leaders 'walk the talk' and lead by example. Lucey (2005) concurs stating that the effective leadership characteristics include leading by personal example and spending time with as many people as possible. This is especially true of project managers.

Marchewka (2009) suggests that project leadership is a function of the environment faced by the project manager. Lucey (2005) and Cleland and Ireland (2007) agree noting leadership is specific to the circumstances in which it occurs or the situation the leader must deal with. Leading project teams often necessitates allowing team members to assume leadership responsibility as a number of roles and activities of leadership can be shared among team members (Pearce et al. 2009).

Day et al. (2004) state most organisations strive for enhanced teamwork from their employees to help achieve corporate goals and competitive advantage. Good team relationships allow team members to give and take advice from one another making it easier to appreciate the team's combined responsibility to the task (Doz & Kosonen 2007). This enhanced team work could not be achieved without team members assuming some form of leadership 'as depending upon the situation, team members can exhibit leadership and then step back when appropriate to allow the designated leader to lead' (Pearce et al. 2009, 234). Wageman, Fisher & Hackman (2009, 192) state 'timing is a vital element of high-quality team leadership' in ensuring that the leadership actions taken help rather than hinder the team.

Wageman et al. (2009) suggest leadership should not be restricted to positions of formal authority as team members can informally provide leadership through influencing fellow team members or business colleagues. W.L. Gore & Associates is an exceptional example where team leadership is taken to a new level (Manz et al. 2009a; Manz, Shipper & Stewart 2009b). The underlying principles of leadership at Gore are 'the importance of social relationships, shared responsibility and influence, teamwork and the development of team members, and ... putting people first within an innovative high performance culture' (Manz et al. 2009b, 240). W.L. Gore & Associates are reliant on two types of teams – teams that emerge for a particular project and established project teams. The leadership approach is termed 'Natural Leadership' where leaders are not designated by an organisational hierarchy but emerge based on their credibility within Gore and their passion for work and hence they attract followers (Deutschman 2004; Manz et al. 2009b). As such all Gore employees participate in the leadership process (Manz et al. 2009a).

There are many aspects to teamwork in an organisation. Leadership in the team environment can take several forms with the most common being a designated team leader. However this does not restrict team members from demonstrating leadership qualities to ensure the team delivers its outcomes. Shared leadership of teams enhances organisational performance as team members have the opportunity to show leadership qualities to better serve their business unit stakeholders.

While the literature on teams and teamwork, project leadership and shared leadership is extensive and well covered, there appears to be limited literature which explores these areas in relation to business strategy execution in an organisational setting which is heavily outsourced. This paper attempts to address this deficit by demonstrating how leadership in a team environment can complement the execution of business strategy.

Research methodology

This single case study pursues an interpretive approach as the intent is to understand the actual context of leadership and business relationships in projects and the implications in executing business strategy from the point of view of the participants. In using an interpretive approach the researcher can gain a much deeper understanding of the area under study and the context in which the study has taken place (Crotty 1998).

By conducting a single in-depth case study the researcher can explore the significant features of the case and to create credible interpretations from the everyday experiences of the participants (Crotty 1998). Hamel et al. (1993, 45) defines a case study as an 'in-depth investigation using different methods to collect information and to make observations. These empirical materials help to understand the object of the study'. A single case study has the ability to increase our understanding of a particular situation (Yin 2003) by providing an in-depth understanding of the context under study.

A large Australian mobile telecommunications company (the Telco) is the focus of this case study. The Telco was chosen as one of the authors has extensive experience in the telecommunications industry which spanned over sixteen years.

A qualitative approach to data collection and analysis was undertaken. The author conducted a series of on-site semi-structured open-ended interviews with seven members of the Telco's Solutions Delivery team as follows:

- the General Manager – Solutions Delivery;
- the head of the Solutions Delivery project management team;
- four senior permanent project managers;
- one contract project manager.

Three themes were investigated during these semi-structured open-ended interviews:

1. the IT department's relationship with the rest of the business;
2. leadership within the Telco;
3. the influence of the leadership capability within the organisation and workplace relationships on the execution of business strategy.

The interviews lasted approximately 30 minutes and were recorded. Each interview was then transcribed in full and a copy of the transcript was made available to each interview participant.

Interview transcripts were analysed in several forms. Firstly thematic analysis was used to identify common themes, by interpreting the detailed account of the interviews and to consolidate the preliminary findings (Attride-Stirling 2001; Morse & Richards 2002). Following this preliminary analysis, units of meaning were extracted from the data to identify the dominant themes. The major themes to emerge from the interviews were the business planning cycle, leadership capabilities and workplace relationships.

Findings

The Telco

In the early 1990s the Telco commenced providing mobile telecommunications services in Australia. By late 2008 the Telco had over four million customers using its voice and data products and services and employed approximately 1400 people.

The following divisions – Finance, Technology, Brand & People, Governance, Marketing, Sales and Customer Operations make up the corporate structure of the Telco. Within this structure, the Technology division consists of five groups: Technology, Strategy & Planning, Solutions Delivery, Network Delivery, IT and Network Operations, Partner Performance and Governance and it is in the division that the IT function resides.

From a technology perspective the Telco is extensively outsourced to global companies who provide outsourced IT (e.g. data centres) and Network services. While most outsourced services are operational, applications development and maintenance (AD&M) is also outsourced.

For the delivery of solutions, there is a project management team consisting of a pool of about 25 to 30 Project Managers (PMs) which is a mix of both permanent employees and contractors. The project management team resides in the Solutions Delivery group of the Technology division and is responsible for projects in the following areas: 1) AD&M projects, 2) Network oriented projects, 3) IT infrastructure projects and 4) company driven marketing proposition projects. As such most projects conducted at the Telco impact the outsourced IT environment.

Telco PMs manage the complete project life cycle. This includes the 'go to market aspects' of the project, including all the interactions between various divisions (marketing, sales and customer support) and the outsource partners, along with the legal, commercial and financial components to deliver the project as a whole to the organisation.

The business planning cycle

Typically projects commence with the creation of a concept paper for the high level design of a solution. This process is undertaken by the Design and Capability component of Solutions Delivery in conjunction with the appropriate business unit. The concept paper then proceeds to the business planning cycle and eventually becomes a component in the yearly Integrated Business Plan (IBP). The IBP is essentially the strategy for the next 12 months. The projects in the IBP then go through a Portfolio process where budget and resources are approved and the management reporting structure for the project is set up.

Some projects that are commenced have not come from the IBP such as a regulatory project, or reacting to what competitors have done. These projects start with executive approval due to the urgency and fast track the project methodology by going straight into a planning mode rather the concept phase. However these projects still require the Portfolio approval to ensure the correct process around budgeting, resourcing and reporting are in place.

There is no business prioritisation of projects. The Portfolio process which reviews all projects and makes informed decision about projects to fund does not prioritise projects. All projects are reviewed on a quarterly basis by the Portfolio group to ensure they still align with the strategy. The discussions from a PM perspective at the Portfolio level concern the realignment of business requirements and what can be delivered in the timeframe rather than will the project continue.

Leadership capabilities

The PM role at the Telco is in essence a leadership role in the creation of a project team consisting of people from across the business and from the various vendors to deliver a specific project or agreed set of project deliverables. Under this structure business units are accountable for tasks, deliverables and resolving issues in their particular area during the project's life cycle while the Telco PM is accountable for the entire project. O'Neill & Kline (2008) examine the shared responsibility for accomplishing team outcomes during the formation of teams. Through this leadership role undertaken by the Telco PM the business unit stakeholders are provided with a view of one project team derived from a core team of appropriate resources.

The leadership style employed by many of the Telco PMs is one of 'leading by example' and identifying and using best practice. Gray & Larsson (2006) and Lucey (2005) both identify leading by example as a common trait of project leadership. However PMs must still allow team members to achieve the desired results and from a leading by example perspective this may mean talking a supporting role while the team members work through the issues.

The Telco PM holds quite a powerful position as they are empowered to deliver a project to the market on time and within budget. When issues impact a project the PM is expected to find a resolution or escalate the issue to ensure everything is done to achieve the business imperative. Each PM has the management approval and the right to challenge people as to why they can't deliver in order to achieve the particular project outcome. This aligns with Manz et al. (2009a) who suggest that empowered leadership allows wider participation in the management process.

Project team members are also empowered to do what is needed to achieve the project outcomes. Most Telco PMs do not micromanage their team, but expect the team to own and resolve issues. However, PMs will guide their team as to the best way forward. Project team leadership is focused on guiding, mentoring and coaching rather than stepping in and taking over. Therefore the leader in the team environment at the Telco is more than a title as it involves active leadership, social processes (mentoring and coaching) and peer persuasion as suggested by Pearce et al (2009)

In regards to strategy execution once the *business planning cycle* has approved the execution a project initiative the governance is set up, the team is set up and the project is tightly managed against deliverables. The majority of strategy initiatives (approx. 70 per cent) follow this method. However the remaining 30 per cent of initiatives are driven or initiated through strong personalities or via an organisational change management approach and are not part of the *business planning cycle*. Regardless of the mode of initiation there is a structure in place to allow that an initiative to be deployed from a business sense providing strong sponsorship is present. To overcome these strong personalities, PMs employ a shared leadership model (Labovitz & Rosansky 1997; Ancona et al. 2009; Pearce et al. 2009) which allows leadership practices to be undertaken by the team to ensure alignment with the goals of the organisation.

Workplace relationships

Project managers deliver their projects through process (the *business planning cycle*) or via relationships. Day Doz & Kosonen (2007) state good relationships in project teams are essential for task completion. The 'challenger brand' culture at the Telco, which is heavily influenced by innovative marketing, favours the relationship approach to project delivery. However this approach brings changes to the IBP produced by the *business planning cycle* and many pressures and challenges to the project managers.

The outsourcing partners play a key role in projects as they are accountable for delivery of the project's product. This is especially evident in the AD&M environment where the outsource partner is responsible for the entire project life cycle and is fully accountable for project delivery. For projects that involve the outsource partners, Telco PMs take on a governance role across a number of projects to ensure the correct interfaces between the Telco and the partner are in place for the appropriate approvals take place. This project delivery method supports Ancona et al. (2009) who assert that most work in organisations is carried out by teams that may operate across departments and in the case of the Telco across multiple companies.

The lack of a prioritisation process (mentioned above under *business planning cycle*) leads to problems when projects get to the delivery stage. Prioritisation then becomes a Telco PM responsibility as they are ultimately accountable for the complete project life cycle. The relationships the PMs have with each other play a huge role in prioritisation of projects. In most cases, prioritisation is based on the skills of the project manager in the areas of communication and influencing, and their experience and maturity within the organisation.

Telco PMs and their teams must build good relationships with their business unit stakeholders. These relationships are based on individual interactions and the team delivering to commitments. Good team relationships are essential for task completion (Day & Kosonen 2007). Team members also show individual *leadership capabilities* as proposed by Wageman et al. (2009) such as influencing, guiding and coercing. Through these actions business unit stakeholders will always get a consistent and aligned message from the project team. This provides a sound foundation to obtain committed business buy-in to projects and business units will overcome their fear that strategy will not be executed correctly.

Discussion

Wageman et al. (2009) posit that timing is a vital element in team leadership. There is no process to stop a project that may have deviated from the strategy other than the work undertaken by the PMs to realign the project deliverables and timeframe to be more in line with the strategy. The timing of these actions is extremely important to ensure the best outcomes for the project and for the Telco. Currently the Portfolio process with the *business planning cycle* approves project funding and undertakes periodic reviews of all projects of to ensure they are still in alignment with the strategy. The *business planning cycle* could easily be expanded to include a prioritisation process as part of the periodic review.

Another issue with the project prioritisation process is new projects that arise due to the need to react to a competitor's product offering, marketplace changes, or regulatory changes. These projects need to be undertaken but as they have not been part of the *business planning cycle* no project planning has taken place. Funds are made available to commence these projects, but resourcing is very difficult. From a management perspective an individual PM can easily be found (as many Telco PMs manage multiple projects), however the remaining aspects of the project (e.g. matrix team formation, project sponsorship etc) are a major concern as most resources are committed to projects that have come from the original *business planning cycle*. In this case a PM must utilise their *leadership capabilities* and rely on their *workplace relationships* to deliver the project outcomes. The *leadership capabilities* displayed in these projects are a function of the environment encountered by the PM (Marchewka 2009) rather than following the corporate processes set out by the *business planning cycle* and the Portfolio group.

It has been recognised that the project management philosophy at the Telco is in need of change. The envisaged project management model for the AD&M area is for the outsource partner's PM to deal directly with the business stakeholders and form sound *workplace relationships* at the operational level and for the Telco PM to assume a purely vendor management role and hence project leadership will become more apparent. This model has not yet matured and currently each project has a strong reliance on the Telco PM to show strong *leadership capabilities* in order to set direction and align people with tasks to ensure project outcomes are achieved (Cleland & Ireland 2007). As such a number of Telco PMs are managing two or more projects concurrently.

To support this there is a very supportive, collaborative and facilitating leadership style through the various levels of the Telco. The *workplace relationship* component is critical in all projects. To enable project success PMs must utilise their *workplace relationships* and have the confidence to question stakeholders and push back issues to the business unit stakeholders and the outsource partners. Telco PMs and project team members must possess *leadership capabilities* such as communication, influencing, facilitation and team development to enable the project to succeed. This is imperative for the PMs and project team members if they are to add value to the project process as suggested by Majchrzak et al. (2005).

Conclusions

This paper has explored leadership and workplace relationships and how these influence the execution of business strategy in an Australian mobile telecommunications company. While the research reported in the paper is part of a larger study, some findings suggest leadership and workplace relationships do influence business strategy execution at the Telco.

The formal *business planning cycle* and the initiation and ongoing review of approved projects enable the successful execution of strategy; however, other factors can impact strategy execution. For example, new projects can surface which have not been through the *business planning cycle*. There is no process in place to prioritise and review the existing project load or determine when these new projects should be scheduled. It is the Telco PMs to re-prioritise the existing project load to accommodate the new projects and secure the appropriate resources. For this to happen it is essential for project managers and team members to use their *workplace relationships* and *leadership capabilities* to ensure all projects are prioritised and adequately resourced.

There are several limitations to this study. Firstly, the sample size is relatively small and may not be representative of other organisations. Secondly all interview participants held leadership positions within the Telco (one general manager and six project managers) and the views of project team members are not presented. Finally, all interview participants were from the Telco's IT unit and therefore no views from the remainder of the organisation are presented.

As mentioned in the introduction section this is research in progress and the paper has been based on a subset of the data captured (Australian project managers). Overall 32 interviews have been conducted in the study on the Telco in Australia, England and New Zealand. The topic of the full study is to investigate 'The Role of Leadership in an Effective IT/Business Relationship'. Currently a draft literature review has been completed and all interviews have been subjected to a preliminary analysis and all Australian interviews have been analysed in more detail to identify dominant themes. A more detailed analysis is required on the interview transcripts and further work is being undertaken on the literature review.

References

Ancona, D; Bresman, H; Caldwell, D. 2009. 'The X-factor: Six steps to leading high-performing x-teams'. *Organisational Dynamics* 38 (3): 217–224.

Attride-Stirling, J. 2001. 'Thematic networks: An analytical tool for qualitative research'. *Qualitative Research* 1 (3): 385–405.

Crotty, M. 1998. *Foundations of Social Research: Meaning and Perspective in the Research Process.* Sydney: Allen & Unwin.

Cleland, D. I.; Ireland, Ireland, L.R. 2007. *Project manager's handbook: Applying best practices across global industries.* New York: McGraw-Hill.

Day, D V; Gronn, P; Salas, E. 2004. 'Leadership capacity in teams'. *The Leadership Quarterly* 15: 857–880.

Doz, Y; Kosonen, M. 2007. 'The new deal at the top'. *Harvard Business Review* 85 (6) (June): 98–104.

Forret, M; Love, M S. 2008. 'Employee justice perceptions and coworker relationships'. *Leadership & Organization Development Journal* 29 (3): 248–260.

Gray, C. F; Larson, E. W. 2006. *Project Management: The Managerial Process*, 3rd ed. Boston: McGraw-Hill/Irwin.

Haggerty, N. 2000. 'Understanding the link between IT project manager skills and project success research in progress'. Proceedings of the 2000 ACM SIGCPR Conference on Computer Personnel Research, Chicago, IL, Retrieved October 1, 2009, from ACM Portal.

Hamel, J; with Dufour, S; Fortin, D. 1993. *Case Study Methods.* Newbury Park, CA: Sage Publications.

Hertel, G; Geisterb, S; Konradtb, U. 2005. Managing virtual teams: A review of current empirical research'. *Human Resource Management Review* 15: 69–95.

Labovitz, G; Rosansky, V. 1997. *The Power of Alignment*. New York: John Wiley & Sons.

Lucey, T. 2005. *Management Information Systems*. 9th edn. London: Thompson Learning.

Majchrzak, A; Malthora, A; John, R. 2005. 'Perceived individual collaboration know-how development through information technology-enabled contextualization: Evidence from distributed teams'. *Information Systems Research* 16 (1): 9–27.

Manz, C C; Pearce, C L; Sims Jr, H P. 2009a. 'The ins and outs of leading teams: An overview'. *Organizational Dynamics* 38 (3): 179–182.

Manz, C C; Shipper, F; Stewart, G L. 2009b. 'Everyone a team leader: shared influence at W. L. Gore & Associates'. *Organizational Dynamics* 38 (3): 239–244.

Marchewka, J T. 2009. *Information Technology Project Management: Providing Measureable Organizational Value*. 3rd edn. Hoboken, NJ: John Wiley & Sons.

Morse, J M; Richards, L. 2002. *Readme First for a User's Guide to Qualitative Research*. Thousand Oaks, CA: Sage Publications.

O'Neill, T A; Kline, T J B. 2008. 'Personality as a predictor of teamwork: A business simulator study'. *North American Journal of Psychology* 10 (1): 65–78.

Pearce, C L; Manz, C C; Sims Jr, H P. 2009. 'Where do we go from here? Is shared leadership the key to team success?'. *Organizational Dynamics* 38 (3): 234–238.

Turner, J R; Müller R. 2003. 'The project manager's leadership style as a success factor on projects: A literature review'. *PM Journal* June: 49–61.

Wageman, R; Fisher, C M; Hackman, J R. 2009. 'Leading teams when the time is right: Finding the best moments to act'. *Organizational Dynamics* 38 (3): 192–203.

Yin, R K. 2003. *Case Study Research: Design and Methods*. 3rd edn. Thousand Oaks, CA: Sage Publications.

Yukl, G. 2002. *Leadership in Organizations*. 5th edn. Upper Saddle River, NJ: Prentice Hall.

Section 3

Managing Socio-Technical Projects

Chapter 11

The impact of sustainability on project management

A J Gilbert Silvius

Utrecht University of Applied Sciences, the Netherlands

Jasper van den Brink

Utrecht University of Applied Sciences, the Netherlands

Adri Köhler

Utrecht University of Applied Sciences, the Netherlands

Sustainability is one of the most important challenges of our time. How can we develop prosperity without compromising the life of future generations? Companies are integrating ideas of sustainability in their marketing, corporate communications, annual reports and in their actions. It is for that reason inevitable that 'sustainability' will find its way into project management methodologies and practices in the very near future. This paper explores the concept of sustainability and its application to project management. After a review of the relevant literature on sustainability, its leading elements are identified. Based on an analysis of the scarce literature on the application of these elements in project management, a working definition of 'Sustainable Project Management' and its concepts are derived. In the last section of the paper, the implications of these concepts for project management processes, reports and competencies are further analysed and related to the leading concepts and standards on project management.

Introduction

Striking a balance between economic growth and social wellbeing has been around as a political and managerial challenge for over 150 years (Dyllick and Hockerts 2002). Concern for the wise use of natural resources and our planet also emerged many decades ago, with Carson's (1962) book *Silent Spring* a landmark. However, with the widespread acceptance of the interconnectedness of these issues, following the 1992 United Nations Rio Earth Summit (Keating 1993), sustainable development became one of the most important challenges of our time.

The recent world crises may even imply that a strategy focused solely on shareholder value is no longer viable. Following the success of Al Gore's 'inconvenient truth', awareness seems to be growing that a change of mindset is needed, both in consumer behaviour and corporate policies. How can we develop prosperity without compromising the life of future generations? Proactively or reactively, companies are looking for ways to integrate ideas of sustainability into their marketing, corporate communications, annual reports and in their actions generally (Hedstrom et al. 1998; Holliday 2001).

Whether this increased attention to sustainability is in itself sustainable can be debated, but some developments indicate that it is. For example, the 'sustainability monitor' of PriceWaterhouseCoopers concludes that investments in projects that are considered sustainable are less prone to the current financial crises as non-sustainable projects (PriceWaterhouseCoopers 2009). Secondly, companies that have a strong sustainability image, like certain banks that include sustainability criteria in their investment policies, show less loss of value than other banks. Thirdly, public organisations are integrating criteria on sustainability into their procurement policies, thereby stimulating companies to be more active in this area.

But how does this increased attention to sustainability find its way to the shop floor? Is sustainability a point of concern there? Is sustainability for example integrated into projects and project management? If organisations 'put their money where their mouth is' on sustainability, it is inevitable that sustainability criteria and indicators will find their way into project management methodologies and practices in the very near future.

This development is recognised by leading professionals in the field of project management. At the 22nd World Congress of the International

Project Management Association (IPMA) in 2008, IPMA Vice-President Mary McKinlay stated in the opening keynote speech that 'the further development of the project management profession requires project managers to take responsibility for sustainability' (McKinlay 2008). Her plea summarised her view of the future development of project management as a profession. In her view, project managers need to take a broad view of their role and to evolve from 'doing things right' to 'doing the right things right'. This implies taking responsibility for the results of the project, including the sustainability aspects of that result. The relationship between project management and sustainability is also explored in academic research (e.g. Eid 2009; Gareis et al. 2009; Taylor 2008, Labuschagne and Brent 2006) as one of the (future) developments in project management.

This paper explores the concept of sustainability and its application to project management. After a review of the relevant literature we will develop a definition of 'Sustainable Project Management'. We will then explore the most familiar concepts of project management to understand if and how sustainability is covered in these standards.

The concept of sustainability

Sustainability in the context of sustainable development is defined by the World Commission on Environment and Development (1987) as 'forms of progress that meet the needs of the present without compromising the ability of future generations to meet their needs'. This broad definition emphasises the aspect of future orientation as a basic element of sustainability. This care for the future implies, among other things, a wise use of natural resources and other aspects regarding the environmental footprint. The 'green' aspect of sustainability is recognised in many other definitions of sustainability. For example the OECD (1990) states that 'the sustainable development concept constitutes a further elaboration of the close links between economic activity and the conservation of environmental resources. It implies a partnership between the environment and the economy.'

Other authors emphasise sustainability in relation to the development of underdeveloped regions. For example, Barbier (1987) links sustainable development to 'increasing the material standard of living of the poor at the "grassroots" level, which can be quantitatively measured in terms of increased food, real income, educational services, healthcare, sanitation and water supply, emergency stocks of food and cash, etc.'

The combination of both social and environmental perspectives can be found in the earlier-mentioned report by the United Nations World Commission on Environment and Development (1987). The report states that, 'in its broadest sense, sustainable development strategy aims at promoting harmony among human beings and between humanity and nature'.

The International Institute for Sustainable Development (2010) elaborates on the generic definitions in a definition more focused on sustainable management of organisations: 'Adopting business strategies and activities that meet the needs of the enterprise and its stakeholders today while protecting, sustaining and enhancing the human and natural resources that will be needed in the future.' Important in this definition is the mentioning of the 'needs of the enterprise and its stakeholders today'. This aspect recognises that without profitability today, care for the environment and humanity cannot be sustained. John Elkington (1997), in his book *Cannibals with Forks: the Triple Bottom Line of 21st Century Business*, identified this as the 'triple bottom line' or 'Triple-P (People, Planet, Profit)' concept: Sustainability is about the balance or harmony between economic sustainability, social sustainability and environmental sustainability.

From the literature and definitions mentioned above, three key elements of sustainability can be identified (Dyllick and Hockerts 2002).

- Sustainability is about integrating economic, environmental and social aspects.
- Sustainability is about integrating short-term and long-term aspects.
- Sustainability is about consuming the income and not the capital.

Sustainability is about integrating economic, environmental and social aspects

This element refers to the triple bottom line or three-P concept as stated by Elkington (1997) and acknowledged by Adams (2006) as the 'three pillars' of sustainability: Social, Environmental and Economic (illustrated in Figure 11.1). The concept suggests that three dimensions are inter-related and therefore may influence each other in multiple ways.

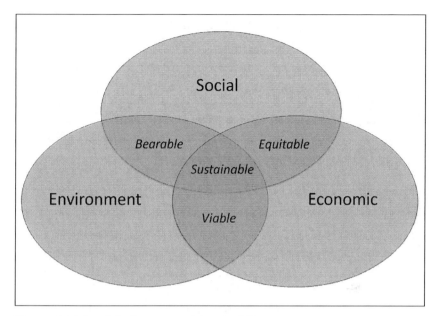

Figure 11.1. The triple-P concept of sustainability

Sustainability is about integrating short-term and long-term aspects

This element focuses attention on the long-term nature of the matter at hand. An important notion in this aspect is that the economic perspective, because of discount rates, tends to value short term effects more than long term effects, whereas social impacts or environmental degradation may not occur before the long-term.

Sustainability is about consuming the income and not the capital

This idea is common in business. From a social or environmental perspective, however, the impact may not be visible in the short-term, causing degradation of resources in the long run. Sustainability implies that 'the natural capital remains intact. This means that the source and sink functions of the environment should not be degraded. Therefore, the extraction of renewable resources should not exceed the rate at which they are renewed, and the absorptive capacity of the environment to assimilate waste, should not be exceeded' (Gilbert et al. 1996).

Sustainability in project management

The concerns about sustainability indicate that the current way of producing, organising, consuming, living, etc. may have negative effects on the future. In short, our current way of 'doing things' is not sustainable. Therefore, some 'things' have to change. And since change in organisations, whether it is a new production plant, a new product, a new business process or a new resource, is in many cases organised as projects (Silvius and Batenburg 2009), it can be concluded that a (more) sustainable society requires projects. In fact, this connection between sustainability and projects was already established by the World Commission on Environment and Development (1987). However, Eid (2009) concludes two decades later that the standards for project management 'fail to seriously address the sustainability agenda'.

When discussing the implications of sustainability for project management, it is of eminent importance to have a clear understanding of the elements of sustainability outlined above. This may be a challenging exercise because the elements are conceptual, rather than practical (Moneva et al. 2006; Pope et al. 2004). The concept of sustainability is understood intuitively, but is not easily expressed in concrete operational terms (Briassoulis 2001). The relationship between sustainability and project management is still an emerging field of study. Literature is scarce, but some first studies and ideas were published in recent years. An overview of publications is provided in Table 11.1.

Some of the studies listed in this table (Labuschagne and Brent 2006; Association for Project Management 2006; Russell 2008) focus on the implications of sustainability for business strategy and policies and thereby on the *content* of projects/changes. More specifically, they focus on the considerations that should be taken into account in defining or managing projects. The studies pay little attention to the implications of sustainability on project management processes and on the competencies of the project manager.

Other studies (Eid 2009; Gareis et al. 2009; Turner & Huemann 2010) focus on the impact of sustainability on the *process* of managing projects/changes. These studies tend to pay little attention to the contribution of projects and project management to sustainability.

In our work (Silvius et al. 2009; 2010) we try to cover both the content aspect of sustainability as well as the process aspect.

Based on the studies mentioned in Table 11.1, the following insights on sustainability in project management can be derived.

Author	Concepts of sustainability			Implications for Project Management
	Triple-P approach	**Integrating short term and long term**	**Consuming income, not capital**	
Labuschagne and Brent (2006)	√	√		Project Managers should take into account the triple-P aspects in the interacting life-cycles of the project, the asset and the product.
APM (2006)	√			Project and Program Managers are well placed to make contributions to Sustainable Management practices at many levels on their projects.
Russell (2008)		√		Corporate Social Responsibility will become increasingly important.
Taylor (2008)		√		Sustainability checklist for project managers.
Eid (2009)	√	√		Project management processes provide leverage points to introduce sustainable development to project management standards.
Silvius et al. (2009)	√	√		Concepts and framework for sustainability indicators in projects.
Gareis et al. (2009)	√	√	√	Directions for further development of project management.
Turner and Huemann (2010)	√	√	√	A framework for considering sustainable development in project management
Silvius et al. (2010)	√	√	√	An overview of concepts and frameworks for integrating sustainability in projects management.

Table 11.1. Studies on sustainability in project management

Sustainability in project management is about integrating economic, environmental and social aspects in the content and management of projects

This insight corresponds with the triple bottom line element of sustainability. Integrating sustainability in project management requires the inclusion of 'People' and 'Planet' performance indicators in the management systems, formats and governance of projects (Silvius et al. 2009). In current project management methodologies, the management of projects is dominated by the 'triple-constraint' variables of time, cost and quality (Project Management Institute 2008). And although the success of projects is most often defined from a more holistic perspective (Thomas and Fernandéz 2007), this broader set of criteria doesn't reflect on the way projects are managed.

The triple-constraint variables clearly put emphasis on the profit 'P'. The social and environmental aspects may be included as aspects of the quality of the result, but they are bound to get less attention.

Sustainability in project management is about considering the full life-cycle of the project

Given the future-orientation of the concept of sustainability, a logical implication is to consider the full life-cycle of a project, from its conception to its disposal. This view is further developed by Labuschagne and Brent (2006). In their work they argue that when considering sustainability in project management the total life cycle of the project (e.g. initiation-development-execution-testing-launch) should be taken into account. But not just the life-cycle of the project is relevant. The project will 'produce' a result, being a change in assets, systems, behaviour, etc. The asset produced should also be considered over its full life cycle. And the life cycle of the product or service that the asset produces should be considered. Figure 11.2 visualises how these life cycles, 'project life cycle', 'asset life cycle' and 'product life cycle', interact and relate to each other. Including sustainability considerations in projects suggests that these three life cycles need to be taken into account.

Because Labuschagne and Brent (2006) include the result of the project in their framework, it is sensitive to the context of the project. Their studies focus on the manufacturing sector in which projects generally realise assets that produce products. In other contexts, the result of a project may not be an asset, but an organisational change or a new policy. The general insight, however, is that sustainability in projects should be considered in relation to results and effect.

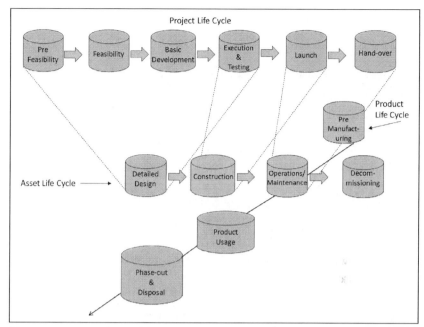

Figure 11.2. Interrelating life-cycles (based on Labuschagne & Brent 2006)

Combining the triple-P element of sustainability and the life-cycle views, the following definition of sustainable project management can be derived: Sustainable Project Management is the management of project-organised change in policies, assets or organisations, with consideration of the economic, social and environmental impact of the project, its result and its effect, for now and future generations.

Implications

The implications of integrating sustainability into project management can be grouped into a number of fields. We identify:

- the impact of sustainability on project management processes;
- the impact of sustainability on measuring, reporting and governing projects;
- the impact of sustainability on project management competencies.

The impact of sustainability on project management processes

This section explores how sustainability could be included in the familiar process standards of project management and what the impact could be. We will consider the inclusion of sustainability in the Project Management

Institute's (2008) *A Guide to Project Management Body of Knowledge (PMBOK Guide)*. Since the 'profit' aspects of sustainability are traditionally addressed in the triple constraint of project management, cost, time and quality, we will focus this analysis on the social and environmental aspects of sustainability.

For the purpose of this paper, the fourth edition of the *PMBOK Guide* (Project Management Institute 2008) was studied for aspects of sustainability. Both the Index and the Glossary do not mention sustainability as a relevant word or term. Also in parts of the guide where a reference to sustainability aspects would be quite logical, this reference is not made. For example Paragraph 1.8, Enterprise Environmental Factors, mentions the organisation's human resources and marketplace conditions as 'internal or external environmental factors that surround or influence a project's success'. But the paragraph fails to more explicitly identify potential social or environmental elements resulting from sustainability policies as factors of influence.

Also, in relation to 'stakeholders', any reference to typical sustainability stakeholders such as environmental protection pressure groups, human rights groups or non-governmental organisations are lacking. In fact, Chapter 10, 'Project Communications Management', also fails to recognise these potential stakeholders when it discusses stakeholder communication.

In the introduction of Chapter 3, 'Project Management Processes', the *PMBOK Guide* mentions a few criteria for a successful project. Here it is mentioned that the project manager should be able to 'balance the competing demands of scope, time, cost, quality, resources and risk' (Project Management Institute 2008). In this section the PMBOK Guide fails to recognise social and environmental aspects as relevant factors in project success.

Also in Chapter 11, 'Project Risk Management', there is no mentioning of ecological and/or social risks.

Does this mean that the *PMBOK Guide* has no eye for sustainability aspects at all? Well, we found two references to aspects of sustainability. One is surprisingly clear. Paragraph 4.1.1., Develop Project Charter, mentions 'Ecological impacts' and 'Social needs' as potential benefits of a project when it discussed the business case. The other reference is more implicit. The processes in the *PMBOK Guide* are derived from the generic project life cycle. In fact, it also mentions the interaction between the project life cycle and a product life cycle in paragraph 2.1.2. Product vs. Project Life Cycle Relationships.

Based on this analysis it can be concluded that the concepts of sustainability are not yet fully included in the project management processes in the *PMBOK Guide*. Obvious areas of impact should be the identification of stakeholders, the criteria for project success and the business case.

This analysis is confirmed by Eid (2009). In his study he asked 36 project management practitioners about their assessment of the impact of sustainable development on project management and on the area of impact. Figure 11.3 shows that in all five of the project management process groups (Project Management Institute 2008), an impact from sustainability is expected.

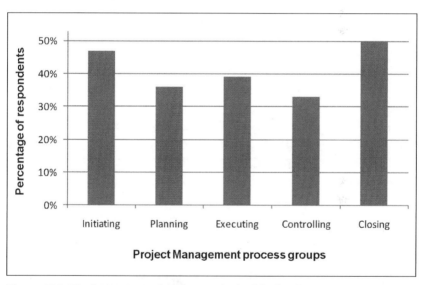

Figure 11.3. The best areas to integrate sustainable development into project management (based on Eid 2009)

The impact of sustainability on measuring and reporting projects

In considering the impact of sustainability on measuring and reporting projects, the conceptual concepts of sustainability should be translated into concrete indicators. An analysis of efforts to do so reveals different approaches to this 'translation'. Various discussions form the basis for these different approaches.

One discussion is between monetary and physical indicators (Turnhout et al 2007; Singh et al. 2009). Many economists argue that all the sustainable effects of the behaviour of a company or a project can be translated into monetary consequences (Coase 1960) The big advantage of this is that all different kind of indicators are expressed in the same way. Critics argue that this leads to an oversimplification of reality.

Another discussion focuses on the difference between biotic and abiotic indicators (Turnhout et al. 2007). Biotic indicators describe direct, biological consequences, e.g. the concentration of plankton in seawater, or the number of birds of prey in a certain area. Abiotic indicators are indirect indicators like the concentration of ozone or the level of pesticide pollution. Biotic indicators are often seen as the most valuable indicators. At the same time their numbers can fluctuate easily. Abiotic indicators are more stable but only measure whether the conditions for a good ecological system are present, not how this ecological system really 'behaves'.

There is an ongoing academic debate about the approaches described above. This debate is fuelled by a lack of knowledge in many areas, specifically when it comes to discussions about the 'planet' indicators (Turnhout et al. 2007). Complex ecological systems are difficult to understand and even more difficult to capture in one or two indicators. According to various authors all these different approaches are not just signs of an intense scientific debate but also show the normative arguments that are part of the discussion. For example, what are the criteria to include or exclude certain indicators? (Niemeijer et al. 2008)

The most well-known set of sustainability indicators based on stakeholder participation is the Global Reporting Guidelines from the Global Reporting Initiative (GRI). The GRI is a set of criteria developed by a wide variety of different stakeholders. Table 11.2 provides an overview of the GRI criteria.

The GRI is used by 1000 to 3000 organisations (Brown et al. 2009; GRI 2009) and it is still becoming more popular. One third of all sustainability reports of the largest 100 companies in various countries in the world are explicitly inspired by the GRI (Brown et al. 2009).

The implication of the goal of sustainability for project management is that this set of indicators is matched with the indicators on which a project is managed. The total set of indicators is probably far too extensive to use in most projects, but a selection of relevant indicators can be very useful for project managers to get a better understanding of the sustainability aspects of their project.

Economic Criteria		Direct Economic Performance
		Market Presence
		Indirect Economic Impact
Environmental Criteria		Materials
		Energy
		Water
		Biodiversity
		Emissions, effluents and waste
		Products and services
		Compliance
		Transport
		Overall
Social Criteria	Labour Practices and Decent Work	Employment
		Labour / Management relations
		Health and Safety
		Training and Education
		Diversity and Equal opportunity
	Human Rights	Investment and Procurement practices
		Non-discrimination
		Freedom of association and collective bargaining
		Child labour
		Forced and compulsory labour
		Disciplinary practices
		Security practices
		Indigenous rights
	Society	Community
		Bribery and corruption
		Public policy
		Anti-competition behaviour
		Compliance core
	Product Responsibility	Customer health and safety
		Products and services labelling
		Market communication and Advertising
		Customer privacy
		Compliance

Table 11.2. Overview of indicators in the Global Reporting Guidelines

The impact of sustainability on project management competencies

This section explores how a concern for sustainability is included in the widely used standards for project management competencies, the International Project Management Association's (IPMA) *Competence Baseline version 3* (ICB3). The ICB3 provides the official definition of the competences expected from project management personnel by the IPMA for certification using the universal IPMA certification system. It is the common framework document that all IPMA Member Associations and Certification Bodies abide by to ensure that consistent and harmonised standards are applied.

In ICB3, the IPMA added two new groups of competences to the baseline: behavioural and contextual. ICB3 now breaks professional project management down into 46 competences that cover the following categories (International Project Management Association 2006):

- technical competences for project management (20 competences);

- behavioural competences of project personnel (15 competences);

- contextual competences of projects, programs and portfolios (11 competences).

An overview of these competences is shown in Table 11.3.

The word 'sustainable' is scarcely used in the ICB3 (International Project Management Association 2006): competence 2.04 Assertiveness talks about 'sustainable relationships to the interested parties' (p. 94) and competence 3.09 Health, Safety, Security, Environment talks about 'security and sustainability' (p. 32).

The content of sustainability, however, is addressed under the key word of 'project context'. This starts in competence 1.3 Project Requirements & Objective, where the conformity to the context conditions is required in addition to achieving the project objectives. The context is later specified in several of the contextual competences: 3.05 Permanent Organisation; 3.06 Business; 3.07 Systems, Products & Technology; 3.08 Personnel management; 3.09 Health, Safety, Security, Environment.

In 3.07 Systems, Products & Technology and 3.09 Health, Safety, Security, Environment the subjects within sustainability (e.g. the systems life cycle management) are well addressed. Also the responsibility (permanent organisations) and some processes (e.g. internal and external audits) and tools (Environmental Impact Study) are mentioned. And the reference to ethics in competence 2.15 implies that at least some social aspects are taken into consideration. Other references to the social aspects of sustainability can be found in element 3.08 Personnel management and 2.14 Values appreciation.

Technical competences	Behavioural competences	Contextual competences
1.01 Project management success	2.01 Leadership	3.01 Project orientation
1.02 Interested parties	2.02 Engagement & motivation	3.02 Program orientation
1.03 Project requirements & objectives	2.03 Self-control	3.03 Portfolio orientation
1.04 Risk & opportunity	2.04 Assertiveness	3.04 Project, program & portfolio orientation
1.05 Quality	2.05 Relaxation	3.05 Permanent organisation
1.06 Project organisation	2.06 Openness	3.06 Business
1.07 Teamwork	2.07 Creativity	3.07 Systems, products & technology
1.08 Problem resolution	2.08 Results orientation	3.08 Personnel management
1.09 Project structures	2.09 Efficiency	3.09 Health, security, safety & environment
1.10 Scope & deliverables	2.10 Consultation	3.10 Finance
1.11 Time & project phases	2.11 Negotiation	3.11 Legal
1.12 Resources	2.12 Conflict & crisis	
1.13 Cost & finance	2.13 Reliability	
1.14 Procurement & contract	2.14 Values appreciation	
1.15 Changes	2.15 Ethics	
1.16 Control & reports		
1.17 Information & documentation		
1.18 Communication		
1.19 Start-up		
1.20 Close-out		

Table 11.3. The project management competences from the ICB3

Although our analysis shows that indications of and references to aspects of sustainability can be found, the full integration of sustainability in project management competences requires a further elaboration of the behavioural and contextual aspects of the ICB3.

As Eid (2009) concluded, 'Project management … knowledge areas fall short of committing to a sustainable approach'.

Conclusion

Projects can make a contribution to the sustainable development of organisations. It should therefore be expected that the concepts of sustainability are reflected in projects and project management. And although some aspects of sustainability are found in the various standards of project management, it has to be concluded that the impact of sustainability is not fully recognised yet. The standards of project management do not completely reflect the different aspects of sustainability that can be derived from the concepts of sustainable development.

Based on the concepts of sustainability, we developed a working definition of Sustainable Project Management:

> Sustainable Project Management is the management of project-organised change in policies, assets or organisations, with consideration of the economic, social and environmental impact of the project, its result and its effect, for now and future generations.

This view of Sustainable Project Management suggests a number of areas in which project management needs to develop further in order to capture the impacts of sustainability planning. These areas are:

- project management processes;
- project management performance indicators;
- project management competencies.

These areas of impact also hold a recommendation for further research.

We suggest the development of a framework that can be used to identify the sustainability aspects and criteria of projects. In this framework the people-planet-profit concept of sustainability should be recognised in such a way that projects can be considered on criteria of 'social sustainability', 'environmental sustainability' and 'economic sustainability'. These criteria or indicators should then be applied on the level of the project itself, and impact on its result (an asset, product or a change) and its effect (what is it that the asset delivers).

It is clear that there is still a lot of work to be done on the implications of Sustainable Project Management and that there is a growing need for expertise, criteria and concepts to practically implement the concept in the management of projects. The consequences are not at all clear yet and may even be underestimated. The definition we developed, however, provides a foundation for further development and operationalisation.

References

Adams, W M. 2006. *The Future of Sustainability: Re-thinking Environment and Development in the Twenty-first Century*. Report IUCN. Available from: http://cmsdata.iucn.org/downloads/iucn_future_of_sustanability.pdf

Association for Project Management. 2006. 'APM supports sustainability outlooks'. Available from: http://www.apm.org.uk/page.asp?categoryID=4.

Barbier, E. 1987. 'The concept of sustainable economic development'. *Environmental Conservation* 14 (2): 101–110.

Briassoulis, H. 2001. 'Sustainable development and its indicators: Through a (planner's) glass darkly'. *Journal of Environmental Planning and Management* 44 (3): 27–409

Brown, H S; Jong, M de; Levy, D L. 2009. 'Building institutions based on information disclosure: Lessons from GRI's sustainability reporting'. *Journal of Cleaner Production* 17: 571–580.

Carson, R. 1962. *Silent Spring*. Boston: Houghton Mifflin.

Coase, R H. 1960. 'The problem of social cost'. *Journal of Law and Economics* 3: 1–44.

Dyllick, T; Hockerts, K. 2002. 'Beyond the business case for corporate sustainability'. *Business Strategy and the Environment* 11: 130–141.

Elkington, J. 1997. *Cannibals with Forks: The Triple Bottom Line of 21st Century Business*. Oxford: Capstone Publishing Ltd.

Gareis, R; Huemann, M; Martinuzzi, A. 2009. *Relating Sustainable Development and Project Management*. Berlin: IRNOP IX.

Gilbert, R; Stevenson, D; Girardet, H; Stern, R, eds. 1996. *Making Cities Work: The Role of Local Authorities in the Urban Environment*. London: Earthscan Publications Ltd.

Global Reporting Initiative (GRI). 2009. Accessed September 2009. Available from: http://www.globalreporting.org/NewsEventsPress/PressResources/PressRelease_14_July_2006_1000GRIReports.htm 21.

International Institute for Sustainable Development (IISD). 2010. Accessed September 2010. Available from: http://www.iisd.org/sd/

Hedstrom G; Poltorzycki S; Stroh P. 1998. 'Sustainable development: The next generation'. *Prism* 4: 5–20.

Holliday C. 2001. 'Sustainable growth, the DuPont way'. *Harvard Business Review* September: 129–134.

International Project Management Association. 2006. *IPMA Competence Baseline version 3.0*. Nijkerk, the Netherlands: IPMA,

Keating, M. 1993. *The Earth Summit's Agenda for Change*. Geneva: Centre for our Common Future.

Labuschagne, C; Brent, A C. 2006. 'Social indicators for sustainable project and technology life cycle management in the process industry'. *International Journal of Life Cycle Assessment* 11 (1): 3–15.

McKinlay, M. 2008. 'Where is project management running to?' Key-note speech, International Project Management Association, World Congress, Rome, Italy.

Moneva, J M; Archel, P; Correa, C. 2006. 'GRI and the camouflaging of corporate sustainability'. *Accounting Forum* 30: 121–137.

Niemeijer, D; de Groot, R S. 2008. 'A conceptual framework for selecting environmental indicator sets'. *Ecological indicators* 8: 14–25

OECD. 1990. *Issues papers: On Integrating Environment and Economics.* Paris: OECD.

Pope, J; Annandale, D; Morris-Saunders, A. 2004. 'Conceptualising sustainable assessment'. *Environmental Impact Assessment Review* 24: 595–616.

PriceWaterhouseCoopers. 2009. *Sustainability Monitor (In Dutch: Duurzaamheidsbarometer), May 2009, measurement 4.* Amsterdam: PriceWaterhouseCoopers.

Project Management Institute. 2008. *A Guide to Project Management Body of Knowledge (PMBOK Guide).* 4ᵗʰ edn. Newtown Square, PA USA: Project Management Institute.

Russell, J. 2008 'Corporate social responsibility: What it means for the project manager'. In Proceedings of PMI Europe Congress, Malta, Philadelphia, PA: Project Management Institute

Silvius, A J G; Batenburg, R. 2009. 'Future development of project management competences'. Paper presented at the 42nd Hawaii International Conference on Systems Science (HICSS), Waikoloa HI, January 2009.

Silvius, A J G; Brink, J. van der; Köhler, A. 2009. 'Views on sustainable project management'. In *Human Side of Projects in Modern Business*, edited by Kähköhnen, Kalle; Kazi, Abdul Samad; Rekola, Mirkka. Helsinki, Finland: IPMA Scientific Research Paper Series.

Silvius, A J G; Brink, J. van der; Köhler, A. 2010. 'The concept of sustainability and its application to project management'. Paper presented at IPMA Expert Seminar Survival and Sustainability as Challenges for Projects, Zurich.

Singh, R K; Murty, H R; Gupta, S K; Dikshit, A K. 2009. 'An overview of sustainability assessment methodologies'. *Ecological Indicators* 9: 189–212.

Taylor, T. 2008. *A Sustainability Checklist for Managers of Projects.* Available from: http://www.pmforum.org/library/papers/2008/PDFs/Taylor-1-08.pdf.

Thomas, G; Fernandez, W. 2007. 'The elusive target of IT project success'. International Research Workshop on IT Project Management (IRWITPM), Association of Information Systems, Special Interest Group for Information Technology Project Management, Montreal, December 9–12.

Turnhout, E; Hisschemoller, M; Eijsackers, H. 2007. 'Ecological indicators: Between the two fires of science and policy'. *Ecological indicators* 7: 215–228.

Turner, R; Huemann, M. 2010. 'Responsibilities for sustainable development in project and program management'. IPMA Expert Seminar Survival and Sustainability as Challenges for Projects, Zurich.

World Commission on Environment and Development. 1987. *Our Common Future.* Great Britain: Oxford University Press.

Chapter 12

The project entity as human activity system and social process

Providing the structural openness to connect with context

Jocelyn Small

TLC Aged Care, Australia

Derek Walker

RMIT University, Australia

This paper focuses on the advantages of viewing projects as a social process. It moves away from traditional views that draw on linear and predictable models of project practice to a perspective that better highlights the complex nature of human interrelations. Findings from recent doctoral research implemented in the Middle East indicate that socio-cultural factors in project contexts affect knowledge creation processes critical to organisational change. The project organisation was viewed as a 'complex adaptive system' with a structurally open project entity facilitating the contextual interconnections necessary for detecting and creating environmental change. Pragmatic knowledge was seen as emergent through human interactions and contributed to the portrayal of the project organisation as a 'becoming' cognitive system whose resilience is dependent upon producing meaning as opposed to processing information. Complexity in project management and theory has traditionally focused on technical and structural aspects of project practice, whereas aligning social systems with nature where disorder and uncertainty prevails provides a better model of social analysis. Working in culturally pluralistic project environments, where multiple realities and disparities in language are commonplace, create challenges to traditional project management practice. Adaptive project management responses seek common ground for understanding through facilitating knowledge flow and meaningful interactions.

Introduction

This paper illustrates how a recent doctoral thesis project initially drew on traditional project management techniques but later found that viewing project practice as a social process provided a more effective way to probe the research question.

Fully describing the work encompassed by the thesis is beyond the scope of this paper. For a complete coverage, readers should refer to Small (2009). Therefore a brief summary of the salient points relevant to this paper is presented to introduce the main focus of this paper; that is the advantage of viewing a project as a social process to allow high level study of a project management (PM) phenomenon. Initially, the thesis was framed as a case study of how a quality assurance (QA) process was introduced to allow international accreditation of a set of study programs and to facilitate the associated change management flow-on implications. When the topic was first framed and the investigation began it was conceived as being a case study of a subset of PM processes – the way that the QA was instigated and how the change management program was planned to be enacted. During the data gathering phase of the research, it became clear that the key issues that appeared to affect the way that this QA project unfolded were not the way that tools and techniques were applied and adopted. Rather, what was significant was the way that the entire context of the situation and the shifting socio-political pressures played a role in the reality of the change management transformation; a reality of the situation that all project team and direct stakeholders faced and experienced. Following on from this realisation, it was decided to abandon a case study research approach that focused on techniques and tools as the unit of analysis to the project environment as being the focus of attention. The investigation was re-conceptualised as being the study of a 'messy situation' involving critical knowledge generation and sharing, and it was decided to employ a soft system methodology (SSM) approach (Checkland 1999; Checkland & Winter 2006). Using an adaptive management approach within a social setting emerged as a critical factor in determining observed outcomes. This enabled a far more relevant and rich method of investigating what was 'happening' inside the project.

Following a discussion of the socio-cultural complexity in project environments, this paper then focuses on the biological nature of social complexity to highlight the relevance of complexity theory in organisational analysis. Next, the conceptual framework employed in the doctoral research is summarised before the notion of projects as complex human activity systems is explored. The final section of the paper presents the realities of project praxis as involving unpredictable, non-linear interrelationships of social process, where the complexity of difference is revealed as the critical factor to be managed for effective outcomes.

Socio-cultural complexity in project environments

Today's work environment has increased in complexity, project outcomes are influenced by a range of subtle social processes triggered by technology altering the pace of business and globalisation is creating a more diverse marketplace. Changes in organisational structures and workplace behaviour have attempted to accommodate such realities (DiTomaso & Hooijberg 1996; Bass & Steidlmeier 1999; Osborn, Hunt & Jauch 2002; Avolio, Gardner, Walumbwa, Luthans & May 2004). Traditional bureaucratic systems and project management processes have tended to impede the rate of response to the dynamics existing in current business environments. This has led to operational shifts to more flexible flatter organisational structures with functional emphases on project-based management (Turner 1999; Hodgson & Cicmil 2006; Hobbs, Aubry & Thuillier 2008) and the portrayal of projects as 'vehicles' or 'vectors' of strategy and competency development (Bredillet 2008). Recent questioning of the application of a mechanistic view of project management (PM), however, has led to a reappraisal of how PM techniques and processes should be applied. This has been accompanied by a focus on the role of knowledge as co-learning through co-enactment of project participants (Weick 1995).

It is the *nature* of projects, in particular, which has come under the spotlight more recently, with changes in thinking about project actuality being associated with a systems approach to organisational analyses. In this shift, projects have been defined, as 'tools' for business (Packendorff 1995; Winter, Smith, Morris & Cicmil 2006); as temporary organisations (Thomas, Clark & Gioia 1993; Lundin & Söderholm 1995; Turner & Müller 2003; Modig 2007); as emerging initiators of organisational learning and change (Kreiner 1992; Bresnen 2006); as objects of organisational innovation (Hobbs et al. 2008); and as language and practice (Lineham & Kavanagh 2006). The traditional view of projects as endeavours which are goal-directed, structured, planned within a time frame and unique (Turner 1999) is being replaced by alternative views of project praxis within in an ontology of becoming (Chia 1995) and as 'an emergent outcome of disparate, ambiguous, political practices' (Lineham & Kavanagh 2006, 55).

Yet, this conceptual movement away from more static models of project practice has not necessarily translated into real change in ways of 'doing' business; an emphasis still remains on finite stages of 'development, implementation and termination' in project management (Söderlund 2004a), with a project ontology being perceived as an entity in a state of 'existence' or being. It is the absence of a strong project management theoretical base which is perpetuating the tendency to still draw upon traditional organisational theory to explain project functionality (Kreiner 1992; Lundin & Söderholm 1995; Turner & Müller 2003; Söderlund 2004a; Modig 2007). Winter et al. (2006, 638) have indicated that 'the conceptual base of project management continues to attract criticism for its lack of relevance to practice'. What is needed is a greater emphasis on the social realities existing within project contexts, particularly given increasing global mobility and diverse human plurality dominating multinational workforces. Through re-directing project theory to re-think relationships between the individual and the organisation (Kreiner 1992), such issues as autonomy and control, self-regulation and change, may be better addressed for improved project practice.

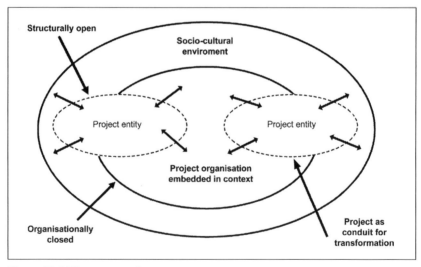

Figure 12.1. The open project structure

This paper has evolved from research completed in the Middle East which was guided by a defined ecological conceptual framework to present the project actuality as an open entity able to facilitate regeneration, reorganisation and renewal for organisational transformation and resilience (Folke 2006; Small 2009). As represented in Figure 12.1, whilst the organisation and project entity *per se* remain 'organisationally closed', the project structure is perceived as open. In this way, the project entity is mutually coupled both with the organisation and the environment actively functioning in forward-directed sense-making activities whilst feeding back interpreted information to the main organisation. The socio-cultural environment was characterised by project team members coming from a range of religious and ethnic backgrounds with all the cultural norms, mind-sets (world views) and assumptions that this implies (Hofstede 1980; House, Javidan, Hanges & Dorfman 2002; Schein 2004).This context was further complicated by the way in which authority, power, influence and legitimacy was perceived by the institutions in which the project took place which was based upon dominant cultural norms of the host organisation. Project practice is thus not only presented as having the potential to contribute to 'solving' problems in the organisational environment, but is able to facilitate change through social processes entailing inquiry and reflection to create knowledge necessary for optimising an organisation's capacity to act.

Such interplay promotes a balanced and circular nature in project existence, akin to metabolic changes in living organisms, ensuring organisational equilibrium is maintained whilst incremental adaptations to contextual change are possible. Visualising the project organisation as being autopoietic in nature, even if only metaphorically, can support the conceptualisation of a project entity existing as potentially ontologically autonomous, yet whose survival or resilience is dependent upon a self-perpetuating relationship with and within an organisational entity.

Bourne (2005, 59; 2009) visualises the existence of hidden energies and influences that can be harnessed by the project manager and project team. Figure 12.2 illustrates her argument of how project managers view various stakeholders and ways to manage projects through looking and reflecting upon their influence through viewing their impact upwards, downwards, sideways and inwards. Her model, adapted from Briner, Hastings and Geddes (1996), was developed to describe the skills set needed by a project manager. Dimension 1 relates to knowledge of how to look forwards and backwards to apply effective PM techniques – this could include applying an appropriate stakeholder engagement strategy. Dimension 2 relates to knowledge of relationships of how to look inwards, outwards and downwards, which is also relevant to the ability to manage relationships with key influencing stakeholders. Dimension 3 skills relate to considering and ensuring that political influence and lobbying is addressed by looking sideways and upwards.

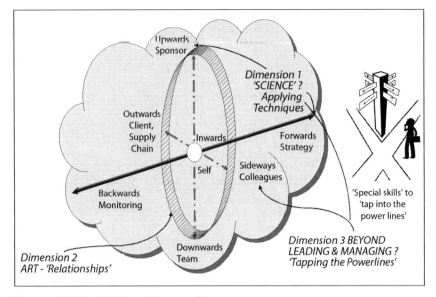

Figure 12.2 Tapping into the powerlines

This is what she refers to as 'tapping into the powerlines' of project stakeholder influence. This provides an example of a sophisticated skill set that specifically recognises the reality of projects and project management of the environmental interfaces, especially socio-cultural complexity aspects. It also stresses co-learning and knowledge generation and sharing in a social setting, it relies more highly on context-specific tacit knowledge held by various parties and the application process and procedural knowledge rather than knowledge *of* these tools and techniques.

The challenge for the project manager in socially complex contexts where cultural disparities exist is to foster the mutually reciprocal interrelationships to underpin a communicative common ground for knowledge creation, sense-making and learning. Another useful technique worth considering, for making sense of the environment in order to deal with the social complexity of disparate stakeholders, is analysis of political, economic, social, technical, environmental and legal (PESTEL) factors. There are a number of tools that can be used for developing plans to deal with uncertainty. Walsh (2005, 120) for example, argues:

> Understanding the performance of firms within a changed environment can be achieved using the combination of a PESTEL analysis, internal resource analysis and the use of scenarios to create a model of a possible environment in which the firm must operate and an investigation of

the strategic implications of that scenario to the firm. Assessing this environment provides insight into the unique changes, the implications these changes have on firms' strategies, and the creation of special techniques required to understand them.

So PESTEL can be used to help picture a 'current reality' for any given stakeholder group as well as aid in planning for a 'preferred future reality'. Other strategic planning tools for enacting change and understanding socially complex abound. A bricoleur approach (Weick 1995) therefore appears appropriate by using traditional PM tools and techniques wherever they may prove useful. There are a range of tools that can help us see a problem, the reality of a complex social setting and ways in which a valid response can be made.

Biological nature of social complexity

Although characteristics of Complex Adaptive Systems (CAS) have been identified by several authors, it is Holland (1995) who has been attributed with defining such systems. He has referred to CAS as being a dynamic network of many agents interacting jointly and in parallel, where the control is dispersed and decentralised and the system's behaviour is determined by individual decision making and coherence being a result of competition and cooperation. Dooley (1996) also suggests that CAS comprise agents as evolving semi-autonomous units who scan, interpret and respond to an unpredictable and changing environment in a competitive manner for survival. These agents both instigate schematic change and interact with other agents exchanging information in nonlinear flows, having determined rules of interaction both internal and external to the system.

These definitions have been informed by earlier biological cybernetics works of Maturana and Varela (1980). Autopoietic theory includes descriptions about complex behaviours and relationships which autonomous organisms have both internally and externally through structural coupling of their systems with environments in which dynamic relationships underpin a multitude of interactions. The theory has been used to frame analysis in relation to complexity of socially constructed organisations and has been identified as being pertinent to organisational knowledge creation and management, particularly in relation to the biological concepts of enacted consciousness and embodied cognition (Baerveldt & Verheggen 1999; Kay 2001; Riegler 2002; Hall 2005; Buchinger 2006; Limone & Bastias

2006; Parboteeah & Jackson 2007). This biological metaphorical way of viewing CAS to seemingly self-organise has been provided by Bonabeau and Meyer (2001, 108) in improving airport baggage handling by studying the way ants cooperate. Three particularly sound adaptive traits can be found from this research that are relevant to good PM practice. These are by the 'swarm' of social insects following a small number of simple rules: flexibility (the colony can adapt to a changing environment); robustness (even when one or more individuals fail, the group can still perform its tasks); and self-organisation (activities are neither centrally controlled nor locally supervised). A further application of the biological metaphor has been evolutionary change. Evolutionary change as a biological process as applied to organisational adaptation has its origins also in the works of Kauffman and Levin (1987), who note the element of conflict in and between components of complex systems:

> many parts and processes must become coordinated to achieve some measure of overall success, but conflicting requirements due to alternative simultaneous optimization goals, or conflicting constraints due to the natures of the different parts and processes to be co-coordinated, limit the end result achieved (p. 12).

Adaptation here is seen as more than predicting elements of future change. Rather, adaptation is seen as incremental responses and mutations to previous environmental contexts balanced with 'local search' procedures seeking contextual perturbations (Kauffman & Levin 1987).

The relevance of CAS to project praxis is focused on their defining properties of instability, emergence and self-organisation, with the 'whole' being irreducible to parts and multiple elements of time and space existing. CAS involve non-linear systems with unpredictable outcomes, irreversible processes and positive feedback loops to reinforce change (Cilliers 2000; Law & Urry 2004; Eijnatten 2004). Such biologically sourced 'chaos', in which certainty can only be found in uncertainty, is also the social reality of an enacted globally complex world; CAS 'constantly seek to adapt to the environmental circumstances in which they find themselves' (Carlisle & McMillan 2006, p. 4) with interrelationships facilitating a reciprocity of creation and adaptation through active innovative behaviour moving learning beyond maintaining stability to shaping change through inquiry.

This creates resilience within the CAS which is measured by the capacity to absorb change and shape change through sensing and adapting to disturbances in the environment (Folke 2006). A biological representation of cognition where the 'knower' is a 'complex agent that is organizing, self-maintaining and structurally determined' (Proulx 2008, 12) extends upon the resilience perspective to portray knowledge as enacted with meaning brought forth through constant evolving interactions. Through recognising cognition as a process of the living, organisational responsiveness as a CAS may thus be seen to reflect the system's capacity to adapt as an emergent entity for transformation.

The main factors which have been noted as characterising CAS as autopoietic entities include self-organising behaviour, structural openness, fractals of other entities, agents interconnected in dynamic interdependent relationships, non-linear processes, patterned dissipative behaviour, emergent entities, positive feedback loops, instability, the whole being irreducible to parts and behaviour which is unpredictable and spontaneous in an environment equally uncertain (Law & Urry 2004; Bloch 2005; Stackman, Henderson & Bloch 2006). Complexity pertaining to organisational systems has been referred to as 'chaotic' with the environmental context being so unpredictable that traditional linear systems of management are considered inadequate in sustaining the organisation (Glass 1996). Whilst the chaotic nature of business practice has been disputed (Cilliers 2000), with it being suggested that 'chaos theory implies that events have a life and logic of their own; there is limited room for intervention' (Tyler 2005, 569), it is the concept of non-random emergence which is relevant for the project organisation as it moves to higher levels of complexity and coherence (Glass 1996). Findings in the research which influenced this paper indicate that project praxis has the potential to facilitate evolving collective action, despite disparities in vision 'sharing' in socially disparate collectives.

It is also suggested in this paper that discussions on 'complexity' in project management have predominantly been in relation to solving organisational problems which are messy, structurally and technically, where goals and project specifications are unclear and elements of performance are convoluted (Williams 2002; Atkinson, Crawford & Ward 2006; Pundir, Ganapathy & Sambandam 2007). The life cycle model of projects and project management has dominated project management theory, with a different conceptual research approach aiming to address calls to focus more on the social nature of complexity in projects practice (Winter et al. 2006; Cooke-Davies, Cicmil, Crawford & Richardson 2007).

Conceptual framework

A socio ecological conceptual framework was therefore defined to philosophically guide and expand upon project management thinking to underpin the research (Figure 12.3). As expressed by Cicmil and Hodgson (2006), there is a 'need to explore how the relationships between individuals and collectivities are being constituted and reproduced in the context of project management, and how asymmetrical power relations create and sustain the social reality of projects'. The assumptions in the defined conceptual framework support the concept of inherent interconnected relationships in project practice, noting projects as social process and as human activity systems in non-linear states of flux and messiness. Postmodernism was found useful in relation to focusing on the importance of individual experience and complexity in human existence as opposed to models of predictability and control, whilst enactivist theory supported the contextually embedded nature of cognition (knowing and understanding).

The problems under study for the thesis were deceptively simple to define. One was 'what is going on in this quality assurance (QA) and accreditation process?' another was 'how are project management (PM) tools and techniques being applied to this messy change management process?'

Figure 12.3 illustrates this framework. The problem was initially framed as being related to implementing a QA project in the Middle East. As the study progressed, however, it became necessary to better understand the rich strands of influence and action that shaped the way the project unfolded. A different view of what was happening was needed. Actions, reactions, ploys, understandings and misunderstandings were seen to be subject to the socio-cultural dynamics at play. It then became more useful to see this the project as a social process rather than a way in which techniques and tools were mechanistically applied. As Figure 12.3 indicates, perceiving the project in this way opened up and challenged traditional assumptions of what was happening inside the project team. A fresh set of conceptual enquiry assumptions presented themselves, leading to a new philosophical way of thinking about project practice.

Ontologically, the nature and structure of the world has been assumed to entail emergent change, evolving processes, transformation and adaptation, complemented by a pragmatic epistemology which views knowledge as enacted cognition, culturally situated and emergent.

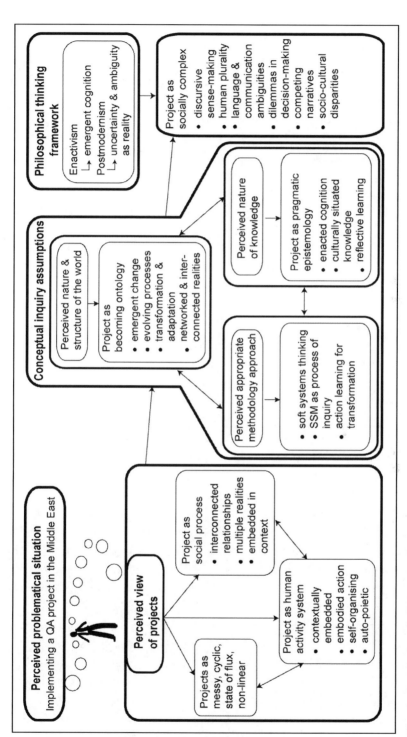

Figure 12.3. Research philosophical conceptual framework

Projects as complex human activity systems

Project management has been described using complexity inspired metaphors (Ivory, Alderman, McLoughlin & Vaughan 2006; Cooke-Davies et al. 2007; Pundir et al. 2007; Richardson 2008) to move thinking from positivist-inspired models of instrumentality and predictability, to conceptualise project practice as entailing dynamic patterned behaviour which is self-organising and co-emergent. The multiple interconnections in the project as a social process involve mutuality in creation and adaptation in environmental contexts. Associating complexity theory with social systems can help focus on the realities of social inter-relatedness in organisational and project practice. The workplace of today is embedded in a globalised emerging context which is culturally diverse and pluralistic in nature. Changes in organisational dynamics, from the blurring of cultural, national and international borders, demand greater consideration be given to the connectedness of action, cognition and context (Pettigrew, Woodman and Cameron 2001b; Orlikowski 2002). The resilience of project organisations resides in the ability to move beyond adaptation in context, to the creation and shaping of the environment through collective activity.

Project management models which align project complexity with structural uncertainty (Williams 1999; Sommer & Loch 2004; Atkinson et al. 2006), without giving consideration to the ongoing social interactions creating the dynamism in projects as complex adaptive systems (CAS) (Whitty & Maylor 2007), only in part contribute to understanding the impact an array of discursive social agendas may have on project outcomes. Organisations and teams as communities of practice, have been identified as CAS (Carlisle & McMillan 2006; Stackman et al. 2006), and viewing projects in the same light is an extension to this concept. Projects as complex adaptive systems do not fit within instrumental life cycle models of projects as 'tools' to manage organisational complexity, rather reside within ecological representations of projects where actors are interconnected with each other and the environment (Ekinsmyth 2002; Söderlund 2004a). Further, as Engwall (2003) argues, projects are not isolated 'islands' but are influenced by the organisational context and the history of social interactions of its participants and are intertwined with the organisations participating. Additionally, projects are (or should be) generally part of a program of projects that fit together to cumulatively deliver a pre-defined benefit (Pellegrinelli 1997) and the level of autonomy of a project from its parent organisation varies according to the complexity of stakeholder involvement (Artto, Martinsuo, Dietrich & Kujala 2008).

It is the human element inherent in projects as social activity systems which implies a complexity due to the individual nature of cognitive elements interacting in numerous and variable ways (Waldrop 1992). The complexity need not assume chaos and disorder, rather should acknowledge the realities of human life as patterned yet discursive and culturally pluralistic. That is, 'organised complexity' where 'the character of the structures showing it depends not only on the properties of the individual elements of which they are composed, and the relative frequency with which they occur, but also on the manner in which the individual elements are connected with each other' (Hayek 1974, 3).

Projects as complex human activity systems refocus the theoretical lens on the individual as the primary element embedded in context, who through being structurally coupled with other individuals and the environment, co-emerge and change through dynamic 'knotted' interactions. Behaviour which contributes to project team survival relies on collective activity which is persistent, creative and sensitive to environmental triggers. Project practice if then conceptualised as an emergent human activity, may be seen to involve coordinated collaborative 'swarming' movements to combine outward 'action and pursuit' with inward regathering and reflective practice (Engeström 2006).

Project actuality therefore has the potential to create connectivity on a global scale through having players working on more than one project at a time or being a member of more than one project at a time; projects with work subcontracted and subcontracted again. The realities of the social processes involved in such interconnected human activity systems will inevitably entail socio-cultural differences originating from disparate historical roots and discursive language underpinnings. Project management in this new era creates challenges where the solution is unlikely to be found in traditional control models of instrumentality. The complexes that exist which are seeing 'an unfolding interplay between language, action and structure has produced a model of managing projects that bears no resemblance to the sanitised world of the project management literature' (Green 2006, 249)

Management of more complex projects, which are described as 'messy' in this paper, moves beyond the controlling paradigm to requiring new and emergent forms of leadership. Such projects are better led through envisioning and anticipating the future for organisational adaptation, though this will need to be tempered with the reality that complexity assumes it is impossible to model or predict a world whose ontology is no longer singular (Law & Urry, 2004). Courtney, Kirkland and Viguerie (1997), for example, nominate four broad levels of uncertainty when dealing with modelling and prediction: a clear-enough future; alternate futures; a range of futures; and true ambiguity of residual uncertainty facing most strategic-decisions. They (Courtney, Kirkland & Viguerie 1997) also offer three strategic postures a company can adopt to plan for the future: shaping it, adapting to it, or reserving the right to play in the future. These adaptations plan to cope with an envisioned future rather than expect to rigidly plan and control for it. Both context-determined and global factors are contributing to the increasingly complex project environment and although these elements have been instrumental in driving an increase in project-based management (Hobbs et al. 2008), the traditional project management models incorrectly assume environmental sense-making can be based on positivist control (Whitty 2005). An enactivist view more ably complements expansive learning through visualising projects as human activity systems to support emergent forms of project management. Further, it depends upon project management actions that 'tap into the powerlines' of the political and social realities that can be perceived as shaping action. Also, project managers need to have an ability to better be aware of and perceive stakeholder politics at work, both in terms of more obvious and visible signals as well as more intangible hidden signals that help to indicate the nature of socio-political influences playing out.

Projects as social process

Emergence as a property of projects as 'complex adaptive systems', reflects the cognitive nature of the entity, with embodied experience serving to produce meaning, and learning being the product which assures organisational resilience. Such a becoming ontology moves beyond the perceived adaptive nature of self-organising project systems where survival involving emergence to sustain a state of 'being' dominates. Projects as social processes involving a complexity of human interrelations fluctuate between stability and instability with uncertainty and unpredictability being exacerbated by the dissipated nature of cognition which emerges from disparate patterns of human connections.

Complexity in the research context did not originate from multi-firm partnerships, international alliances, cross-cultural partnerships or joint ventures as has been identified in other project research (Loosemore & Al Muslmani 1999; Gupta & Govindarajan 2000; Clark & Geppert 2006; Bresnen 2007; Ambos & Schlegelmilch 2008; Grisham & Walker 2008). Rather project complexity arose from and within the project entity comprising a multiplicity of expatriate workers interconnected and embedded within an Arabic socio-cultural and political context. The 'real' project actuality provided an insight into the social nature and ecology of project practice, revealing a complexity created by social-cultural differences which emerged as critical to project praxis.

Findings supported the call for scholars to 'pay closer attention to the relationships between projects and their environments' (Söderlund 2004b, p. 664) and shifted the emphasis from structured 'one-size-fits-all' project management models, to focusing on strategic adaptive approaches to working with projects as socially complex processes. The unpredictable nature of the project trajectory created the demand for exploration into complexity arising from the social interactions that exist in project practice (Winter et al. 2006) to enable different conceptualisations from the more rational and finite models of project management.

The interconnected and dynamic relationships existing in and between all project components and the environment create volatility in an era of uncertainty, where realities of the individualism being promoted in today's world of 'late modernity' (Höijer, Lidskog & Uggla 2006) are compounded by characteristic innovative, creative and risk-taking behaviours.

Privileging the autonomy in project practice that is needed to facilitate a greater transparency in communication for learning and change amongst socially diverse project players was missing within the research organisation. The complexity arising from social differences and the ambiguities in decision making were compounded by systems of governance which perpetuated bureaucratic methods of control. Managing multiplicities of part-whole relationships within the project context called for an emergent form of leadership, one which not only evolved in adaptive response to changing social dynamics, but one whose strategy recognised and accommodated for the fluid nature of all interconnected components. This can be supported by ideas of project management using expert intuition in particular (Leybourne & Sadler-Smith 2006; Leybourne 2009) and even adopting a muddling through approach (Lindblom 1959; Cates 1979; Lindblom 1979; Hällgren & Wilson 2007). In such approaches realistic coping mechanisms are adopted in place of the folly of rigid planning in highly uncertain circumstances which has long been cautioned against in complex, dynamic settings where agility and adaptive skills need to be applied to reach broad goals and milestones (Andersen 1996; 2008).

Project leaders, like national and global leaders, are facing social contexts which are 'highly complex, constantly changing and difficult to interpret'

(Zagorsek, Jaklic & Stough 2004, 16). Cognitive realities are culturally specific and emergent as the social make-up of the environment changes. This calls for flexible, non-concrete strategic approaches to guide the project as social process towards learning for effective change and adaptive organisational resilience. The multiplicity of factors which impinge on project praxis in reality are frequently outside the bounds of individual control. Yet the first step in moving forward, whilst acknowledging an ontology of becoming, is to recognise the value inherent in existent human plurality. The ambiguities which will arise from human interconnections within disparate social contexts are the project actuality. It is the development of an organisation's capability to assimilate and accommodate for these differences which can be effected through projects, as their adaptive nature provides the structural openness necessary for promoting the contextual interconnectedness which is integral to learning, making sense and bringing forth new worlds of meaning.

Conclusions and implications for project management theory and practice

The paper briefly explained how the change in conceptualisation of the researched situation from a traditional 'tools and techniques' study to a socio-political process study and how this yielded far richer insights. This we argue, illustrates a distinct advantage of viewing a project of this kind as a social process in order to better understand what forces shaped outcomes. This has direct implications for the study of PM practice.

The paper also provided a theoretical basis for viewing the project this way and offered some explanatory power to better understand PM praxis in this light. Traditional command and control techniques were argued to be counterproductive in such circumstances. PM becomes a highly intuitive and organic function when compared to traditional machine models of praxis.

The implication for PM practice is not to abandon traditional PM approaches where they can be applied in less complex and demanding situations but to open up the possibility of taking more adaptive approaches in more complex project environments. Seeing projects as complex socio-political adaptive systems-situations rather than an opportunity to apply more static rules and heuristics, provides greater scope for co-learning *about* the project situation and its contextual nuances. Such an approach reveals a more emergent strategy which can be followed based on more general milestones or goals that are manoeuvred towards using adaptive coping approaches rather than application of strict management means.

References

Ambos, B; Schlegelmilch, B. 2008. 'Innovation in multinational firms: Does cultural fit enhance performance?' *Management International Review* 48 (2): 189–206.

Andersen, E S. 1996. 'Warning: Activity planning is hazardous to your project's health!' *International Journal of Project Management* 14 (2): 89–94.

Andersen, E S. 2008. *Rethinking Project Management – An Organisational Perspective.* Harlow, UK: Pearson Education Limited.

Artto, K; Martinsuo, M; Dietrich, P; Kujala, J. 2008. 'Project strategy: Strategy types and their contents in innovation projects' *International Journal of Managing Projects in Business* 1 (1): 49–70.

Atkinson, R; Crawford, L; Ward, S. 2006. 'Fundamental uncertainties in projects and the scope of project management'. *International Journal of Project Management* 24: 687–698.

Avolio, B J; Gardner, W L; Walumbwa, F O; Luthans, F; May, D R. 2004. 'Unlocking the mask: A look at the process by which authentic leaders impact follower attitudes and behaviours.' *The Leadership Quarterly* 15: 801–823.

Baerveldt, C; Verheggen, T. 1999. 'Enactivism and the experiential reality of culture: Rethinking the epistemological basis of cultural psychology.' *Culture Psychology* 5 (2): 183–206.

Bass, B M; Steidlmeier, P. 1999. 'Ethics, character and authentic transformational leadership behaviour.' *The Leadership Quarterly* 10 (2): 181–217.

Bloch, D. P. 2005. 'Complexity, chaos, and nonlinear dynamics: A new perspective on career development theory.' *The Career Development Quarterly* 53: 194–207.

Bonabeau, E; Meyer, C. 2001. 'Swarm intelligence: A whole new way to think about business.' *Harvard Business Review* 79 (5): 106–114.

Bourne, L. 2005. 'Project relationship management and the stakeholder circle'. Ph.D. thesis, Graduate School of Business, Melbourne, RMIT University.

Bourne, L M. 2009. *Stakeholder Relationship Management.* Farnham, Surrey, UK: Gower.

Bredillet, C. 2008. 'Learning and acting in project situations through meta-method (MAP) a case study: Contextual and situational approach for project management governance in management education.' *International Journal of Project Management* 26: 238–250.

Bresnen, M. 2006. 'Conflicting and conflated discourses? Project management, organisational change and learning.' In *Making Projects Critical*, edited by Hodgson D; Cicmil, S. New York: Palgrave Macmillan: 68–89.

Bresnen, M. 2007. 'Deconstructing partnering in project-based organisation: Seven pillars, seven paradoxes and seven deadly sins.' *International Journal of Project Management* 25: 365–374.

Briner, W; Hastings, C; Geddes, M. 1996. *Project Leadership.* 2nd edn. Aldershot, UK: Gower.

Buchinger, E. 2006. 'The sociological concept of autopoiesis: Biological and philosophical basics and governance relevance.' *Kybernetes* 35 (3/4): 360–374.

Carlisle, Y; McMillan, E. 2006. 'Innovation in organizations from a complex adaptive systems perspective.' *Emergence: Complexity and Organization* 8 (1): 2–9.

Cates, C. 1979. 'Beyond muddling: Creativity.' *Public Administration Review* 39 (6): 527–532.

Checkland, P. 1999. *Systems Thinking, Systems Practice.* Chichester, UK: John Wiley & Sons Ltd.

Checkland, P; Winter, M. 2006. 'Process and content: Two ways of using SSM.' *The Journal of the Operational Research Society* 57 (12): 1435–1441.

Chia, R. 1995. 'From modern to postmodern organizational analysis.' *Organization Studies* 16 (4): 579–604.

Cicmil, S; Hodgson, D. 2006. 'Making projects critical: An introduction.' *Making Projects Critical*, edited by Hodgson D; Cicmil, S. New York: Palgrave Macmillan: 1–25.

Cilliers, P. 2000. 'What can we learn from a theory of complexity?' *Emergence* 2 (1): 23 33.

Clark, E; Geppert, M. 2006. 'Socio-political processes in international management in post-socialist contexts: Knowledge, learning and transnational institution building.' *Journal of International Management* 12 (3): 340–357.

Cooke-Davies, T J; Cicmil, S; Crawford, L; Richardson, K. 2007. 'We're not in Kansas anymore, Toto: Mapping the strange landscape of complexity theory, and its relationship to project management.' *Project Management Journal* 38 (2): 50–61.

Courtney H, Kirkland J, Viguerie P. 1997. 'Strategy under uncertainty.' *Harvard Business Review*. 75 (6): 66–79.

DiTomaso, N; Hooijberg, R. 1996. 'Diversity and the demands of leadership.' *Leadership Quarterly* 7 (2): 163–187.

Dooley, K. 1996. 'A nominal definition of complex adaptive systems.' *Chaos Network* 8 (1): 2–3.

Eijnatten, F. M. 2004. 'Chaordic systems thinking: Some suggestions for a complexity framework to inform a learning organization.' *The Learning Organization* 11 (6): 430–449.

Ekinsmyth, C. 2002. 'Project organization, embeddedness and risk in magazine publishing.' *Regional Studies* 36 (3): 229–243.

Engeström, Y. 2006. 'From well-bounded ethnographies to intervening in mycorrhizae activities.' *Organization Studies* 27 (12): 1783–1793.

Engwall, M. 2003. 'No project is an island: Linking projects to history and context.' *Research Policy* 32 (5): 789–808.

Folke, C. 2006. 'Resilience: The emergence of a perspective for social-ecological systems analyses.' *Global Environmental Change* 16 (3): 253–267.

Glass, N. 1996. 'Chaos, non-linear systems and day-to-day management.' *European Management Journal* 14 (1): 98 – 106.

Green, S. 2006. 'The management of projects in the construction industry: Context, discourse and self-identity'. In *Making Projects Critical*, edited by Hodgson, D; Cicmil, S. New York: Palgrave Macmillan: 232–251.

Grisham, T; Walker, D. 2008. 'Cross-cultural leadership.' *International Journal of Managing Projects in Business* 1 (3): 439–445.

Gupta, A K; Govindarajan, V. 2000. 'Knowledge flows within multinational corporations.' *Strategic Management Journal* 21: 473–496.

Hall, W P. 2005. 'Biological nature of knowledge in the learning organisation.' *The Learning Organisation* 12 (2): 169–188.

Hällgren, M; Wilson, T L. 2007. 'Mini-muddling: Learning from project plan deviations.' *Journal of Workplace Learning* 19 (2): 92–107.

Hayek, F A von. 1992[1974]. 'The pretence of knowledge'. In *Nobel Lectures, Economics 1969–1980*, edited by Lindbeck A. Singapore: World Scientific Publishing Co.

Hobbs, B; Aubry, M; Thuillier, D. 2008. 'The project management office as an organisational innovation.' *International Journal of Project Management* 26 (5): 547–555.

Hodgson, D; Cicmil, S. 2006. 'Are projects real? The PMBOK and the legitimation of project management knowledge'. In *Making Projects Critical*, edited by Hodgson, D; Cicmil, S. New York: Palgrave Macmillan: 29–50.

Hofstede, G H. 1980. *Culture's Consequences: International Differences in Work-Related Values*. Beverly Hills: Sage.

Höijer, B; Lidskog, R; Uggla, Y. 2006. 'Facing dilemmas: Sense-making and decision-making in late modernity.' *Futures* 38: 350–366.

Holland, J. 1995. *Hidden Order: How Adaptation Builds Complexity*. Reading, MA:

Addison-Wesley.

House, R; Javidan, M; Hanges, P; Dorfman, P. 2002. 'Understanding cultures and implicit leadership theories across the globe: An introduction to project GLOBE.' *Journal of World Business* 37 (1): 3–10.

Ivory, C; Alderman, N; McLoughlin, I; Vaughan, R. 2006. 'Sense-making as a process within complex projects'. In *Making Projects Critical*, edited by Hodgson, D; Cicmil, S. New York: Palgrave Macmillan: 316–334.

Kauffman, S; Levin, S. 1987. 'Towards a general theory of adaptive walks on rugged landscapes.' *Journal of Theoretical Biology* 128 (1): 11–45.

Kay, R. 2001. 'Are organizations autopoietic? A call for new debate.' *Systems Research and Behavioural Science* 18: 461–477.

Kreiner, K. 1992. 'The postmodern epoch of organization theory.' *International Studies of Management and Organization* 22 (2): 37–52.

Law, J; Urry, J. 2004. 'Enacting the social.' *Economy and Society* 33 (3): 390–410.

Leybourne, S; Sadler-Smith, E. 2006. 'The role of intuition and improvisation in project management.' *International Journal of Project Management* 24 (6): 519–535.

Leybourne, S A. 2009. 'Improvisation and agile project management: A comparative consideration.' *International Journal of Managing Projects in Business* 2 (4): 519–536.

Limone, A; Bastias, L E. 2006. 'Autopoiesis and knowledge in the organization: Conceptual foundation for authentic knowledge management.' *Systems Research and Behavioural Science* 23: 39–49.

Lindblom, C E. 1959. 'The science of 'muddling through'.' *Public Administration Review* 19 (2): 79–88.

Lindblom, C E. 1979. 'Still muddling, not yet through.' *Public Administration Review* 39 (6): 517–526.

Lineham, C; Kavanagh, D. 2006. 'From project ontologies to communities of virtue'. In *Making Projects Critical*, edited by Hodgson, D; Cicmil, S. New York: Palgrave Macmillan: 51–67.

Loosemore, M; Al Muslmani, H S. 1999. 'Construction project management in the Persian Gulf: inter-cultural communication.' *International Journal of Project Management* 17 (2, April): 95–100.

Lundin, R A; Söderholm, A. 1995. 'A theory of the temporary organization.' *Scandinavian Journal of Management* 11 (4): 437–455.

Maturana, H; Varela, F. 1980. *Autopoiesis and Cognition: The Realization of the Living*. Dordrecht, Holland: Reidel.

Modig, N. 2007. 'A continuum of organizations formed to carry out projects: Temporary and stationary organization forms.' *International Journal of Project Management* 25: 807–814.

Orlikowski, W J. 2002. 'Knowing in practice: Enacting a collective capability in distributed organizing.' *Organization Science* 13 (3): 249–273.

Osborn, R N; Hunt, J G; Jauch, L R. 2002. 'Towards a contextual theory of leadership.' *The Leadership Quarterly* 13: 797–837.

Packendorff, J. 1995. 'Inquiring into the temporary organization: New directions for project management research.' *Scandinavian Journal of Management* 11 (4): 319–333.

Parboteeah, P; Jackson, T W. 2007. 'An autopoietic framework for organisational learning.' *Knowledge and Process Management* 14 (4): 248–259.

Pellegrinelli, S. 1997. 'Program management: Organising project-based change.' *International Journal of Project Management* 15 (3): 141–149.

Pettigrew, A; Woodman, R W; Cameron, K S. 2001b. 'Studying organizational change and development: Challenges for future research.' *Academy of Management Journal* 44 (4): 697–713.

Proulx, J. 2008. 'Some differences between Maturana and Varela's theory of cognition and constructivism.' *Complicity: An International Journal of Complexity and Education* 5 (1): 11–26.

Pundir, A; Ganapathy, L; Sambandam, N. 2007. 'Towards a complexity framework for managing projects.' *Emergence: Complexity and Organization* 9 (4): 17–25.

Richardson, K. 2008. 'Managing complex organizations: complexity thinking and the science and art of management.' *Emergence: Complexity and Organization* 10 (2): 13: 1–18.

Riegler, A. 2002. 'When is a cognitive system embodied?' *Cognitive Systems Research* 3: 339–348.

Schein, E H. 2004. *Organisational Culture and Leadership*. 3rd edn. San Francisco: Jossey Bass.

Small, J. 2009. 'The emergent realities of project praxis in socially complex project environments'. Ph.D. thesis. Melbourne: RMIT University, Australia.

Söderlund, J. 2004a. 'Building theories of project management: Past research, questions for the future.' *International Journal of Project Management* 22 (183–191.

Söderlund, J. 2004b. 'On the broadening scope of the research on projects: A review and a model for analysis.' *International Journal of Project Management* 22: 655–667.

Sommer, S C; Loch, C H. 2004. 'Selectionism and learning in projects with complexity and unforeseeable uncertainty.' *Management Science* 50 (10): 1334–1347.

Stackman, R W; Henderson, L S; Bloch, D P. 2006. 'Emergence and community: The story of three complex adaptive entities.' *Emergence: Complexity and Organization* 8 (3): 78–91.

Thomas, J B; Clark, S M; Gioia, D A. 1993. 'Strategic sensemaking and organizational performance: Linkages among scanning, interpretation, action and outcomes.' *Academy of Management journal* 36 (2): 239–270.

Turner, J. R. 1999. *The Handbook of Project-Based Management*. London: McGraw-Hill Company.

Turner, J R; Müller, R. 2003. 'On the nature of the project as a temporary organization.' *International Journal of Project Management* 21: 1–8.

Tyler, L. 2005. 'Towards a postmodern understanding of crisis communication.' *Public Relations Review* 31: 566–571.

Waldrop, M. 1992. *Complexity: The Emerging Science At The Edge Of Order And Chaos*. New York: Touchstone.

Walsh, P R. 2005. 'Dealing with the uncertainties of environmental change by adding scenario planning to the strategy reformulation equation.' *Management Decision* 43 (1): 113–122.

Weick, K E. 1995. *Sensemaking in Organizations*. Thousand Oaks, CA: Sage.

Whitty, S J. 2005. 'A memetic paradigm of project management.' *International Journal of Project Management* 23: 575–583.

Whitty, S J; Maylor, H. 2007. 'And then came complex project management'. Paper presented at 21st IPMA World Congress on Project Management, Cracow, Poland, 18–20 June.

Williams, T. 1999. 'The need for new paradigms for complex projects.' *International Journal of Project Management* 17 (5): 269–273.

Williams, T. 2002. *Modelling Complex Projects*. London: Wiley.

Winter, M; Smith, C; Morris, P; Cicmil, S. 2006. 'Directions for future research in project management: The main findings of a UK government-funded research network.' *International Journal of Project Management* 24: 638–649.

Zagorsek, H; Jaklic, M; Stough, S J. 2004. 'Comparing leadership practices between the United States, Nigeria and Slovenia: Does culture matter?' *Cross Cultural management* 11 (2): 16–34.

Chapter 13

Motivating construction organisations through incentives

A case study for client-side project managers

Timothy M Rose

Queensland University of Technology, Australia.

Karen Manley

Queensland University of Technology, Australia.

Client-side project managers face challenges in motivating project organisations to pursue exceptional design and construction performance. One approach to improving the motivation of project organisations is by offering a financial incentive reward for the achievement of voluntary performance standards above the minimum required standard. However, little investigation has been undertaken into the features of a successful incentive system as a part of an overall procurement strategy. In response to a lack of information available to client-side project managers tasked with the initial design of an incentive system, the paper explores motivation under a successful incentive and identifies key learnings for client-side project managers to consider when designing incentives. Our findings are based on the results of a large Australian case study which is interpreted against a conceptual framework based on both economic and psychological perspectives of motivation. The results suggest that motivation towards incentive goals is influenced by the value the project organisations place on the incentive reward as a commercial opportunity to increase their profit margins. However, perhaps more important are the relationship management processes that promote commitment to the project; and pride in the achievement of project goals. In the case study, these processes intensified the direct motivational effect of the incentive reward on offer. The findings also highlight the importance of ensuring that incentive goals and performance measurement processes remain relevant to the organisations throughout a project to continuously encourage motivation under changing project conditions.

Introduction

Many contractual arrangements between construction clients and contractors are confrontational, reflecting considerable mistrust and leading to high contractor premiums to cover significant risk levels (Zaghloul & Hartman 2003). More effective use of contracting options such as financial incentives can improve the balance between the allocation of risk and reward for performance gains (Howard et al. 1997). A key objective of incentive contracting is to provide the opportunity for contractors to earn additional profit for higher performance (Bower et al. 2002). Generally, financial incentives aim to align the motivations of interdependent project stakeholders within a temporary project organisation. This is achieved through client gain-sharing, that is, by providing the contractor and/or consultants a share in the client's success from the project.

Financial incentives can be combined with any type of base construction contract and can be designed to reward the achievement of an infinite range of project objectives. Generally, incentives motivate a contractor by:

- The method of payment of the contract price, which encourages the contractor to meet cost objectives, where overruns or delays will cause the contractor additional expense. Lump sum contracts penalise the contractor if fixed costs increase, as profit margins are diminished (Levine and Rickman 2000).

- A profit sharing (cost-plus) incentive arrangement, where the actual cost savings can be distributed between the client and the contractor in predetermined ratios (Arditi and Yasamis 1998).

- A performance bonus for meeting performance targets based on one or more client goals (Bower et al. 2002).

Although, penalties can act as a strong motivator to prevent failure to comply with the contract conditions, to ensure that an adversarial relationship does not develop between the contracting parties, the incentive systems should focus on positive incentives, rather than penalties (Lahdenpera & Koppinen 2003). Another argument in favour of the balanced use of positive incentive systems is that penalties will only encourage a contractor and/or consultant to deliver the minimum contract specification, where positive incentives aim to encourage performance above the minimum.

A key objective of financial incentives is motivation towards cost containment. Cost containment rewards are one of the most widely used forms of incentive and can be applied to either fixed price, or modified cost reimbursable (cost-plus) contracts, depending on how the incentive is structured (Russell 2003). Generally, under a cost-plus incentive arrangement, the client's target cost is introduced into a reimbursable contract and acts as the fulcrum around which the cost containment mechanism is driven, where savings achieved below the target cost are split between the contractor and client based on a predetermined share profile (Broome & Perry 2002). The aim of this arrangement is to motivate the contractor and client to work together to minimise actual costs, as the contractor is able to maximise their profit margin by sharing the benefits of reduced project cost, and the client is motivated to minimise the total cost paid out (Broome & Perry 2002).

One of the most common forms of financial incentive is a performance bonus which can be integrated into a wide range of contract types, including standard lump sum and cost reimbursable contracts. Simply, performance bonus incentives aim to motivate the contractor by providing them with a financial bonus that is additional to their prescribed fee for exceeding minimum acceptable levels of performance (Washington 1997). Generally, performance is evaluated *ex ante* and the reward is distributed from a separate client bonus pool specified at the start of a project. As the financial incentive is drawn from a separate bonus pool, there is a wide range of performance areas that can rewarded, including schedule, environmental, quality, safety and design performance targets. However, important to the success of bonus incentives are specific, mutually agreed and measurable targets. If the output deliverables cannot be well defined, then an incentivised contract should not be pursued (HM Treasury 1991). The downside to such arrangements is that they can be time consuming to establish goals and benchmarks; and measurement processes need to be clearly defined and specified to prevent ambiguity.

Although positive financial rewards offer potential to promote motivation towards incentive goals, they can be challenging to design and implement. A key consideration for client-side project managers (referred to henceforth as 'client managers') in the context on a construction project is how the bonus or profit sharing reward will be distributed, that is to say, who are the reward recipients and will the reward be fairly distributed to those who have contributed to the performance gains? To effectively assess the optimal balance, client managers need to consider the possibility of individual- and/ or team-based incentives and how performance will be measured across the various vertical and horizontal levels in a project.

This challenge is further compounded by the one-off nature of construction projects and the 'blurring of the lines' of performance contribution due to the high levels of task interdependency. The construction product supply chain is commonly characterised by disjointed relationships between contracting parties (Rahman & Kumaraswamy 2004), where a large team is brought together on a one-off basis. As such, there can be limited scope to build cohesive team relationships over time. As a project can be viewed as a temporary organisation with its own social system (Gareis 2008), the dynamics and social complexity between construction stakeholders provide further challenges for client managers when designing an incentive mechanism.

The ability of a social system to provide constructive dynamics in such a complex environment is influenced on its ability to develop complexity of its own in areas such as project organisation, culture and context dimensions (Gareis & Huemann 2008). These issues suggest that client managers tasked with the initial design and implementation of incentives require a clear understanding of not only the incentive mechanism, but also the organisational and social context in which it is implemented. Consideration must be given to the incentives interaction with other procurement initiatives and the social and productive repercussions of its differential impact across the supply chain. For example, what happens if contractors are rewarded, but subcontractors are not?

Although the design of incentive systems is generally context dependent, client managers can benefit from the development of broad guidelines on how to incorporate incentives in their projects and how procurement initiatives can support their incentive design to improve the effectiveness of the project organisation to meet incentive objectives.

Conceptual framework

The previous section highlighted the challenges faced by construction client managers when designing incentive systems. Despite these significant challenges, little information is available to managers on what should be considered when designing financial incentives as a part of an overall procurement strategy. Arguably, there is a general assumption in the construction management literature that financial incentives automatically promote motivation with little regard to the context in which they are applied. However, research undertaken by Bresnen and Marshall (2000) shows that reliance primarily on extrinsic rewards such as incentives as a motivator can be construed by contractors and consultants as a 'calculative' approach, where such organisations are deemed to be motivated by short-term economic self-interest. In response, the findings stress the importance of understanding the limits of financial rewards to generate more intense forms of motivation and suggest the overall procurement approach needs to be complementary to the reward's intention, although Bresnen and Marshall provide little detail about how this might be achieved. This paper responds to this gap in the literature by exploring what supporting mechanisms and incentive design configurations may produce a well-rounded approach to promoting team motivation towards voluntary project goals.

Given the lack of research into the impact of incentives on motivation in construction, a conceptual framework was developed, based on theoretical insights, to identify the 'motivation drivers' that impact on incentive goal motivation. By identifying these drivers, conclusions can be drawn about the impact of financial incentives on motivation and the types of project initiatives that should be considered by client managers when designing incentives as a part of an overall procurement approach.

The case study interprets the motivation drivers according to a conceptual framework developed by Rose (2008). This framework represents the first time that both economic and psychological perspectives of motivation have been integrated to investigate financial incentives in a project-based environment. Figure 13.1 provides a summary of the main features of the model.

According to the conceptual framework, project-based motivation towards voluntary incentive goals is determined by the features of (i) the financial incentive design and; (ii) the supporting procurement initiatives. Within these features lie specific motivation drivers that can be uncovered by exploring two broad motivation indicators developed from a review of the organisational motivation literature: (1) goal commitment; and (2) organisational justice.

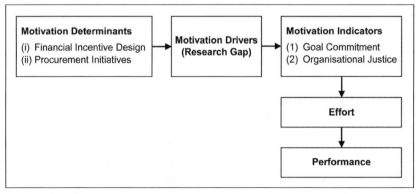

Figure 13.1. Conceptual framework summary – motivation on construction projects

These two indicators were used to identify the motivation drivers that impacted on the effectiveness of the financial incentive mechanism and the related procurement initiatives. In the case of this research, the first indicator, goal commitment (Hollenbeck & Klein 1987) refers to the sustained determination and motivation to try for the performance goal associated with the incentive. Key antecedents of goal commitment are those that impact on *the attractiveness of goal attainment* and those that impact on the *expectancy of goal attainment* (Hollenbeck & Klein 1987). Thus, positive drivers linked to this indicator improved the attractiveness of goal attainment and the stakeholders' expectancy that incentive goals could be achieved.

The second broad indicator, organisational justice, relates to the fairness of compensation systems for work performed. Simply, justice theories can predict how groups may behave based on the perceived levels of fairness in an organisational environment. Key antecedents of organisational justice (Colquitt 2001) are those that impact on 1) distributive justice, or the fairness of the reward on offer relative to the effort required to achieve; 2) procedural justice, or the fairness and transparency of procedures linked to incentive distribution decisions; and 3) interactional justice, or the underlying treatment and communication processes between project stakeholders, influencing mutual trustworthiness. These framework constructs represent a theoretical contribution to the construction management literature and proved instructive during the empirical phase of this project-based research. Rose (2008) provides further information on the theoretical background to the framework.

Methods

A case study methodology was chosen to explore the research question: 'What are the specific project drivers that impact on motivation towards voluntary financial incentive goals?' This was seen as the best method given the complexity of project environments and the need for in-depth understanding of the dynamics surrounding project-based motivation in order to effectively scope and identify drivers. This case study method promised to result in more valid and reliable findings than a broader quantitative approach. The case study presented in this paper was selected in a purposive manner, as it represents an example of the successful design and implementation of a financial incentive system as part of the overall project procurement approach.

Case study findings were triangulated across the following data sources: semi-structured face-to-face interviews, project and contractual documentation (including project briefs and minutes from meetings), industry publications and a site visit. Extensive preliminary data were collected, which helped shape the questions asked during the interviews, as did the conceptual framework shown in Figure 13.1. The interviewees comprised eight senior managers; two from each of four key stakeholder types (client, head contractor, consultants and subcontractors) who were heavily involved in the procurement and delivery of the case project. All interviews were in-person and ranged from 60 to 90 minutes duration, based on structured and unstructured questions. Raw interview data was analysed using content analysis. This involved manually aggregating and categorising responses from the interview transcripts and the secondary data to identify the key motivation drivers. The identification and refinement of driver categories was achieved by inductive coding. The primary data amounted to approximately 8000 words contained in interview transcripts. The coding process involved interpretation of each interviewee's transcript and each coding category was revised and refined until clear lines could be drawn between the motivation drivers. Initially, key themes associated with the broad motivation indicators were categorised into features of (i) the financial incentive design and; (ii) the supporting procurement initiatives. Once all project data had been allocated in this way, each theme was revisited and driver patterns were refined. Distinct patterns were separated into coding categories and allocated motivation driver labels. The goal was to define coding categories that captured the breadth of interview experience, whilst limiting the categories to key concerns.

Care was taken to identify driver categories that covered all instances, were limited in number and were mutually exclusive. Due to the subjective nature of content analysis, an 'expert panel' was formed to test content analysis accuracy and ensure inadvertent bias was minimised. The category allocations of the three expert panel members reflected over 80 per cent accuracy, providing evidence of the reliability of the coding.

Case project details

The project involved the design and construction of a large-scale extension to a convention centre situated in the central business district (CBD) of Adelaide, South Australia. The original budget for this project was approximately AU$85 million (increased to AU$92 million near the conclusion of the project). This was a landmark building project for the state government client, as the upgraded centre was expected to significantly contribute to the state's economy.

The project involved increasing the capacity of an existing convention centre by 110 per cent, providing approximately 7000 square metres of new multipurpose exhibition, banqueting and pre-function facilities. The project site covered more than 1.2 hectares with a total building floor space of more than 21,000 square metres. The centre was designed to meet new multi-venue operational requirements, based on international convention centre standards and to accommodate more than 6600 guests with undercover parking for 1350 vehicles. The duration of the project was approximately 22 months, from 1999 to 2001.

A major goal of the project was to achieve the target completion date, as the client had made a commitment to host a major international convention in the new venue in late 2001. Other project goals included meeting all functionality and design requirements set out in the project brief (including environmental and safety goals), defects-free by completion date, limiting errors and omissions in construction documentation, minimising industrial disputes, minimising injuries and meeting the client budget.

The general procurement approach was a Managing Contractor – Construction Management (MC-CM) arrangement. This was the first time a 'relationship-based' MC-CM procurement approach had been used by the South Australian Government. They chose this approach because it allowed them complete control over the design. It also allowed them to manage construction costs through variation payments to the managing contractor and consultants. The disadvantage of this form of control was that the client took on the majority of the cost risks associated with the design (and design discrepancies) and construction. It was expected that, as the managing contractor was appointed under a fee arrangement to provide input into the design process and manage the construction trade packages, it would improve the constructability of the design, potentially decreasing design-construction integration risks.

The procurement approach also included a comprehensive relationship management process. This aimed to further mitigate the design and construction risks taken on by the client, through closer integration of the project team (the managing contractor and consultants were directly contracted to the client throughout the project) and improved decision-making and problem resolution processes. It also established shared project goals against which performance could be assessed.

The management structure was a 'construction management' arrangement, with managing contractor and key subcontractors involved in design development and documentation. A unique feature on this project was the abolition of the traditional hierarchical structure. A 'round table' approach saw key representatives from each project organisation form an Integrated Management Team (IMT) and Project Control Group (PCG). There were monthly IMT and PCG meetings, where open and honest communication was encouraged, in an equitable environment. The IMT and PCG were established after the managing contractor was appointed, near the end of the schematic design stage, under a price and non-price criteria selection model. The IMT involved senior executive representatives, while the PCG involved management representatives from the client, end-users, cost manager and consultant and managing contractor organisations. The IMT reported directly to the government minister responsible for the project, while the PCG reported to the IMT. Any issues that could not be resolved by the PCG were referred to the IMT.

The managing contractor and early key subcontractors were brought into the design process early, during design development and documentation, to fast track the commencement of the construction stage and improve constructability. A relationship consultant was appointed during the project's conceptual stage to establish and formalise the management structure and facilitate relationship workshops and ongoing relationship coaching. This approach aimed to foster team commitment to the project goals. All project parties were contractually obliged to 'act in good faith'.

The financial incentive system was intended to reward the contractor for efficiently managing the client's risks, above their standard construction management fee. The client did not wish to include risk penalties such as liquidated damages, which they saw as contradictory to relationship management principles. The positive performance-based incentive aimed to reward three main areas of project performance: innovation contribution, contingency savings and ready-for-use completion. As a part of the 'value strategy', a financial incentive was offered to the managing contractor to seek innovative value-adding design and construction options. The managing contractor could propose innovations that would achieve cost-savings and/or program savings while preserving functionality and quality. The innovation would then be approved by the client representatives and the net benefit of the innovation would be shared on the basis that:

- 50 per cent was placed in a managing contractor's program and cost savings incentive pool;
- 50 per cent was retained by the client to reinvest in the project.

As the client managers needed to manage the government's design and construction risks, they were motivated to promote innovative ideas and retain as much from the incentive pool as possible. The incentive was designed so that 50 per cent of the accumulated incentive pool would be paid to the contractor if they achieved the 'ready-for-use' target completion date. However, if they failed to achieve this date, the contractor forfeited their portion of the accumulated incentive pool amount. By project completion, approximately AU$2 million in savings was achieved from innovations by the managing contractor. As the managing contractor achieved the 'ready-for-use' completion date, 50 per cent of this (AU$1 million) was distributed to them as an incentive reward payment.

Despite the overall success of the project in achieving the design and quality objectives, problems with budget overruns were experienced. It was initially believed that the project budget of AU$85 million was sufficient to achieve project objectives, including the design and construction program. Despite robust management of design and construction, however, the project team came to the consensus that, due to rising 'actual' project costs attributed to a rising cost of construction across the building sector, it was unlikely that they would complete the project under the agreed specification within the original budget. Joint team efforts to bring costs down were unsuccessful in capturing sufficient savings and it was agreed the original budget was inadequate to meet the scope of works. An open-book review of the project budget followed and the client agreed to an increase of approximately AU$7 million to the budget to avoid having to compromise on construction outcomes.

The managing contractor and finishing subcontractors were involved in a special incentive arrangement – the 'acceleration' agreement – which was implemented late in the construction stage near the conclusion of the project, after the above problems were uncovered and it appeared unlikely that the project would be finished by the target completion date under the original budget. The client proposed the acceleration agreement (as a part of the revised budget) to fast-track project completion. The managing contractor and their subcontractors were required to complete the final scope of works by the target 'ready-for-use' completion date to receive the AU$1.2 million bonus (plus management fees). The managing contractor was offered an AU$220,000 management fee to manage the final works; if they did not achieve the target completion date, they would forfeit their management fee. Also, the finishing subcontractors were offered extra payment to fast track completion of their trade packages. The completion date was achieved and the bonus was distributed between the contractor and finishing subcontractors, which allowed a scheduled international convention to be held.

By the conclusion of the project in late 2001, the project participants had achieved all of the project objectives, including the jointly-agreed revised project budget. The project team also produced a wide range of innovative design features that significantly improved the developed design in terms of building functionality and aesthetics. The project was considered a success by the project team, including the client. This success was partly attributed to the financial incentive design, but also to the procurement initiatives that motivated the project team to strive for the project goals maximising the impact of the incentive approach on team motivation. These initiatives are discussed in the following section.

Motivation drivers

The motivation drivers that were nominated by interviewees as contributing to the successful achievement of incentive goals on the project are examined here. These drivers emerged from the case interviews, which were based on background data and the two motivation indicators shown in Figure 13.1: goal commitment and organisational justice. Again, following Figure 13.1, the identified drivers are discussed under two broad classes: (i) those motivation drivers that were associated with effective design of the incentive system, and (ii) those associated with the procurement initiatives that positively supported the incentive approach on the case project. Discussion of the motivation drivers below provides guidance for client managers in designing procurement approaches that incorporate similar financial incentive arrangements. Although the case study found no major negative project aspects arising from the procurement initiatives, negative aspects of the incentive design were raised and these are also discussed to aid in the design of optimal incentive systems in future projects of similar nature.

Financial incentive design

Although the amount of incentive reward on offer had a motivating effect, the design of the reward mechanism featured some elements that amplified this effect and some that constrained it. This suggests that incentives do not necessarily need to be large, but they do need to be strategically applied. For instance, the introduction of an acceleration agreement late in the construction stages of the project promoted goal commitment (cited by seven of the eight interviewees) by improving the expectancy the incentive could be achieved. It also gave the managing contractor access to the innovation incentive pool, as the 'ready-for-use' completion date then became achievable. According to managing contractor representatives, the managing contractor was rewarded with their share of the innovation incentive pool through the introduction of the acceleration agreement, which 'brought reality back' to the overly ambitious budget, restoring fairness in the incentive reward distribution, thus reinstating distributive justice.

Despite the positive nature of the acceleration agreement as a part of the incentive design that promoted goal motivation, injustices in how the incentive reward was distributed across the project team and confusion over the ambiguous nature of the 'innovation contribution' measurement had negative impacts on team motivation. Although those who had shared in the incentive reward valued it, seven of the eight interviewees perceived that the exclusion of the consultants from this incentive de-motivated the consultants and resulted in less value delivered from innovation than might otherwise have been the case. Also, according to five of the eight interviewees, the measurement of performance under the innovation incentive was unclear. According to these interviewees, there were disputes over how an 'innovation contribution' was defined and how it was measured in terms of cost savings. This resulted in perceptions of procedural injustice.

Procurement initiatives

Five project procurement initiatives were found to support the financial incentive approach applied in the case project. They are: 1) an equitable risk profile; 2) project organisation structure; 3) value-based tender; 4) relationship workshops; and 5) future work opportunities.

1) Equitable risk profile

According to the client and managing contractor representatives, the modified MC-CM contract provided the framework for an equitable allocation of design and construction risk under the project conditions and the relationship management approach. These interviewees believed that the equitable contract risk profile promoted incentive goal commitment, where the client was willing to trust the managing contractor to manage their risks associated with program and budget overrun, rather than insisting they carry all design and construction risk. This allowed the managing contractor the financial flexibility to put resources into meeting the incentive goals and therefore improved their expectancy that they could achieve these goals. These interviewees also believed that the project's contract risk profile promoted trust and interactional justice, that is the managing contractor valued the client's decision to share the construction risks under the collaborative culture of the relationship-based procurement approach.

2) Project organisation structure

According to five of the eight interviewees, the project's organisation structure (realised through the IMT and PCG monthly meetings) was a positive motivation driver towards the achievement of the incentive goals. The project organisation structure was perceived to improve the team's ability to control their performance, thus improving the expectancy that the project stakeholders could attain the incentive goals, promoting goal commitment. These interviewees also perceived that the Integrated Management Team and Project Control Group monthly meetings assisted the team in dealing justly with project issues such as the inaccuracies in the project budget.

3) Value-based tender

Seven of the eight interviewees said that selecting the managing contractor and subcontractors on a value-based multi-criteria tender selection process (including non-price) promoted commitment to the incentive goals. According to these interviewees, this commitment was due to the recognition of, and respect for, their ability to perform in a high-risk project. They felt inherent obligations to prove the client had been right to select them, motivating them towards the key project goals (operationalised through the incentive system). The emphasis placed on a value-based tender selection supported the relationship-based approach, where the project parties were partly selected for their demonstrated ability to embrace collaborative arrangements, and to select harmonious project team personnel on whom the client could rely to manage the project risks.

4) Relationship workshops

Seven of the eight interviewees stated that the relationship workshops after tender selection developed a collaborative team culture which helped them to achieve the incentive goals and to minimise the impact of the project budget deficits. This driver was directly attributed to an increase in the attractiveness of goal attainment, thus promoting goal commitment. The relationship workshops were also perceived to be a promoter of interactional justice, in that the client representatives were receptive to, and respectful of, the significance of the contractor's role in the project and the importance in forming a close working relationship. The motivation induced through the project relationships was also promoted through the potential for future work opportunities and the desire to uphold reputation.

5) Future work opportunities

Another positive motivation driver was the potential for future work with the client (cited by five of the eight interviewees) and the importance placed on upholding reputation and market position in the government building sector. These representatives believed that this driver increased their incentive goal commitment, as the achievement of the project goals in a high-profile building project would improve their business reputation, potentially leading to future work opportunities, thus increasing the attractiveness of goal attainment.

Conclusion

These results suggest that the client's addition of the acceleration agreement near the end of the project reinvigorated motivation towards the incentive goals by improving the chances to receive the financial reward. This driver strongly impacted on the goal commitment and organisational justice indicators. Yet, there were perceived injustices in how the incentive was distributed (excluding the design consultants from the incentive distribution) and in the interpretation of 'innovative contributions' (ignoring design ideas). The case results suggest that overall motivation may have been improved if the incentive system had rewarded the entire design team for innovation contributions and not just the managing contractor. This finding emphasises the strength of team based incentives when it is difficult to define performance contribution from individual stakeholder organisations.

Although there were negative aspects of the incentive system on the project, these did not critically affect performance, as innovative cost savings were identified and the 'ready-for-use' completion date was achieved. The results suggest the reason for this was the dominance of positive drivers such as the introduction of an acceleration agreement, the equitable contract conditions and the relationship formed through the initial workshops.

As Figure 13.2 illustrates, motivation towards the incentive was critically supported by the features:

- the flexible incentive arrangement and client's responsiveness to the changing project conditions, which allowed the introduction of an acceleration agreement – significantly improving the reward participants' chances to achieve the 'ready-for-use' completion date and gain access to the innovation incentive pool;

- the Managing Contractor (Construction Management) contract that was perceived to be equitable by the contractors, supporting the ethos of the relationship management approach;

- the relationship management strategy that promoted collaboration and teamwork through the initial relationship workshops and the motivation induced by the potential for future work opportunities if the project was delivered successfully;

- the open-book tender for the managing contractor and subcontractors, with the majority of selection based on non-price criteria;

- the 'round table' design and construction management structure established in the monthly IMT and PCG meetings.

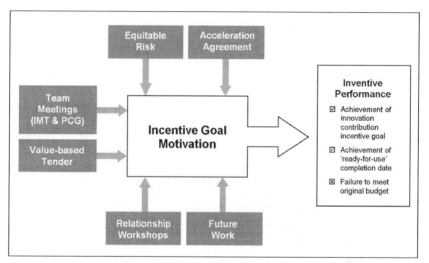

Figure 13.2. Case project motivation drivers

In the case project, motivation towards the incentive goals was strongly influenced by the following factors: 1) the value project stakeholders placed on the incentive reward as a commercial opportunity to increase their profit margins; and 2) the quality of the project and relationship management processes that promoted commitment and loyalty to the project, and pride in the achievement of project goals. These processes intensified the direct motivational effect of the incentive reward on offer.

The findings support the general argument that the effective design of a project in the early stages requires the establishment of technical project plans, but also recognition that the project is a complex social system influenced by relationships within an organisational setting (Gareis, 2008). The framework employed to distil these findings represents advancement of knowledge in the field of construction project management. Prior to this research, there was a general misguided assumption that the use of incentives translates into heightened motivation regardless of the context of application (Bresnen & Marshall 2000). This assumption was rejected by the authors and Figure 13.1 postulate the existence of motivation determinants within incentive design and associated procurement initiatives, which result in motivation drivers. Background literature review suggested the nature of such determinants and fieldwork was conducted to identify motivation drivers. Hence the research gap shown in Figure 13.1 has been filled. The results here indicate that motivation in a complex social organisation such as a construction project is not straightforward and is influenced by numerous vertical and horizontal organisational drivers. The identification of such drivers confirms the value of the conceptual framework and provides it with more detail, thus enhancing its policy value.

In summary, client managers should focus on maximising the impact of financial incentives systems so that stakeholders genuinely value the financial reward on offer and the incentive goals are perceived as achievable. The results also emphasise the importance of situating the incentive within a complementary suite of inter-related project procurement initiatives that promote its positive nature in recognition of high performance. Without doing so, incentive recipients may perceive the incentive's intention as calculative and potentially hostile under an unjust procurement approach. Future quantitative research is recommended to extend the validity of findings presented here and to shed further light on how to design incentives as a part of a broader construction procurement approach. In the meantime, this case study has filled a gap in the literature by providing one view of the drivers of motivation on construction projects. The study has also contributed to theory by confirming the value of the conceptual framework shown at Figure 13.1 to assist in understanding the nature of project motivation. The benefit of integrating both economic and psychological perspectives of motivation has been demonstrated for the first time in a construction project environment.

References

Arditi, D; Yasamis, F. 1998. 'Incentive/disincentive contracts: Perceptions of owners and contractors'. *Journal of Construction Engineering and Management* 124 (5): 361–373.

Bower, D; Ashby, G; Gerald, K; Smyk, W. 2002. 'Incentive mechanisms for project success'. *Journal of Management in Engineering* 18 (1): 37–43.

Bresnen, M; Marshall, N. 2000. 'Motivation, commitment and the use of incentives in partnerships and alliances'. *Construction Management and Economics* 18: 587–598.

Broome, J; Perry, J. 2002. 'How practitioners share fractions in target cost contracts'. *International Journal of Project Management* 20: 59–66.

Colquitt, J. A. 2001. 'On the dimensionality of organizational justice: A construct validation of a measure'. *Journal of Applied Psychology* 86 (3): 386–400.

Gareis, R. 2008. 'Project start process'. In *The Gower Handbook of Project Management*, 4th edn, edited by Turner, J R. Aldershot: Gower: 547–568.

Gareis, R; Huemann, M. 2008. 'Maturity models for the project oriented company'. In *The Gower Handbook of Project Management*, 4th edn, edited by Turner, J R. Aldershot: Gower: 183–210.

H M Treasury. 1991. *Guidance No. 58: Incentivisation*. London: Her Majesty's Stationary Office.

Hollenbeck, J R; Klein, H J. 1987. 'Goal commitment and the goal-setting process: Problems, prospects and proposals for future research'. *Journal of Applied Psychology* 72 (2): 212–220.

Howard, W E; Bell, L C; McCormick, R E. 1997. 'Economic principals of contractor compensation'. *Journal of Management in Engineering* 13 (5): 81–89.

Lahdenpera, P; Koppinen, T. 2003. 'Charting of incentive payment bases for multiobjective construction projects'. In Proceedings of the Joint International Symposium of CIB Working Commissions, Singapore, 2003: 481–493.

Levine, P L; Rickman, N. 2000. *Public Sector Procurement: Lump Sum Payments or Optimal Contracts?* Regulation Initiative (LBS) Working Paper no. 36. Surrey: University of Surrey.

Rahman, M M; Kumaraswamy, M M. 2004. 'Contracting relationship trends and transitions'. *Journal of Management in Engineering* 20 (4): 147–161.

Rose, T M. 2008 'The impact of financial incentive mechanisms on motivation in Australian large non-residential building projects'. Ph.D. thesis. Brisbane: Queensland University of Technology

Russell, S H. 2003. 'Contract types: An exposition of cost – price relationships in a new paradigm'. *Journal of Cost Analysis and Management* Summer: 43–57.

Washington, W N. 1997. 'Some new approaches to reward contracting'. *Acquisition Review Quarterly* Summer: 253–261.

Zaghloul, R; Hartman, F. 2003. 'Construction contracts: The cost of mistrust'. *International Journal of Project Management* 21 (6): 419–424.

Chapter 14

The project as a social system

Identifying key players to ensure outcome realisation

Ofer Zwikael

The Australian National University, Australia

John Smyrk

The Australian National University, Australia

The importance of projects to improve operations management continues to gain wide acceptance. However, as projects are often perceived as a process aimed at generating a unique output, this paper develops a model that is focused on outcome realisation. The model is validated using a triangular research design research. Firstly, a quantitative study involving 102 managers shows that a funder's focus on achieving target outcomes contributes to project success. Outcome and output definition and project plan development and control are found to mediate this relationship. The results indicate that although senior managers do not normally influence project results directly, they have an indirect effect on the eventual levels of success by clearly defining, analysing and validating the relationship between project outcomes and outputs. Secondly, we use a case study to validate the suggested model. Thirdly, a literature analysis shows that the suggested approach is in alignment with recent trends in research. We develop an outcome based project theory and define a new project role – that of project owner – to support new processes within this methodology.

Introduction

The importance of projects for organisational competitive advantage and national growth continuously increases (Lewis et al. 2002). However, despite their importance, most projects fail to achieve their stated goals (Leach 2005; Shenhar & Dvir 2007; Love et al. 2008; Zwikael & Globerson

2004). In response, scholars have explored ways to increase project success rates by analysing the causes of failure (Johnson et. al. 2001), identifying critical success factors (Pinto & Slevin 1987; Cooke-Davies 2002), establishing project success criteria (Müller & Turner 2007), repositioning the role of project managers (Webber & Torti 2004) and developing project management methodologies and frameworks (Kerzner 2006; Project Management Institute 2008; OGC 2007; International Project Management Association 2006). However, largely, these endeavours have not been fruitful in increasing project success rate (Lewis et al. 2002, Zwikael, 2008).

This paper suggests a different approach to addressing the problem of high project failure rates, by going back to the basics of ensuring that projects are implemented in accordance with their only purpose – to deliver value for the funding organisation. In contrast to the accepted output-based practice, we describe an alternative outcome-focused approach to the way organisations perceive and manage projects and validate this approach using a triangulated research design based on a quantitative field study, a qualitative case study and a comparison of the suggested approach with the recent project management literature.

The purpose of projects

While some question whether project management is a profession (Jones 2008), there is little doubt that projects are a core area of work for most organisations and of intense interest to many internal and external stakeholders. This is because projects are central to the realisation of organisational benefits such as reduced operating costs, increased revenue, increased market share and enhanced product/service quality. A key feature of a project is that it has unique target benefits to achieve (Kerzner 2009). Hence, a project can be viewed as a form of investment in which outlays are made today with the intention of realising a flow of benefits over some future timeframe. The person (or entity) approving those outlays is identified below as the 'funder'.

Common perceptions of projects

In practice, instead of being benefit-focused, project management is often perceived as an output-delivery exercise that ends with the implementation of a 'unique product or service' (Project Management Institute 2004). A new bridge, an upgraded software system or a suggested new procurement process are all examples of outputs. Table 14.1 summarises some definitions of 'project' in recent literature. Most of these definitions accept output delivery as the main purpose for project execution. We propose that approaches, which view output-production as the objective of a project, are flawed.

Source	Project definition	Output-focused terms included in the definition
Project Management Institute 2004	Temporary endeavour undertaken to create a unique product or service	Product or service
Meredith and Mantel 2006	A specific, finite task to be accomplished	Task
Lewis 2000	A project is a one-time, multitask job that has clearly defined starting and ending dates, a specific scope of work to be performed, a budget and a specific level of performance to be achieved	A job with scope of work to be performed
International Project Management Association's Competence Baseline 2006	Time and cost constrained operation to realise a set of defined deliverables up to quality standards and requirements	Deliverables

Table 14.1. Project definitions focused on output delivery

These definitions primarily reflect an operational view: the work of a project consumes resources, (generically identified as inputs) to execute processes resulting in an output. When linked in a diagram these same three elements provide us with a conceptual view of a project, as is shown in Figure 14.1. This representation is known in the Operations Management discipline as the Input-Process-Output (IPO) model (Chase et al. 2006; Krajewski & Ritzman 2005; Russell & Taylor 2005). It is also often applied to projects (e.g. Project Management Institute 2008), as being a special type of process (Koskela & Howell 2002). Such a view is consistent with the proposition that operations management is an allied discipline to project management (Kwak & Anbari 2008).

The focus on outputs in the project management discipline is consistent with Turner's claim that 'scope management is the raison d'être of Project Management' (Turner 1993). As a result, most project management research and practice is focused on the delivery of project outputs with agreed quality on time and within budget (Johnson et al. 2001; Project Management Institute 2008).

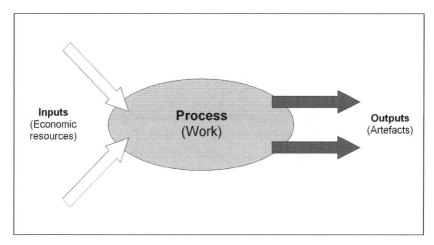

Figure 14.1. The input-process-output (IPO) model of a project

Weaknesses in current perceptions of projects

Many scholars criticise current project management methodologies and the lack of a robust theory. For example, Shenhar and Dvir (1996) argue, 'most research on the management of projects is relatively young and still suffers from a scanty theoretical basis and a lack of concepts'. Meredith (2002) claims that the project management literature is often characterised by frameworks unrelated to previous literature and non-rigorous research methods. Reasons for the relative immaturity of much of the material appearing in the project management literature include claims that it is practitioner-driven (Jugdev 2004) and reliant on 'war stories' (Meredith 2002). Other criticisms relate to the extensive use of normative (rather than positive) approaches (Lipsey & Lancaster 1956; Budzinski 2008) and appeal to lists of factors derived from surveys of project practitioner opinions, rather than empirical research grounded in theory (Packendorff 1995). Bygstad and Lanestedt (2009) support this view by showing that project management methodologies are rarely used 'as is' in Germany and Switzerland, but usually modified or adapted before application. Increasingly, there have been calls for improved theory generation through the adoption of research designs that build on existing literature to develop models for rigorous, evidence-based testing in industry (Meredith 2002).

More specifically, because most current project management approaches are focused on output delivery, they tend to ignore the realisation of benefits (Fraser 2003; Carden & Egan 2008; Remenyi et al. 1997). However, despite the fact that projects are funded with the express intention of generating a stream of benefits, there is a paucity of benefit management tools to support an alternative approach (Ashurst et al. 2008). Another related issue is widespread confusion between outcomes and outputs (Nogeste & Walker 2005). Consequently, a number of approaches that claim to be outcomes-oriented may simply be variants of an outputs based approach (e.g. PRINCE2, Office of Government Commerce 2007).

A consequence of these problems is that there is often little encouragement for organisations to seek, measure and manage explicit benefits from projects, and an expectation that they should be satisfied with outputs. As a result, Young and Jordan (2008) conclude, 'Project managers must recognise the limitations of project methodologies and allow projects to focus on project success rather than project management success even though they cannot be accountable for the realisation of outcomes/benefits'.

Characteristic	Output	Outcome
Intention	What is to be delivered?	What is the objective?
Form	Artefact	Measurable end effect
Specification	Set values for all critical fitness-for-purpose features	Set seven attributes (characteristics)
Labelling	Noun	Participial adjective
Creation mechanism	Production or delivery	Generation or realisation
Certainty	Production can be guaranteed	Generation cannot be guaranteed
Manageability	Production can be controlled	Generation can only be influenced
Measurement	Through fitness-for-purpose features measured in quality tests	Through one or more agreed measures with agreed units and dimensions
Tangibility	Outputs are tangible	Outcomes are intangible (but measurable)
Appearance	Impossible without execution of process	In certain cases possible – even if process is not executed
Lead time	Available immediately after process is executed	Delayed until after execution of the process

Table 14.2. Outputs versus outcomes

To ensure that benefits are realised from projects, key stakeholders have to accept that, in addition to outputs, another sort of result, relating to end-effects, must be recognised. This paper identifies these as outcomes and is primarily concerned with target outcomes – those that provide the rationale for producing a project's outputs. Because outputs take the form of artefacts ('things'), they are properly described as tangible. Outcomes, on the other hand, take the form of measurable effects and so are classified as intangible. Outcomes in general, and target outcomes in particular, can always be expressed as a change in the value of a variable associated with an end-effect, for example: 'reduced waiting times', 'increased market share' and 'compliance with legislation'. Table 14.2 summarises the major differences between outputs and target outcomes.

Because an outcome represents a change for the organisation, its labelling should also emphasise this expected change. As a result, the wording used in the titles of outcomes will frequently begin with a participial adjective (loosely an '–ed' word such as 'increased' or 'decreased'). For example, consider a project that is being proposed to reduce traffic congestion in a city's CBD. Outputs from the exercise include a cross-city tunnel, changes in the configuration of existing city streets, a tolling system, a suite of management/maintenance processes and a new business unit to operate the facility. Candidate target outcomes could include 'reduced accident rates' and 'reduced travel times'.

An alternative project approach

The drawbacks of current project management approaches suggest that an alternative approach is required: one that focuses on outcome realisation, rather than output delivery. An outcome-focused approach is also supported by leading scholars in recent studies (e.g. Kerzner 2009; Turner 2006; Shenhar & Dvir 2007). This view indicates that meeting objectives, realising benefits and effecting change represent the real rationale for a project.

The definition of a project

Support for an outcome based project approach can be found in the increasing prominence of benefits and outcomes in new definitions of 'project' in the recent literature, as is presented in Table 14.3. While traditional definitions focused on output delivery (see Table 14.1), an analysis of these newer definitions show that, in general, they accept that projects are a means to creating change and achieving agreed goals. Interestingly, an outcome based definition suggested as far as half a century ago, has, unfortunately, been ignored since: 'A project is an organisation unit *dedicated to the attainment of a goal* [our emphasis]' (Gaddis 1959).

Source	Project definition	Outcome-focused terms included in the definition
Turner 2006	Temporary organisation to which resources are assigned to do work to bring about beneficial change	Change
Gray & Larson 2006	A complex, non-routine, one-time effort limited by time, budget, resources and performance specifications designed to meet customer needs	Needs
Shenhar & Dvir 2007	A temporary organisation and process set up to achieve a specified goal under the constraints of time, budget and other resources	Goal
Pinto 2007	A unique venture with a beginning and end, conducted by people to meet established goals within parameters of cost, schedule and quality	Goal
Kerzner 2006	Any series of activities and tasks that have a specific objective to be completed within certain specifications	Objectives
Project Management Institute 2008	Temporary endeavour undertaken to create a unique product, service or a result	Result

Table 14.3. Recent project definitions focused on outcome realisation

In addition to the support lent from the recent project management literature, outcome realisation is also recognised as an important part of organisational modelling. For example, the Logic Model (Savaya & Waysman 2005), which integrates planning, evaluation and action in organisations, suggests a sequence of steps to achieve a desirable impact. This sequence includes inputs, activities, outputs and outcomes, which finally lead to some form of beneficial effect. In the logic model outcomes are defined as specific changes in program participants' behaviour, knowledge, skills, status and level of functioning.

The project model

This section supports an outcome-oriented project approach with a new definition of a project and an accompanying conceptual model. Following the significant shift in emphasis from outputs to outcomes, the proposed definition for a 'project' in this paper is: 'A unique process intended to achieve target outcomes'. This definition suggests that the IPO model presented in Figure 14.1 be modified by expanding the three components that are already there (inputs, process and outputs). The new structure represents the ITO model of a process, as shown in Figure 14.2. The ITO model is so-named because it seeks to explain how *inputs* on the left are *transformed* into *outcomes* on the right (Smyrk 1995).

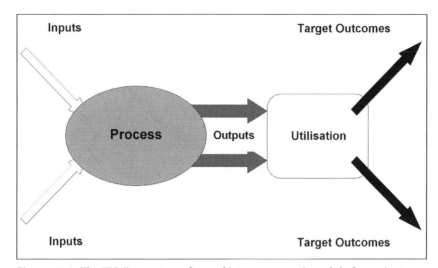

Figure 14.2. The ITO (inputs transformed into outcomes) model of a project

The left hand half of the ITO model is simply the IPO model – to which has been appended a utilisation mechanism and a flow of target outcomes. The 'left-to-right' chronology implied by the IPO model in Figure 14.1 can now be extended in the following way: the project's outputs are eventually delivered to someone who then utilises them in a way that subsequently generates target outcomes. The entities that utilise a project's outputs in such a way as to generate target outcomes are called the project's customers. While every execution of a process has an IPO model, not all executions of all processes have target outcomes. This is a relatively common situation with operational processes. All projects, on the other hand, do have target outcomes, because they are designed to effect some intended change. In the left-hand (IPO) part of the ITO model, the link between outputs and the process is an example of strong causality (Hicks 1979). This means that the outputs will exist if, and only if, the process is executed. In business, we treat processes as controllable and so are willing to guarantee outputs.

The chronology that underpins the ITO model can be made a little more explicit by showing a horizontal timeline. Under this view, the 'work' part of the model (represented by the process ellipse) would have defined start and finish dates, obtained notionally by dropping perpendiculars from the left and right hand extremities of the ellipse onto the X-axis, as shown in Figure 14.3. T_1 represents the date on which the work of producing the project's outputs begins, while T_2 indicates the date on which this work is complete. The difference between these two dates is the duration of the work required to produce the project outputs. This is the traditional duration of a project. However, the real duration of a project is longer, as the project finishes after utilisation has begun (when a flow of outcomes has been secured), as indicated by T_3.

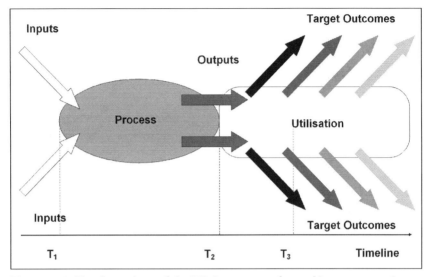

Figure 14.3. The chronology of the ITO (inputs transformed into outcomes) methodology

Figure 14.3 shows the most general situation whereby utilisation takes place over an indefinite period into the distant future.

Some forms of target outcome tend to appear regularly in real life projects – suggesting that there may be an underlying taxonomy. A generic list of target outcomes would include changes in such variables as: incidents/events (count), sales (count/revenue), risk exposure, compliance and operational output quality (error/reject rates).

Under the new model, accountability for outputs remains with the project manager, but the question of accountability for target outcomes now needs to be answered. At first brush it would appear that the funder is self-accountable. While a view could be taken that achievement of target outcomes is the business of the funder and no-one else, the issue is complicated by the circumstances under which a funding decision is made. Two common situations surrounding the acceptance of a business case are particularly noteworthy. The first is where the idea for a project (and an associated business case) has come from someone other than the funder (often called the project 'champion'). In that case, the funder could well hold the champion accountable for the outcomes that he/she has claimed as benefits in the business case. The second is where the funder is too busy to play an active day-to-day role in the conduct of the project. In that case, someone would have to be appointed to look after the funder's interests. (There is, of course, a third scenario involving a combination of the two situations outlined here – which would still require the participation of someone other than the funder). Whether filled by the project champion or by another player altogether, a new role emerges whenever a business case is accepted and a new project begins. This new role is identified here as that of project owner, who becomes the funder's agent.

An example of the new project model

The following project example demonstrates the use of the ITO model. A project is executed by the Department of Transport to improve the quality of line-marking on national roads. As illustrated in Figure 14.4, the five ITO components for this project may be:

1. Inputs – funds and labour, measured in dollars and working hours.

2. Process – mark lines. The efficiency of this process can be measured in lane km per dollar invested.

3. Output – pavement lines, measured in km of fully marked lane.

4. Utilisation – compliant (or non-compliant) behaviour on the part of the driver. This behaviour (which would take the form of acknowledgement by the driver of the lines on the pavement), could be measured in km (or proportion of distance) driven within marked lanes.

5. Target outcomes – for example, decreased accident rates, measured in serious crashes per year and increased traffic flow, measured in vehicles per hour.

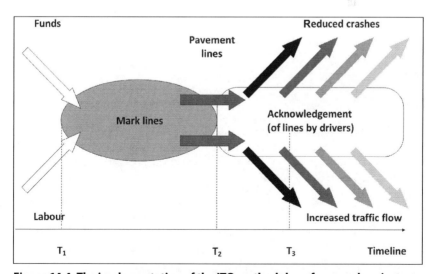

Figure 14.4. The implementation of the ITO methodology for a road project

Model validation

In this section, we employ a concurrent mixed method design (Jick 1979; Sackett & Larson 1990; Scandura & Williams 2000; Yin 1984; Patton 2002), which uses a triangular approach to validate the project model: a quantitative questionnaire, qualitative case study and literature analysis.

Model validation: a quantitative field study

In order to validate the importance of the outcome-focused approach, the following hypotheses have been proposed.

The research model

Based on the ITO model and the project management literature, a research model has been developed. As can be seen in Figure 14.5, the model assumes that the project process is triggered by a desire to realise certain outcomes and is then driven by their importance. This, in turn leads through outcome and output definition, project planning and execution to project success.

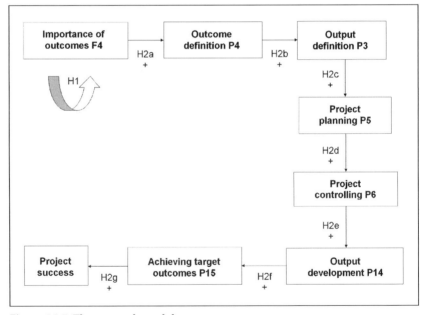

Figure 14.5. The research model

Research hypotheses

The first hypothesis states that outcomes drive projects (Fraser 2003; Carden & Egan 2008; Remenyi et al. 1997) and hence their achievement is critical to a project funder and triggers the whole project process.

H$_1$: Achieving target outcomes is the most important factor to a project funder

Assuming the acceptance of the first hypothesis, the second hypothesis states that the core importance of outcomes drives several project processes towards project success. The level of importance of outcomes and the clear definition of outcomes and outputs are all directly derived from the ITO model. Hence, we raise the following hypotheses:

H2a: The importance of outcomes realisation to a project funder is positively correlated with the definition of outcomes (according to the ITO model outcomes have to be clearly defined).

H2b: The definition of outcomes is positively correlated with the definition of outputs (according to the ITO model outputs have to be defined to support outcome realisation).

The management literature suggests strongly that, work in organisations has to first be planned, then controlled (Chase et al. 2006; Kerzner 2009). In addition, project management studies have proved that high quality planning, through controlling project execution, contributes to successful delivery of project outputs (e.g. Pinto & Slevin 1988; Zwikael & Globerson 2004). Hence, we assume that planning and later, controlling, are essential for successful output execution.

H2c: The definition of outputs is positively correlated with the development of a project plan.

H2d: Project planning is positively correlated with project controlling.

H2e: Controlling a project is positively correlated with output development.

Finally, the ITO model identifies the project owner as accountable for outcome realisation. Hence, the assignment of a project owner (to ensure that output delivery results in realised outcomes) is another essential factor in the model:

H2f: The development of outputs is positively correlated with achieving target outcomes.

H2g: Achievement of target outcomes is positively correlated with project success.

Research methodology

Based on these hypotheses, a questionnaire was developed and distributed to 102 project managers, program managers, project officers and project funders in Asia Pacific countries. 29 responses came from India, 16 from New Zealand, 15 from Australia and the rest from different Asia Pacific countries. 20.2 per cent of responses came from software organisations, 19.0 per cent from services, 11.9 per cent from engineering, 13.1 per cent from government and 8.3 per cent from production organisations. Project duration ranged between two and 60 months with an average of 15.6 months. 55.4 per cent of the projects were executed for an internal funder within the same organisation, while 44.6 per cent of the projects were undertaken for an external organisation. 89 per cent of responses were male and 11 per cent female.

Data collected from these questionnaires include: (1) the relative importance of various project management factors (described in Table 14.5) to the project funder using a five point Likert scale (see the questionnaire structure in Table 14.4); (2) level of effort invested in the same factors using a similar five point Likert scale; (3) organisational and project characteristics; (4) project success, measured as the level of funder satisfaction with the project on a scale of one to five (Zwikael & Sadeh, 2007) and; (5) the person accountable for outcome realisation in the last completed project.

Project Management Factor	Not important			Extremely important	
Developing a list of agreed outputs (deliverables)	1	2	3	4	5
Developing a list of agreed target outcomes (benefits)	1	2	3	4	5

Table 14.4. Example of the project questionnaire: importance of project management factors to the project's funder

Result: the importance of target outcomes in a project context

In order to test the first research hypothesis, which argues that outcome realisation has the highest importance to funders (and hence represents the trigger for a project), we analysed the relative importance of various factors to the projects' funders. Table 14.5 presents the ranked list of factors, including the mean of each project management factor on a one (low) to five (high) scale.

Project Management Factors – a ranked list	Importance to Funder (1–5 scale)
Achieving target outcomes (benefits)	3.98
Approving a business case	3.92
Developing a business case	3.91
Developing a list of agreed outputs (deliverables)	3.91
Producing outputs (deliverables)	3.91
Developing a list of agreed target outcomes (benefits)	3.84
Effective communications with stakeholders	3.70
Controlling the project	3.68
Developing a project plan	3.61
Managing project risks	3.53
Assigning a person accountable for target outcomes (benefits) achievement	3.46
Support provided by senior managers	3.40
Assembling a suitable project team	3.19
Updating the project plan	3.17
Managing the project team	3.09
Developing the project team	2.70

Table 14.5. The ranking of project management factors as are important to funders and as practices by project managers

This analysis shows that achieving target outcomes is the most important factor for project funders with a mean of 3.98. An additional statistical analysis shows that the 95 per cent confidence interval is (3.78, 4.18), which means that the importance of achieving target outcomes to a funder is significantly higher than most other project management factors. While the other factors also have very high scores, they too relate to outcomes – in particular, development/approval of the business case (where outcomes are defined) and development/production of outputs (that directly support outcome realisation). The importance of outcomes and their related processes to the projects' funders allows us to accept the first research hypothesis, (which claims that achieving target outcomes is the most important factor to a project funder).

Results: validating the research model

A second set of research hypotheses, which includes the factors required to transfer target outcomes to project success, has been used to validate the research model. In order to test these hypotheses, we analysed the correlations among all project management factors included in the research model. For each pair of factors, Table 14.6 presents the Pearson correlation and significance level (in brackets). A one-tailed test was used, as the hypotheses assume positive correlations among all variables.

	F4-Importance of developing target outcomes	P4-Developing a list of agreed target outcomes	P3-Developing a list of agreed outputs	P5-Developing a project plan	P6-Controlling a project	P14-Producing outputs	P15-Achieving target outcomes	Project success
F4-Importance of developing target outcomes	1.000	.414** (.000)	.392** (.000)	.125 (.119)	.137 (.198)	.242* (.011)	.443** (.000)	.234* (.016)
P4-Developing a list of agreed target outcomes		1.000	.609** (.000)	.294** (.002)	.399** (.000)	.183* (.042)	.533** (.000)	-.083 (.228)
P3-Developing a list of agreed outputs			1.000	.490** (.000)	.600** (.000)	.519** (.000)	.443** (.000)	.269** (.007)
P5-Developing a project plan				1.000	.674** (.000)	.387** (.000)	.227* (.016)	.225* (.020)
P6-Controlling a project					1.000	.534** (.000)	.396** (.000)	.110 (.160)
P14-Producing outputs						1.000	.576** (.000)	.400** (.000)
P15-Achieving target outcomes							1.000	.317* (.002)
Project success								1.000

Table 14.6. Correlations among research variables
* p≤0.05; **p≤0.01

These results show large and significant levels of correlation among all pairs of the factors in question: significance level for all five relationships tested in hypotheses is below (or very close to) 0.01. However, as the research model includes several mediating effects, we have also conducted a test for mediation (Baron & Kenny, 1986) for all meditating variables. Table 14.7 shows the results of three mediating tests conducted for each of the six sets of mediating relationships included in the model. For each set results include the identification of the independent, mediating and dependent variables and the significance level of the slopes in three regression tests.

Independent variable (X1)	Mediating variable (X2)	Dependent variable (Y)	Significance level X1→X2	Significance level X1→Y	Significance level (X1,X2)→Y	Mediating effect confirmed?
F4	P4	P3	.000**	.000**	F4:.069 ns P4:.000**	Yes
P4	P3	P5	.000**	.005**	P4: 0.956 ns P3:.000**	Yes
P3	P5	P6	.000**	.000**	P3:.000** P5:.000**	Partially
P5	P6	P14	.000**	.000**	P5:.696 ns P6:.000**	Yes
P6	P14	P15	.000**	.000**	P6:.211 ns P14:.000**	Yes
P14	P15	Project success	.000**	.000**	P14:.006 P15:.152 ns	No

Table 14.7. Tests for mediator effects in the model
* $p \leq 0.05$; **$p \leq 0.01$; ns: not significant

The results in Table 14.7 confirm the mediating effects for the bulk of the model. These results confirm the sequence of events occur in projects, as observed by the ITO model. However, in order to ensure that not only isolated parts of the model are validated separately for each mediator variable, we also analysed the effect of predecessor variables on each process. The reason for this is to ensure that each additional process has significant contribution to the suggested model. Hence, we have conducted a set of regression runs with a new dependent variable at a time, whereas previously analysed processes become controlled variables, as is summarised in Table 14.8.

Independent variable	Controlled variable	Dependent variable	R-squared value	Significance value
F4	-	P4	0.414	F4: 0.000**
P4	F4	P3	0.394	P4: 0.069 P4: 0.000**
P3	F4, P4	P5	0.245	F4: 0.437** P4: 0.893 P3: 0.000**
P5	F4, P4, P3	P6	0.559	F4: 0.248 P4: 0.374 P3: 0.001** P5:0.000**
P6	F4, P4, P3, P5	P14	0.398	F4: 0.128 P4: 0.015* P3: 0.002** P5:0.927 P6:0.003**
P14	F4, P4, P3, P5, P6	P15	0.561	F4: 0.020* P4: 0.000** P3: 0.093 P5:0.307 P6:0.459 P14: 0.000**
P15	F4, P4, P3, P5, P6, P14	Project success	0.351	F4: 0.159 P4: 0.002** P3: 0.028* P5:0.024* P6:0.0852 P14: 0.242 P15:0.012*

Table 14.8. Tests for controlling effects in the model
* p≤0.05; **p≤0.01; ns: not significant

The fact that the last added independent variable has more significant values than those of the controlled variables for all regression runs described in Table 14.8 supports the suggested model and with the support of previous results (see Tables 14.6 and 14.7) allows us to accept all H_2 sub-hypotheses that support the suggested research model.

Model validation: a qualitative case study

PSMA is an Australian company that supplies value-added spatial information generated from raw data obtained from various agencies across the country. This information is packaged as datasets such as Transport & Topography (which is concerned with road, rail, air infrastructure, parks and water bodies). PSMA's clients are firms who develop products and services that present the data in meaningful and useful ways. In 2003, the company saw a gap in the market for an authoritative geocoded address index covering the whole country. A project entitled G-NAF was commissioned to fill this gap.

In terms of the research model, G-NAF can be characterised in the following way:

Outcomes: PSMA saw that an increase in the levels of commitment amongst its customers to the company's product sets was critically important to achievement of its strategic business goals. This objective was then expressed as two defined outcomes – the numbers of organisations committed to G-NAF as their source of national address data and the number of projects undertaken by organisations to enhance their products/services/processes by exploiting G-NAF.

Outputs: The project was scoped in terms of five major outputs: a geocoded national address file, a set of agreed custodial licensing arrangements (involving data-suppliers), a distribution strategy, a new business unit to manage ongoing G-NAF-related operations and a product maintenance strategy.

Planning: After the business case for G-NAF was accepted, a detailed project plan was assembled including a work breakdown structure, schedules of milestones, resource plans and so on.

Output development: The project was executed in accordance with the project plan. PSMA's Chief Operating Officer was appointed as project manager and the CEO as project owner.

Assessing project success: When all outputs from the project had been delivered and implemented, a formal closeout workshop was conducted to assess the success of the project under eight performance criteria (such as adherence to budget). The results of that exercise, together with later analysis of client records, indicated that G-NAF had been successful.

Dan Paull, the CEO of PSMA Australia Limited has concluded this project by saying: 'there is no doubt that the use of the ITO model played a significant role in success of the project to develop G-NAF. It provides sharp clarity of the essential components of a project and how they logically interlock to deliver the outcomes sought. With this framework in place, it is easier to monitor progress of the project, manage contingencies and respond to opportunities in a very dynamic environment. It is scalable, so as not to bind a project up in unnecessary bureaucracy and aide significantly in communicating the what, how, when and why to the project team and stakeholders.'

Model validation: project success measures

As part of the validation exercise, we have analysed the alignment of project success dimensions appearing in the recent project management literature with the suggested outcome focused approach. For example, unlike the output based project management methodology presented in the Project Management Institute's (2008) *PMBOK Guide*, the recent PRINCE2 methodology (Office of Government Commerce 2007) offers a benefit based view of project management. However, while acknowledging the importance of outcome realisation, PRINCE2 does not provide practical tools to manage project outcomes.

In addition, it has been found that many project success measures in the literature also focus on outcome realisation, as is suggested in this paper. These results are summarised in Table 14.8.

The analysis in Table 14.8 shows high level of relationship between the two lists. This analysis also suggests that a variety of different success dimensions can all be considered under the title of 'desirable outcomes', as varies among projects, for example 'increased business opportunities for the future'.

Literature source	Success dimension
Dvir and Lechler 2004	The satisfaction of the project funder ('customer' in the original terminology of their paper).
Dvir et al. 2003	Funder benefits – success from the funder's point of view ('customer' in the original terminology of the paper)
Dvir et al. 2003	Benefits to the parent organisation
Dvir et al. 2003	Benefits to the community and national infrastructures
Kerzner 2009	With acceptance by the funder ('customer' in the original terminology of the book)

Table 14.8. Project success dimensions with relation to outcome realisation

Conclusions

Common definitions of projects (for example, Project Management Institute 2004; International Project Management Association 2006) and supporting practices focus on output delivery. As a result, most projects end when the primary output has been delivered and project success is measured according to time and cost overruns and quality of this output. For a long time, there have been suspicions that this view might be flawed (Shenhar &Dvir 1996; Meredith 2002; Packendorff 1995; Fraser 2003). Turman (1986), for example, predicted, 'the days when we could define success in terms of cost, schedule and technical objectives are gone'. Similarly, Turner and Müller

(2003) criticise that 'classical definitions of projects are not wrong, just incomplete'. Others (e.g. Shenhar & Dvir 1996; Turner 2006) claim that most research literature on the management of projects suffers from a scanty theoretical basis and a lack of concepts.

This paper identifies additional problems with current project management approaches. For example, it argues that output achievement, even with high quality, short time and low cost, while a necessary condition to project success, is not a sufficient condition (Thorp 1998). Also, because 'benefits are not delivered or realised by the project manager and project team' (Cooke-Davies 2002), there is a need for a new project role to be accountable for benefit realisation.

The new project approach proposed in this paper emphasises project outcomes that, in turn, support organisational benefits. This approach can be argued to be part of the 'success' research school of project management (Bredillet 2008) and is aligned with recent benefit realisation models (e.g. Baccarini 1999; Simon & Herbert 1976; Ashurst et al. 2008; Ward & Daniel 2006; Peppard et al. 2007; OGC 2007) and project-strategic fit models (Benko & McFarlan 2003; Zwikael & Linenberg 2000). However, as this paper involves the analysis of only one case study, future research can focus on validation of the suggested approach in different project contexts. More specifically, because we have not addressed quantitative validation of the utilisation process itself, future studies may benefit from measuring utilisation of project output and their contribution to achieve project success.

This paper has also suggested the ITO model to support project modelling, an additional project phase and a new accountable person (project owner) to support outcome realisation and a tool to define and validate outcomes and outputs (the Utilisation Map). This approach has been validated using triangulated design (Jick 1979; Sackett & Larson 1990; Scandura & Williams 2000; Yin 2003), involving a quantitative questionnaire, qualitative case study and literature analysis.

Reflecting back on the evolution of project management in the past few decades, this paper shows that from an early goal-oriented approach (Gaddis 1959), the orientation has changed to a dominant delivery based approach. We think that the establishment of project management professional organisations serving the community of project managers (e.g. Project management Institute and the International Project Management Association) during the 1960's and their significant growth since has changed the focus of this profession from projects to project managers. We believe that while focus on project managers' processes is still essential, an outcome-based wider view on projects is also required on the organisational level. Yet, we do not accept the approach according to only programs have to deal with outcomes, while projects should maintain their focus on output delivery. As a result, both projects and programs should deliver both outputs and outcomes that are related to the organisational strategic plan.

This paper establishes a closer link between projects and organisational goals. Not only does the discussion propose an approach to give projects a role that is more goal-oriented, but it also suggests project management processes that are more meaningfully linked with organisational benefits and strategy. In particular, it is argued that, in order to achieve benefits from projects, funders should define target outcomes and tangible outputs, project managers should plan and work towards output delivery that is supportive of benefit realisation and project owners should lead an outcome realisation process to ensure benefits are secured.

References

Ashurst, C; Doherty, N F; Peppard, J. 2008. 'Improving the impact of IT development projects: The benefits realization capability model'. *European Journal of Information Systems* 17 (4): 352–370.

Baccarini, D. 1999. 'The logical framework method for defining project success'. *Project Management Journal* 30 (4): 25–32.

Baron, R M; Kenny, D A. 1986. 'The moderator-mediator variable distinction is social psychological research: Conceptual, strategic, and statistical considerations'. *Journal of Personality and Social Psychology* 51: 1173–1182.

Benko, C; McFarlan, F W. 2003. *Connecting the Dots: Aligning Projects with Objectives in Unpredictable Times.* Boston, MA: Harvard Business School Press.

Bredillet, C N. 2008. 'Exploring research in project management: Nine schools of project management research'. *Project Management Journal* 39 (3): 2–5.

Budzinski, O. 2008. 'Monoculture versus diversity in competition economics'. *Cambridge Journal of Economics* 32 (2): 295–324.

Bygstad, B; Lanestedt, G. 2009). 'ICT based service innovation – A challenge for project management'. *International Journal of Project Management* 27 (3): 234–242.

Carden, L; Egan, T. 2008. 'Does our literature support sectors newer to project management? The search for quality publications relevant to non-traditional industries'. *Project Management Journal* 39 (3): 6–27.

Chase, R B; Jacobs, FR; Aquilano, N J. 2006. *Operations Management for Competitive Advantage.* 11th edition. Boston, MA: Irwin McGraw Hill.

Cooke-Davies, T. 2002. 'The "real" success factors on projects'. *International Journal of Project Management* 20: 185–190.

Dvir, D., Lechler, T., 2004. Plans are nothing, changing plans is everything: the impact of changes on project success. *Research Policy* 33, 1–15.

Dvir, D; Lipovetsky, S.; Shenhar, A J; Tishler, A. 2003. 'What is really important for project success? A refined, multivariate, comprehensive analysis'. *International Journal of Management and Decision Making* 4 (4): 382.

Fraser, I. 2003. 'Benefits realisation: Balancing outputs with outcomes'. Project Insight –

Managing Projects to Realise Strategic Initiatives Conference, Sydney, Australia.

Gaddis, P O. 1959. 'The project manager'. *Harvard Business Review* 32 (May–June): 89–97.

Gray, C F; Larson, E W. 2006. *Project Management – The Managerial Process.* 3rd edn. McGraw-Hill.

Hicks, J R. 1979. *Causality in Economics.* New York: Basic Books, Inc.

International Project Management Association. 2006. *IPMA Competence Baseline, Version 3.* Nijkerk, the Netherlands: IPMA.

Jick, T D. 1979. 'Mixing qualitative and quantitative methods: Triangulation in action'. *Administrative Science Quarterly* 24: 602–611.

Johnson, J; Karen, D; Boucher, K C; Robinson, J. 2001. 'Collaborating on project success'. *Software Magazine*, February/March.

Jones, D A. 2008. 'Project management is not a profession and why we shouldn't legislate'. Australian Institute of Project Management annual conference, Canberra, Australia.

Jugdev, K. 2004. 'Through the looking glass: Examining theory development in project management with the resource-based view lens'. *Project Management Journal* 35 (3): 15–26.

Kerzner, H. 2006. *Project Management: A Systems Approach to Planning, Scheduling and Controlling.* 9th edn. Hoboken, N.J: John Wiley and Sons.

Kerzner, H. 2009. *Project Management: A Systems Approach to Planning, Scheduling and Controlling.* 10th edn. New York: John Wiley and Sons.

Koskela, L; Howell, G. 2002. 'The underlying theory of project management is obsolete'. In Proceedings of the PMI Research Conference: Seattle, 14–17 July: 293–302.

Krajewski, L J; Ritzman, L P. 2005. *Operations Management.* Upper Saddle River, NJ: Prentice Hall.

Kwak, Y H; Anbari, F T. 2009. 'Analyzing project management research: Perspectives from top management journals'. *International Journal of Project Management* 27 (5) 435–446.

Leach, L P. 2005. *Critical Chain Project Management.* 2nd edn. Boston, US: Artech House.

Lewis, J. P. 2000. *The Project Manager's Desk Reference.* 2nd edn. New York: McGraw-Hill.

Lewis, M W; Welsh, M A; Dehler, G E; Green, S G. 2002. 'Product development tensions: Exploring contrasting styles of project management'. *The Academy of Management Journal* 45 (3): 546–564.

Lipsey, R; Lancaster, K. 1956. 'The general theory of second best'. *Review of Economic Studies* 24 (1): 11–32.

Love, P E D; Edwards, D J; Irani, Z. 2008. 'Forensic project management: An exploratory examination of the causal behaviour of design-induced rework'. *IEEE Transactions on Engineering Management* 55 (2): 234.

Meredith, J R; Mantel S J. 2006. *Project Management – A Managerial Approach.* 6th edn. Hoboken, NJ: John Wiley and Sons.

Meredith, J. 2002. 'Developing project management theory for managerial application: The view of a research journal's editor'. Paper presented at PMI Frontiers of Project Management and Research Conference. Seattle, Washington.

Müller, R; Turner, R. 2007. 'The influence of project managers on project success criteria and project success by type of project'. *European Management Journal* 25 (4): 298.

Nogeste, K; Walker, D H T. 2005. 'Project outcomes and outputs: making the intangible tangible'. *Measuring Business Excellence* 9 (4): 55–68.

Office of Government Commerce (UK) (OGC). 2007. *Managing Successful Programs.* Norwich, UK: The Stationery Office.

Packendorff, J. 1995. 'Inquiring into the temporary organization: New directions for project management research'. *Scandinavian Journal of Management* 11 (4): 319–333.

Peppard, J; Ward, J; Daniel, E. 2007. 'Managing the realization of business benefits from IT investments'. *MIS Quarterly Executive* 6 (1): 1–11.

Pinto, J K. 2007. *Project Management – Achieving Competitive Advantage*. New Jersey: Pearson.

Pinto, J K; Slevin, D. P. 1987. 'Critical factors in successful project implementation'. *IEEE Transactions on Engineering Management*. EM-34, February: 22–27

Project Management Institute. 2004. *A Guide to the Project Management Body of Knowledge (PMBOK Guide)*. 3rd edn. Newtown Square, PA: Project Management Institute.

Project Management Institute. 2008. *A Guide to the Project Management Body of Knowledge (PMBOK Guide)*. 4th edn. Newtown Square, PA: Project Management Institute.

Patton, M. Q. 2002. *Qualitative Research and Evaluation Methods*. 3rd edn. Thousand Oaks, CA: Sage Publications Inc.

Remenyi, D; White, T; Sherwood-Smith, M. 1997. 'Information systems management: The need for a post–modern approach'. *International Journal of Information Management* 17 (6): 421–435

Russell, R S; Taylor, B W. 2005. *Operations Management*. Prentice Hall.

Saarinen, T. 1990. 'Systems development methodology and project success'. *Information and Management* 19: 67–75.

Sackett, P R; Larson Jr, J R. 1990. 'Research strategies and tactics in industrial and organization psychology'. In *Handbook of Industrial and Organizational Psychology*, edited by Dunnette, M D; Hough, L M. Palo Alto, CA: Consulting Psychologists Press: 419–489.

Savaya, R; Waysman, M. 2005. 'The logic model: A tool for incorporating theory in development and evaluation of programs'. *Administration in Social Work* 29 (2): 85–103.

Scandura, T A., Williams, E A., 2000. 'Research methodology in management: Current practices, trends, and implications for future research'. *Academy of Management Journal* 43 (6): 1248–1264.

Shenhar A; Dvir, D. 1996. 'Toward a typological theory of project management'. *Research Policy* 25: 607–32.

Shenhar, A J; Dvir, D. 2007. 'Project management research-the challenge and opportunity'. *Project Management Journal* 38 (2): 93–99.

Simon, H. 1976. *Administrative Behavior*. 3rd edn. New York: The Free Press.

Smyrk, J. 1995. 'The ITO model: A framework for developing and classifying performance indicators'. Paper presented at the International Conference of the Australasian Evaluation Society. Sydney, Australia.

Thorp, J. 1998. 'How about focusing on benefits too?' *Computing Canada* 24 (42): 32.

Turman, J. 1986. 'Success modelling: A technique for building a winning team'. Proceedings of PMI annual seminar and symposium, Montreal: 94–108.

Turner, J R. 1993. *The Handbook of Project-Based Management*. London: McGraw-Hill.

Turner, J R. 2006. 'Editorial: Towards a theory of project management: The nature of the project'. *International Journal of Project Management* 24: 1–3.

Turner, J R; R. Muller. 2003. 'On the nature of the project as a temporary organization'. *International Journal of Project Management* 21 (1): 1–8.

Ward, J; Daniel, E. 2006. *Benefits Management*. Chichester: John Wiley and Sons.

Webber, S S; Torti, M T. 2004. 'Project managers doubling as client account executives'. *The Academy of Management Executive* 18 (1): 60–71.

Yin, R K. 1984. *Case Study Research: Design and Methods.* Thousand Oaks, CA: Sage Publications.

Young, R; Jordan, E. 2008. 'Top management support: Mantra or necessity?' *International Journal of Project Management* 26: 713–725.

Zwikael, O. 2008. Top management involvement in project management: exclusive support practices for different project scenarios. *International Journal Of Managing Projects In Business* 1 (3): 387–403

Zwikael, O; Sadeh, A. 2007. 'Planning effort as an effective risk management tool'. *Journal of Operations Management* 25 (4): 755–767.

Zwikael, O; Globerson, S. 2004. 'Evaluating the quality of project planning: a model and field results'. *International Journal of Production Research* 42 (8): 1545–1556.

Zwikael, O; Globerson, S. 2006. 'From critical success factors to critical success processes'. *International Journal of Production Research* 44 (17): 3433–3449.

Zwikael, O; Linenberg, Y. 2000. 'Improving the project alignment with the business' drivers'. Paper presented at the 3rd European Project Management Conference, Jerusalem, Israel.

Chapter 15

Research methods for wicked projects

Andrew Finegan

University of Adelaide, Australia

Many complex projects have wicked problem components, which if they are significant, can transform the project into a wicked project. Such projects cannot be viewed in scientific, reductionist terms. Rather, any research investigation must be able to address the combined complexity and diversity that manifests within the project. For example, multiple stakeholders with widely differing viewpoints, constraints that are continuously changing and disagreement over the desired project outcomes. This indicates that flexible, open-ended, participative, collaborative and adaptive approaches are needed to investigate wicked projects.

This paper reviews, with relevant project management examples, a number of systems thinking and action research related techniques and methodologies that are recommended to assist understanding where there is unstructured and poorly defined complexity. These techniques include system dynamics modelling, action research and action learning, soft systems methodology, grounded theory, and actor network theory. Not only will these techniques assist in better understanding wicked projects, they can also be used to provide a framework for a suitable research design.

Introduction

A topical theme in the project management literature has been the trends, direction and methodological issues of project management research. Crawford and Pollack (2004) have mapped the hard and soft dimensions of project management. However, concern has been expressed by Smyth and Morris (2007) that familiarity encourages the mechanistic application of positivist and empirical methods. Major trends in project management research have been examined by Crawford et al. (2006) and their findings include the observation that the influence of systems thinking has increased, with an interest in complexity and emergence.

Winter et al. (2006), in presenting the main findings of their study of future directions in project management research, emphasise the pervasive impact of greater complexity of projects and programs across all industry sectors. Associated issues with such a complex project include multiple stakeholders with different agenda and expectations, multiple theories, practices and discourses, changing project requirements and constraints within a dynamic, ever changing project environment. Faced with this, Winter et al. (2006, 647) identify 'the need for a range of creative research strategies, designs and methods'.

This paper argues that there is a particular group of complex projects – wicked projects that have wicked problems (Rittel & Weber, 1973) as major components – that especially benefit from the application of a variety of research approaches, especially those that incorporate systems thinking concepts. Seeking creative, systems thinking-based examples of project management, five broad groups have been identified and discussed using specific examples.

Wicked problems and wicked projects

The term wicked problems as applied to organisations is attributed to Rittel and Weber (1973) who identified a class of problem in the design of planning that is difficult to define, has no stopping rules and no ultimate 'best solution'. Wicked problems can take a multitude of forms and can be found in many different organisations and environments. Many examples are found in public administration; Brown and Brudney (2003) give illicit drug use, neighbourhood deterioration and juvenile delinquency; and Waddock and Walsh (1999) give school reform, children in poverty and children in legal difficulties, as examples of wicked problems with inter-organisational complexity.

The Australian Public Service Commission (2007) identifies diverse policy issues that include climate change, obesity, indigenous disadvantage and land degradation as wicked policy problems. Part of the challenge of wicked problems is that it is very difficult to fully appreciate the nature of the problem. Therefore wicked problems are rarely 'solved'; rather the task is to design a more or less effective solution that is based upon how the problem has been defined (Pacanowsky 1995). Similarly, Becker (2002) observes that wicked problems are typically made up of a dense web of interconnecting factors, making it difficult to understand how one decision will influence decisions in other area. Also, wicked problems arise in the dynamic and uncertain environments where considerable risk is generated. Therefore, considerable conflict is often associated with wicked problems, especially where 'good outcomes' are traded off against 'bad outcomes' within the same value system.

Shurville and Williams (2005) define wicked projects – projects with wicked problem components – as; 1) Difficult to define, that defining the nature of the problem is the main problem, and 2) Containing a large social and political part. In a case study of project definition, Whelton and Ballard (2002) suggest that project teams need to focus upon how stakeholder organisations operate and how their value sets are developed. Discussing project procurement, Callender et al. (2006) observes that wicked problems have no rational basis, are difficult to define within a boundary and represent highly complex, intractable practical problems. They further state that the challenge is making sense of wicked problems.

Wicked projects and systems thinking

Focusing upon the organisation complexity of projects, a soft, people-based approach is recommended by Brown and Brudney (2003) as being able to provide structure and a collaborative response to wicked problems. Gao et al. (2002) proposes that the systems sciences, including soft systems thinking, should be used to support the different levels and phases of knowledge management. Similarly, Gustafsson (2002) recommends using a holistic open systems approach to deal with inter-related complexity and wicked problems.

Given the impact of viewpoints and stakeholders in creating wicked problems, stakeholder analysis is also recommended. Bryson et al. (2002) show how stakeholder analysis is useful in transforming wicked problems into solvable problems. Stakeholder analysis to deal with wicked problems is also suggested by Savage et al. (1991). Such analysis needs to address the power, intentions and values of both the organisation and key stakeholders. Finegan (1994), Neal (1995) and Green (1999) emphasise the potential for using systems thinking techniques in the early stages of projects, to help the various stakeholders achieve a common understanding of the problem situation.

More specifically, Crawford et al. (2006) observed the influence of systems dynamics, while Smyth and Morris (2007) comment on the role of grounded theory as an interpretive and sense making approach to project management research. Williams (1999) suggests that systems dynamics modelling can be used together with soft systems methodology.

Exploring the theme of systems thinking as a broad framework for project management research, this paper now examines selected examples of project management research that have used system dynamics modelling, action research and action learning, soft systems methodology, grounded theory and actor network theory.

System dynamics modelling (SD)

Systems dynamics (SD) developed originally by Forrester (1961), is a methodology for studying and managing complex social systems, especially those found in business. The key to systems dynamics is that only the study of the whole system – with special attention to feedback systems – will lead to correct results. There is a wide range of applications using this methodology, however most SD models are created in four stages (Albin 1997):

1. Conceptualisation: Define the purpose of the model, define the model boundary and identify key variables, describe the behaviour or draw the reference modes of the key variables, and diagram the basic mechanisms – the feedback loops – of the system.

2. Formulation: Convert feedback diagrams to level and rate equations, and estimate and select parameter values.

3. Testing: Simulate the model and test the dynamic hypothesis, test the model's assumptions, and test model behaviour and sensitivity to perturbations.

4. Implementation: Test the model's response to different policies, and translate study insights to an accessible form.

A strong case for the application of computer modelling using SD in project management is made by Sterman (1992) and Pauley and Ormerod (1998). In a detailed discussion of the complexity associated with large construction projects, Sterman (1992, 9) argues that SD models are useful in dealing with 'the dynamic complexity created by the interdependencies, feedbacks, time delays, and nonlinearities in large scale projects'. It is further claimed that both hard data and soft qualitative knowledge can be incorporated into SD models, that 'the skilled modeller uses all available information sources to specify the relationships in the model' (Sterman 1992, 10).

Describing the cycle of activities in the analysis of major problems in mining projects, Pauley and Ormerod (1998) found that 'graphical systems-dynamics packages provided an appropriate mix of high-level modelling features that people could understand easily. It is particularly interesting to note that the studies undertaken by Pauley and Ormerod (1998) incorporated systems dynamics together with soft systems methodology, queuing theory, Ishikawa diagrams, cognitive maps and value chain analysis. Similarly, addressing the need for new paradigms for complex projects, Williams (1999) recommends using soft systems methodology to capture the soft ideas in a project, together with systems dynamics to create holistic, top-down models.

In *Modelling Complex Projects*, Williams (2002) provides a detailed and practical description of the application of systems dynamic modelling to project management. This describes the use of SD models before the commencement of a project, at the start of a project, during the projects and after project completion. Furthermore, in a study of project overruns, Williams (2005) used SD modelling in project post-mortem analysis. Describing a clear progression from cognitive maps, to cause maps, to influence diagrams to SD models, this systemic modelling provided insightful explanation as to why some projects severely overran. Williams (2005, 501) observes that the SD models 'demonstrate how behaviour arises that would not be predicted from the analysis of individual parts of the project and, thus, show how traditional decomposition models in some circumstances can be inadequate'. Popular SD modelling applications currently available include Stella/iThink, Powersim and Vensim (Williams 2002; Eberlein 2009). Williams (2002) provides examples of a variety of SD models that have been generated using Powersim.

Action research and action learning (AR/AL)

The major study of future directions for project management research undertaken by Winter et al. (2006) identifies the need for creative research strategies, including action research and action learning. These closely related approaches have also been adopted for project management research by Ala-Risku and Karkkainen (2005), Kenny (2003), Ottosson (2003), Walker *et al.* (2008), Nogeste (2008), Bourne and Walker (2006), Sankaran and Tay (2007) and Sankaran et al. (2009).

Action research (AR) is described by Sankaran et al. (2009) as collaborative inquiry undertaken by people concerned with a problematic situation. It often uses a cyclical process to better understand the nature of the problem before attempting a solution. Consistent with systems thinking, the research process is emergent and responds to the situation. AR can use a variety of methods to develop understanding as the process moves towards acting to achieve a solution.

Similarly, action learning (AL) is based upon the simple cycle where participants plan, act, observe and reflect. As with AR, this is often undertaking as repeated iterations of the cycle. Collaboration is an important aspect of AL, with small groups working together on tasks or problems. To be effective in AL, Ellis and Phelps (1999) recommend that the participating groups need to include:

- involvement of individuals with technological skill specialisation and other specialists;
- sharing of experiences and ideas between participants;
- involvement of other staff working in the project area.

Therefore both AR and Al is based upon individuals and groups who seek to understand problem situations through a cycle of critical reflection, followed by application of what is learnt to future action (Kenny 2003). AL is generally suited to where individuals are working for their own professional growth, whereas AR is seen as providing a more formal framework for research, from planning to data collection, analysis and final publication.

The combination of AR and AL is a popular approach applied to project management research in a number of variations. Ala-Risku and Karkkainen (2006) describe using the 'innovative action research (IAR)' approach to develop a solution for managing problems in material logistics in construction projects. A combination of AL and AR is applied to innovation and strategic change projects by Kenny (2003). Also focusing upon innovation and change in projects, Ottosson (2003) argues that 'participation action research (PAR)' reveals important information about projects that do not run smoothly due to misunderstanding between managers and the project team.

The role of AR and AL is the subject of close scrutiny by Walker et al. (2008) in a study of academic-practitioner research undertaken within doctorial programs in North America, Australia and Europe. In these cases, much of the project management research that was undertaken involved reflection and action research/learning. This focus is a result of the importance of reflective learning as an integral part of the doctoral programs. The doctoral candidates developed 'an extremely deep level of reflection, testing cause and effect links, action learning and development of the kind of wisdom one sees in proficient performers and virtuosos' (Walker et al. 2008, 182). Research examples include the development of project management solutions using a dual cycle AR model (Nogeste 2008) and the development of a tool for measuring and visualising stakeholder influence in projects (Bourne & Walker 2006).

A further four examples of doctoral research projects that apply action research techniques to project management are described by Sankaran and Tay (2007) and Sankaran et al. (2009). In two of these cases soft systems methodology (SSM) is used to 'help researchers use a systems approach more effectively towards achieving a solution in an AR project' (Sankaran et al. 2009, 195).

Soft systems methodology (SSM)

Soft systems thinking is an interpretive approach that is strongly influenced by Vickers' (1968, 59, 176) description of the importance of appreciative systems in dealing with human complexity. Checkland (1999) and Checkland and Scholes (1990) have attempted to transform these ideas from systems theory into a practical methodology that is called Soft Systems Methodology (SSM).

SSM concepts are based on practical application and experience in a wide variety of complex managerial systems. The methodology is designed to allow the human element of such systems, which is typically unstructured and poorly defined, to be incorporated into system design work. It may be used to analyse any problem or situation, but it is most appropriate where the problem 'cannot be formulated as a search for an efficient means of achieving a defined end; a problem in which ends, goals, purposes are themselves problematic' (Checkland 1999, 316). SSM encourages investigators to view organisations from a cultural perspective. Therefore the component parts that are human beings determine the essential characteristics of organisations. These 'people components' can attribute meaning to their situation and define their own purpose for the organisation. SSM is particularly suited to sense-making, which suggests its suitability for wicked problems and wicked projects.

A major body of project management-related research work has been undertaken by Crawford et al. (2003), Crawford and Pollack (2004), and Pollack (2005) and Pollack (2007) that examines the concept of hard and soft projects, and the value of adopting systems thinking, and especially SSM as a research framework. However, Pollack (2007) emphasises that no one paradigm, perspective or approach is appropriate to all the situations found in project management research.

Sense-making of a project management transformation process, based upon SSM model development, is described by Crawford and Costello (2000). Applying SSM to sense-making is also a theme in the study of participatory policy analysis, identified as a wicked problem, by Geurts and Joldersman (2001). Other project management related topics where

SSM has been used include study of problem structuring (Winter 2006; Pollack 2007), knowledge and collaborative work in projects (Vat 2005), wicked problems in geographical information systems projects (Balram & Dragicevic 2006), decision support in complex situations (Petkov et al. 2007), and organisational transformation (Morcos & Henshaw 2009).

A Ph.D. research program undertaken by Maqsood (2006) incorporated two phases, model development using grounded theory, and SSM as a knowledge management tool. In this role it was used to undertake a series of case studies to identify organisational knowledge gaps within process, people and technology. In this research SSM was very effective in eliciting useful information and explicit knowledge, and creating associated knowledge artefacts (Maqsood & Finegan 2009).

Grounded theory (GT)

Another popular qualitative research approach that has been applied to project management is grounded theory (GT). Developed by Glaser and Strauss (1967), it can be described as a methodology to generate or discover theory grounded in data. This can be particularly useful to build a theoretical framework in a research area where there has been little or no previous study. It is also very useful in the analysis of the organisational context of projects. Huang et al. (2001) describe GT as being both iterative and comparative. The iteration occurs as movement between concept and data and the comparison is across the types of evidence.

Grounded theory is strongly recommended by Huang et al. (2001) for applications in complex project settings. The case study that they describe used GT to understand the nature and processes of knowledge integration that occur during the implementation of an enterprise resource planning (ERP) project. In another information technology related project, Hoda et al. (2008) have used GT to deal with the complexity in understanding the issues in agile project management. In adopting GT as the research approach, Hoda et al. (2008, p. 220) observe that 'we must not bind ourselves to any preconceived notions and allow important categories to emerge through the iterations of interviews. Therefore, we plan to proceed by conducting a pilot study to understand the real issues within the agile project management area and then improve our list of questions to focus more on the important categories in succeeding interviews'.

Focusing upon the complexity of project organisations several studies have been conducted using GT. A study of 12 project management offices (PMOs) in four different organisations is described by Aubry et al. (2008; 2009). GT was used to analyse the PMOs, and the study shows that 'organisational tensions are among the primary drivers behind the implementation and reconfiguration of the PMOs' (Aubry et al. 2009, 146). Another example is six case studies of the role of improvisation in the project management of strategic change. In this investigation Leybourne (2006) used GT to analyse the processes, routines and mechanisms used to implement change within the study organisations. GT has also been used to describe and understand the relational interaction processes found in project networks. In this study Larson and Wikstrom (2007, 333) took the view 'that people create social realities through their own interpretations as well as through individual and collective action' and found that 'research strategies based on grounded theory ... have their strength in accuracy, but are weak in terms of simplicity' (Larson & Wikstrom 2007, 349).

Responding to scepticism about GT as a research method, Georgieva and Allen (2008) have specifically examined the suitability of grounded theory in project management research. This study of best practices in project management provides a comprehensive example of how to use GT to address a specific but complex research question in project management. The complexity is reflected in the content of the outcomes, that 'Motivation, knowledge transfer and managing awareness are inextricably linked together. They and their properties ... constitute elements of project management best practice as a result of this research. Future research should build on this to clarify their interlinked roles and discover other properties of project management best practice' (Georgieva and Allen 2008, 50).

Actor network theory (ANT)

An alternative approach to understanding complexity is provided by actor network theory (ANT). This approach is based upon the sociology of scientific knowledge and views networks as processes – not structures – that are composed of actors; human, natural and technological (Blackburn, 2002). Cecez-Kecmanovic and Nagm (2008, 198) observe that ANT 'enables analysis of the conditions, constraints and modification of agency within networks that intertwine the humans, culture, language, artefacts and technology (and many other things)', and that it encourages the researcher to '"follow the actors", let them tell their own stories, use their own vocabularies and unfold their own meanings, while tracing the emergence of relations in heterogeneous actor-networks'.

ANT has been applied as a research methodology to a limited number of project management cases. Blackburn (2002) has used ANT to study what project managers do and how they understand and talk about their activity. This approach was able to better understand the power of project management tools to place and maintain the project manager at the centre of the project. It also focused upon maintaining the temporary project organisation, that constant reinforcement was needed to keep the project intact as well as on track. Markowski and Csosz (2008) have also applied ANT to complex issues in project management – in this case the management and mapping of controversies in projects. In another example ANT provided Cecez-Kecmanovic and Nagm (2008) with a technique for better understanding of the development and evaluation of information systems project proposals.

A particularly complex socio-technical project – PALETTE (Esnault et al. 2006) – used ANT successfully as the means to develop a participatory design process. This study describes how an actor-network was built, identifying and enrolling over thirty different types of actors. The resulting methodology encouraged the active participation the diverse group of stakeholders in the design process.

Other approaches

There is a wide variety of additional tools and techniques that may be applicable to the wicked project situation – for example concept mapping and blue sheeting. However, to conclude this review of project management research techniques, brief mention will be made of three multi/meta-methodologies; total systems intervention, critical systems thinking and systems of systems (SoS).

Total systems intervention (TSI) is described by Jackson (2001, 238) as a practical meta-methodology that 'was based upon a sophisticated form of pluralism in which methodologies adhering to different paradigms were to be used in the same intervention on the same problem situation. Providing practical guidelines and a critique of different systems approaches, TSI has been applied in difficult project settings to improve interventions and enable learning (Clarke & Lehaney 1997; Pauley & Ormerod 1998; Jackson 2001; Pollack, 2007).

Critical systems thinking (CST) has been recommended by Midgley (1996), Jackson (2001), Pollack (2007) and Remington and Pollack (2007) as being relevant to complex socio-technological project settings. Describing CST as a modification of TSI, Jackson (2001) suggests that it is essentially about using to advantage, and in a coherent way, all the different management science methodologies, tools and techniques, according to their strengths and weaknesses in dealing with complex societal systems.

The concept of a system of systems (SoS) was the subject of a study by Jackson and Keys (1984). More recently, the field of system of systems engineering (SoSE) has developed in to response to very large systems engineering and integration projects, specifically the challenge of integrating complex meta-systems (Keating et al. 2003). Techniques for managing system of systems projects is an emerging theme that is being addressed by researchers who include Sauser and Boardman (2006), Lane and Boehm (2007) and Ireland (2009). All the indications are that this is an emerging theme in complex project management-related research.

Comparative analysis

Technique	Contribution to Wicked Projects
SDM – System Dynamics Modelling	The resultant models can provide an improved understanding by mapping the dynamic complexity of the project. This includes the tracing of causal chains and the specification of relationships. SDM can also be used to produce a post-mortem analysis of the project.
AR/AL – Action Research/ Action Learning	Assist in a better understanding of dynamic processes and assist the management of innovation and change. It can also be used for developing tools to support project management, for example a tool to measure and visualise stakeholder influence.
SSM – Soft Systems Methodology	Good at helping to better understand what to do about 'the mess'. It can be incorporated into stakeholder and requirements analysis. SSM also has applications as a tool for gap analysis and in the creation of artifacts of knowledge.
GT – Grounded Theory	Assist in the analysis of organisational contexts and the analysis of relational interaction processes and issues in complex projects.
ANT – Actor Network Theory	Assist in tracing the relations in actor-networks, managing and mapping controversies in projects and encourage active participation and communication between different stakeholders.

Table 15.1. Summary of techniques and their contribution to understanding wicked projects

An essential response to wicked projects is to actively seek to discover the alternative ways of dealing with wicked problems. Rittel and Weber (1973) advise that every trial counts. Therefore a significant advantage to applying a variety of systems thinking approaches is that, being based upon different theoretical concepts, they are more likely to result in a broader set of useful alternatives. Table 15.1 provides a summary of the selected techniques and the contribution they could make to a wicked project.

This table illustrates two important considerations. Each technique has particular strengths in helping to understand wicked problems. Secondly, no one technique can provide all the knowledge and learning needed to respond to wicked problems. Therefore, depending upon the nature of a project, a variety of techniques should be the basis of discovering the alternative responses to the wicked problems.

Conclusion

A key message of this study is that as project management researchers we have many choices in our research designs. There is no best approach, especially where we are attempting to deal with wicked problems. However, some approaches are better suited to particular types of problems. For example: action research and action learning are indicated where deep reflection is important; and soft systems methodology where sensing-making and problem structuring are challenges. However, all the approaches that were discussed were able to address the issues of inter-related complexity, which is at the heart of understanding wicked problems.

A useful theme that emerges from examination of the different examples is that researchers are definitely not limited to using one research design approach for a specific study of wicked problems in a wicked project. This suggests many opportunities for further research using combinations of two or more methodologies, particularly when applied to wicked problem situations. System dynamics modelling together with softer techniques for problem structuring, and a greater use of actor network theory, are examples of options that promise interesting outcomes.

References

Ala-Risku, T; Kärkkäinen, M. 2006. 'Material delivery problems in construction projects: A possible solution'. *International Journal of Production Economics*: 19–29.

Albin, S. 1997. *Building a System Dynamics Model Part 1: Conceptualization*, Cambridge, MA: Massachusetts Institute of Technology.

Aubry, M; Hobbs, B; Thuillier, D. 2008. 'Organisational project management: An historical approach to the study of PMOs'. *International Journal of Project Management* 26: 38–43.

Aubry, M; Hobbs, B; Thuillier, D. 2009. 'The contribution of the project management office to organisational performance'. *International Journal of Managing Projects in Business* 2 (1): 141–148.

Australian Public Service Commission. 2007. *Tackling Wicked Problems: A Public Policy Perspective.* Commonwealth of Australia, Canberra.

Balram, S; Dragicevic S. 2006. 'Modeling collaborative GIS processes using soft systems theory, UML and object oriented design'. *Transactions in GIS* 10 (2):199–218

Becker, F. 2002. 'Organisational dilemmas and workplace solutions'. *Journal of Corporate Real Estate* 4 (2): 129–149.

Blackburn, S. 2002. 'The project manager and the project-network'. *International Journal of Project Management* 20: 199–204.

Bourne, L; Walker, D H T. 2006. 'Using a visualising tool to study stakeholder influence – two Australian examples'. *Journal of Project Management* 37 (1): 5–21.

Brown, M M; Brudney, J L. 2003. 'Learning organizations in the public sector? A study of police agencies employing information and technology to advance knowledge'. *Public Administration Review* 63 (1): 30–43.

Bryson, J M; Cunningham, G L; Lokkesmoe, K J. 2002. 'What to do when stakeholders matter: The case of problem formulation for the African American men project of Hennepin County, Minnesota'. *Public Administration Review* 62 (5): 568–584.

Callender, G; Vinsen, K; Jamieson, D; Brown, J. 2006. 'Wicked problems in procurement: a model for software acquisition'. In *Conference Proceedings: Creating & Managing Value in Supply Networks,* edited by Croom, S. Oxford, UK.

Cecez-Kecmanovic, D; Nagm, F. 2008. 'Understanding IS projects evaluation in practice through an ANT inquiry'. Paper presented at 19th Australasian Conference on Information Systems – Understanding IS Projects Evaluation in Practice, 3–5 Dec 2008, Christchurch, NZ.

Checkland, P B. 1999. *Systems Thinking, Systems Practice.* Chichester, UK: John Wiley & Sons.

Checkland, P B; Scholes, J. 1990. *Soft Systems Methodology in Action.* Chichester: John Wiley & Sons.

Clarke, S; Lehaney, B. 1997. 'Total systems intervention and human inquiry: The search for a common ground'. *Systems Practice* 10 (5): 611–34.

Crawford, L; Costello, K. 2000. 'Towards a transferable methodology for managing strategic change by projects'. In *IRNOP IV Conference – Paradoxes of Project Collaboration in the Global Economy: Interdependence, Complexity and Ambiguity,* edited by Crawford, L; Clarke, C F. Sydney, Australia: University of Technology, Sydney

Crawford, L; Costello, K; Pollack, J; Bentley, L. 2003. 'Managing soft changes in the public sector'. *International Journal of Project Management* 21 (6): 443–448.

Crawford, L H; Pollack, J. 2004. 'Hard and soft projects: A framework for analysis'. *International Journal of Project Management* 22 (8): 645–653.

Crawford, L H; Pollack, J B; England, D. 2006. 'Uncovering the trends in project management: Journal emphases over the last 10 years'. *International Journal of Project Management* 24: 174–184.

Eberlein, B. 2009. *System Dynamics Software Info,* Ventana Systems, Inc. Accessed 27 September 2009. Available from: http://www.vensim.com/sdmail/sdsoft.html

Ellis, A; Phelps, R 1999. 'Staff development for online delivery: A collaborative team-based action learning model'. In *Responding to Diversity: The 16th Annual Conference of the Australasian Society for Computers in Learning in Tertiary Education* (ASCILITE), Dec 5–8, Brisbane, edited by Winn, J.: 71–82.

Esnault, L; Vermeulin, F; Zeiliger, R. 2006. 'On the use of actor-network theory for developing web services dedicated to communities of practice'. Paper presented at the 1st International Workshop on Building Technology Enhanced Learning solutions for Communities of Practice (TEL-CoPs'06), EC-TEL Conference, October 1–4, 2006, Greece.

Finegan, A. 1994. 'Soft systems methodology: An alternative approach to knowledge elicitation in complex and poorly defined systems', *Complexity International* 1.

Forrester, J. 1961. *Industrial Dynamics*. Cambridge, MA: MIT Press.

Gao, F; Li, M; Nakamori, Y. 2002. 'Systems thinking on knowledge and its management: Systems methodology for knowledge management'. *Journal of Knowledge Management* 6 (1): 7–17.

Georgieva, S; Allan, G. 2008. 'Best practices in project management through a grounded theory lens'. *EJBRM* 6 (1): 43–52

Geurts, J; Joldersma, C. 2001. 'Methodology for participatory policy analysis'. *European Journal of Operational Research* 128: 300 – 310.

Glaser, B; Strauss, A. 1967. *The Discovery of Grounded Theory*. Chicago: Aidine.

Green, S D. 1999. 'A participative research strategy for propagating soft methodologies in value management practice'. *Construction Management and Economics* 17 (3): 329–340.

Gustafsson, C. 2002. 'From concept to norm – an explorative study of office design management from an organizational perspective'. *Facilities* 20 (13): 423–431.

Hoda, A; Noble, J; Marshall, S. 2008. 'Agile project management'. Paper presented at the New Zealand Computer Science Research Student Conference, April 14, 2008, Christchurch, New Zealand.

Huang, J; Newell, S; Pan, S L; Galliers, R D. 2001. 'Knowledge integration processes within the context of enterprise resource planning (ERP) systems implementation'. Paper presented at ECIS 2001: The 9th European Conference on Information Systems – Global Co-operation in the New Millennium, Bled, Slovenia.

Ireland, V. 2009. 'Identifying and managing uncertainty and emergence'. In *The Human Side of Projects in Modern Business, Scientific Research Papers*, edited by Kahkonen, Kalle; Kazi, Abdul Samad; Rekola, Mirkka. The Project Management Association of Finland in association with VTT Technical Research Centre of Finland.

Jackson, M. 2001. 'Critical systems thinking and practice'. *Journal of Operational Research* 128 (2): 233–244.

Keating, C; Rogers, R; Unal, R; Dryer, D; Sousa-Poza, A; Safford, R; Peterson, W; Rabadi, G. 2003. 'System of systems engineering'. *Engineering Management Journal* 15 (3): 36–45.

Kenny, J D J. 2003. 'A research based model for managing strategic educational change and innovation projects'. Proceedings of HERDSA Conference 2003, 6–9 July 2003, Christchurch, New Zealand: 333–342.

Lane, J; Boehm, B. 2007. 'System of systems cost estimation: Analysis of lead system integrator engineering activities'. *Information Resources Management Journal* 20 (2): 23–32.

Larson, M; Wikström, E. 2007. 'Relational interaction processes in project networks: The consent and negotiation perspectives'. *Scandinavian Journal of Management* 23: 327–352.

Leybourne, S A. 2006. 'Improvisation within the project management of strategic change: Some observations from UK Financial services'. *Journal of Change Management* 6 (4): 365–381.

Maqsood, T. 2006. 'The role of knowledge management in supporting innovation and learning in construction'. Ph.D. thesis. Melbourne: RMIT University.

Maqsood, T; Finegan, A D. 2009. 'A knowledge management approach to innovation and learning in the construction industry'. *International Journal of Managing Projects in Business*, 2 (2): 297–307.

Markowski, K; Csosz, S. 2008. 'Emerging controversies in project management and their impact on the dynamics between project practitioners, consultants and researchers'. 22nd IPMA World Congress – Project Management to Run, November 9–11 2008, Rome, Italy.

Midgley, G. 1996. 'The ideal of unity and the practice of pluralism in systems science'. In *Critical Systems Thinking: Current Research and Practice*, edited by Flood, R L; Romm, N R A. New York: Plenum

Morcos, M; Henshaw, M. 2009. 'A soft systems methodology for transforming organisations to product-service systems (application in defence and construction industry)'. In Proceedings of the 7th Annual Conference on Systems Engineering Research, 20th – 23rd April 2009, Loughborough University, UK.

Neal, R A. 1995. 'Project definition: the soft-systems approach'. *International Journal of Project Management* 13 (1): 5–9.

Nogeste, K. 2008. 'Dual cycle action research: A professional doctorate case study'. *International Journal of Managing Projects in Business* 1 (4): 566–585.

Ottosson, S. 2003. 'Participation action research – a key to improved knowledge of management'. *Technovation* 23: 87–94.

Pacanowsky, M. 1995. 'Team tools for wicked problems'. *Organizational Dynamics*, 23 (3): 36–52.

Pauley, G; Ormerod, R. 1998. 'The evolution of a performance measurement project at RTZ'. *Interfaces* 28 (4): 94–118.

Petkov, D; Petkova, O; Andrew T; Nepal, T. 2007. 'Mixing multiple criteria decision making with soft systems thinking techniques for decision support in complex situations'. *Decision Support Systems* 43 2007): 1615–1629.

Pollack, J B F. 2005. 'Project pluralism: Combining the hard and soft paradigms in IS/IT strategy development in the NSW public sector'. Ph.D. Thesis. Sydney: University of Technology.

Pollack, J. 2007. 'The changing paradigms of project management'. *International Journal of Project Management* 25 (3): 266–74.

Remington, K; Pollack J. 2007. *Tools for Complex Projects*. Aldershot, UK: Gower Publishing.

Rittel, H; Webber, M. 1973. 'Dilemmas in a general theory of planning'. *Policy Sciences* 4: 155–169.

Sankaran, S; Tay, B H. 2007. 'Are interpretive and critical research methods useful for research in project management?'. In *AIPM 2007: Setting the Standard: Proceedings of the AIPM National Conference 2007*, edited by Earl, G; Tam, V; Milner, S; Remington, K; Tupicoff, A; Tucker, R Sydney, Australia: AIPM: 1–13.

Sankaran, S; Tay, B H; Orr, M. 2009. 'Managing organizational change by using soft systems thinking in action research projects'. *International Journal of Managing Projects in Business* 2 (2): 179 – 197.

Sauser, B; Boardman, J. 2006. 'From prescience to emergence: taking hold of system of systems management'. Paper presented at 27th American Society for Engineering Management National Conference, October 26–28, Huntsville, AL.

Savage, G T; Nix, T W; Whitehead, C J; Blair, J D. 1991. 'Strategies for assessing and managing organizational stakeholders'. *Academy of Management Executive* 5 (2), 61–75.

Shurville, S; Williams, J. 2005. 'Managing in-house development of a campus-wide information system'. *Campus-Wide Information Systems* 22 (1): 15–27.

Smyth, H J; Morris, P W G. 2007. 'An epistemological evaluation of research into projects and their management: Methodological issues', *International Journal of Project Management* 25 (4): 423–436.

Sterman, J D. 1992. *System Dynamics Modeling for Project Management.* Cambridge, MA: Sloan School of Management, Massachusetts Institute of Technology.

Vat, K H. 2005. 'Modeling human activity systems for collaborative project work: An IS development perspective'. *Journal of Issues in Informing Science and Information Technology* 2: 49–65.

Vickers, G. 1968. *Value Systems and Social Process.* London, Penguin Books

Waddock, S A; Walsh, M. 1999. 'Paradigm shift: Towards a community-university community of practice'. *The International Journal of Organizational Analysis* 7 (3): 244–264.

Walker, D H T; Anbari, F T; Bredillet, C; Söderlund, J; Cicmil, S; Thomas, J. 2008. 'Collaborative academic/practitioner research in project management: Examples and applications'. *International Journal of Managing Projects in Business* 1 (2): 1–21.

Whelton, M; Ballard, G. 2002. 'Wicked problems in project definition'. Paper presented at the 10th annual conference of the International Group for Lean Construction, Gramado, Brazil, August 6–8, 2002.

Williams, T M. 1999. 'The need for new paradigms for complex projects'. *International Journal of Project Management* 17 (5): 269–273.

Williams, T. 2002. *Modelling Complex projects.* London, UK: Wiley

Williams, T. 2005. 'Assessing and moving on from the dominant project management discourse in the light of project overruns'. *IEEE Transactions on Engineering Management* 52 (4): 497–508.

Winter, M. 2006. 'Problem structuring in project management: An application of soft systems methodology (SSM)'. *Journal of the Operational Research Society* 57 (7): 802–812.

Winter, M; Smith, C; Morris, P W G; Cicmil, S. 2006. 'Directions for future research in project management: The main findings of a UK government-funded research network'. *International Journal of Project Management* 24 (8): 638–649.

Contributors

Editors

Dr Henry Linger is Deputy Director of the Centre for Organisational and Social Informatics (COSI) and the Knowledge Management Research Program (KMRP) in the Faculty of Information Technology at Monash University. He is also a Research Associate at the Defence Science and Technology Organisation (DSTO), contributing to research in social learning and organisational transformation. Henry has a Bachelor of Engineering degree and a PhD in Knowledge Management. He conducts research in the area of knowledge work, knowledge management, organisational learning and the design of ICT systems to support such activity. His research involves national and international collaborations and has been conducted across a broad range of domains including defence, meteorology, epidemiology, immunology and clinical and management aspects of healthcare. His current research focuses on knowledge-based practices managing emergent issues in complex projects, the development of dynamic capabilities for adaptive organisations, and the application of knowledge management to climate change policy development and implementation.

Dr Jill Owen is a key player in the teaching and research of Project Management within the School of Business at University of New South Wales, Canberra Campus. Her research focuses on the project as a vehicle for organising work and on the role of knowledge-based practices and informal processes in influencing how an organisation operates. This complements the contemporary shift of emphasis from the traditional focus on the technical processes of projects to the idea of projects as primarily social constructs that can be considered as social systems. Jill has published in refereed journals and conferences at both the national and international level.

Authors

Professor Emeritus Erling S Andersen
BI Norwegian School of Management, Norway

Shawn D Belling
University of Wisconsin–Platteville, USA

Dr James Connor
University of New South Wales at the Australian Defence Force, Australia

Associate Professor Ken Dovey
University of Technology, Sydney, Australia

Dr Andrew Finegan
University of Adelaide, Australia

Professor Andrew Gemino
Simon Fraser University, Canada

Associate Professor Robert A Hunt
Macquarie University, Australia

Dr Catherine P Killen
University of Technology, Sydney, Australia

Dr Louis Klein
Systemic Excellence Group & Humboldt-Viadrina School of Governance, Germany

Adri Köhler
University of Applied Sciences Utrecht, the Netherlands

Paul TM Leong
Auckland University of Technology, New Zealand

Dr Henry Linger
Monash University, Australia

Dr Karen Manley
Queensland University of Technology, Queensland, Australia.

Chui-Ha (Tracy) Ng
RMIT University, Australia

Paul O'Connor
RMIT University, Australia

Dr Jill Owen
University of New South Wales at the Australian Defence Force Academy, Australia

Dr Simon Poon
University of Sydney, Australia

Dr Blaize Horner Reich
Simon Fraser University, Canada

Dr Timothy M Rose
Queensland University of Technology, Australia

Associate Professor Shankar Sankaran
University of Technology, Sydney, Australia

Dr Chris Sauer
University of Oxford, UK

Professor A J Gilbert Silvius
University of Applied Sciences Utrecht, the Netherlands

Alan Sixsmith
University of Technology, Sydney, Australia

Dr Jocelyn Small
TLC Aged Care, Australia

John Smyrk
The Australian National University, Australia

Dr Felix B Tan
Auckland University of Technology, New Zealand

Jasper van den Brink
University of Applied Sciences Utrecht, the Netherlands

Professor Derek Walker
RMIT University, Australia

Michael Young
University of New South Wales at the Australian Defence Force Academy, Australia

Dr Raymond Young
University of Canberra, Australia

Associate Professor Ofer Zwikael
The Australian National University, Australia